Life on the Levels

Voices from a Working World

This book is dedicated to Judy, Tom and Sophie Willoughby.

Life on the Levels

Voices from a Working World

TONY ANDERSON

Photographs by CHRIS WILLOUGHBY

with additional photographs by SOPHIE WILLOUGHBY

BIRLINN

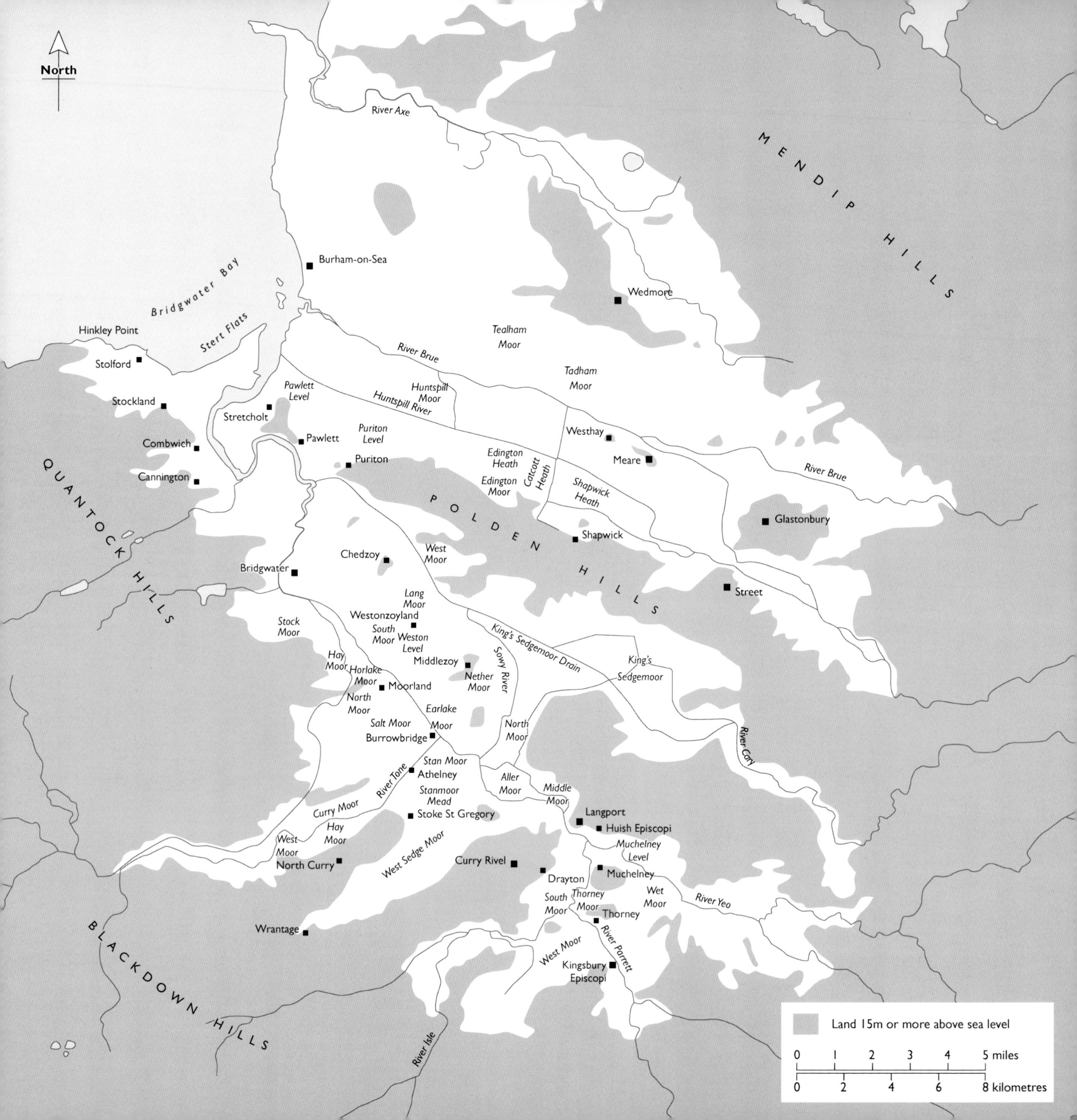
North
River Axe
MENDIP HILLS
Burham-on-Sea
Wedmore
Bridgwater Bay
Stert Flats
Hinkley Point
Stolford
Stockland
Stretcholt
Pawlett Level
Tealham Moor
River Brue
Tadham Moor
Huntspill Moor
Huntspill River
Pawlett
Puriton Level
Puriton
Combwich
Cannington
Westhay
Meare
River Brue
Edington Heath
Catcott Heath
Edington Moor
Shapwick Heath
Glastonbury
QUANTOCK HILLS
POLDEN HILLS
Shapwick
Chedzoy
West Moor
Bridgwater
Street
Lang Moor
Westonzoyland
Stock Moor
South Moor
Weston Level
King's Sedgemoor Drain
King's Sedgemoor
Hay Moor
Horlake Moor
Middlezoy
Nether Moor
Sowy River
Moorland
North Moor
Earlake Moor
Salt Moor
Burrowbridge
North Moor
River Cary
Stan Moor
Athelney
River Tone
Aller Moor
Middle Moor
Stanmoor Mead
Curry Moor
Stoke St Gregory
Langport
Huish Episcopi
Hay Moor
West Moor
North Curry
West Sedge Moor
Curry Rivel
Muchelney Level
Drayton
Muchelney
South Moor
Thorney Moor
Wet Moor
River Yeo
Thorney
Wrantage
River Parrett
West Moor
Kingsbury Episcopi
BLACKDOWN HILLS
River Isle
Land 15m or more above sea level
0 1 2 3 4 5 miles
0 2 4 6 8 kilometres

Contents

Acknowledgements i
Introduction ii

Chapters:

The Mouth of the Parrett 2
Tony Brewer & Brendon Sellick, Mud Horsemen
Bob Thorne, Salmon Fisherman

The Peat Moors 32
Albert Bush, Peat Worker
Richard Roland & Andrew Roland, Peat Producers
(with David Durnam and George David)
Matthew & Minnie Wall, Farmers & Peat Producers

Farming 52
Ray Darby, Traditional Dairy Farmer
Ralph Baker, Progressive Farmer
David Baker, Organic Farmer

Conservation 80
John Humphrey & Harry Paget-Wilkes, RSPB Wardens
Trevor Wall, The Levels and Moors Partnership

Withies 100
Len Meade, Basket Maker
Michael Musgrove, Withy Grower

Industry 118
Maud Gould, Shoes
Chris Tinnion, Sheepskin

Strapping, Cider & Eels 134
Dickie Macey, Strapper
Donald Coate, Dairyman & Cider Maker

A Life on the Levels 146
Cuthbert Hurd

Bibliography 161

Glossary 162

First published in 2006 by
Birlinn Ltd
West Newington House
10 Newington Road
Edinburgh EH9 1QS

www.birlinn.co.uk

Text copyright © Tony Anderson 2006
Photographs © Chris Willoughby & Sophie Willoughby

All rights reserved. No part of this publication may be reproduced, stored or transmitted in any form without the express written permission of the publisher.

ISBN10: 1 84158 504 1
ISBN13: 978 1 84158 504 8

British Library Cataloguing-in-Publication Data
A catalogue record for this book is available from the British Library

Edited by Elizabeth Carr
Design by Andrew Sutterby

Printed and bound by Compass Press, China

Acknowledgements

First and foremost I would like to thank all the people who appear in this book, who gave of their time so generously and talked so eloquently about their lives on the Levels and Moors of Somerset: David Baker, Ralph Baker, Tony and Eirwen Brewer, Albert Bush, Donald Coate, Ray Darby, George David, Henry Durnam, Maud Gould, John Humphrey, Cuthbert Hurd, Dickie Macey, Len Meade, Michael and Ellen Musgrove, Harry Paget-Wilkes, Andrew Roland, Richard Roland, Brendon Sellick, Chris Tinnion, Bob Thorne, Matthew and Minnie Wall, Trevor Wall.

I must also thank, for their help and advice: Richard Clark of Clarks Shoes, Tom Clark, Bob 'Rufus' Heard, Henry Hurd, David Macey, Anne Coate, Paddy Mounter, Duncan Speakman, Ed Hooper, John Nash of the Watchet Maritime Museum, David Bromwitch from Taunton Library and David Walker from the Glastonbury Rural Life Museum. I must also thank Judy Willoughby for permission to use Chris Willoughby's splendid photographs of life on the Levels.

Introduction

The idea for this book was conceived back in 1980 when I first started to interview friends and neighbours on the Levels and Moors of Somerset. All of them seemed to have a story to tell about the way in which their lives had been shaped by this very particular and peculiar environment. My friend and fellow dweller on the Parrett, the photographer Chris Willoughby, had already started an extensive photographic record here; many of his photographs were later shown in various exhibitions, including ones locally at the Glastonbury Rural Life Museum and in the exhibition room at the Brewhouse Theatre, Taunton. By some strange process of transformation, all this work eventually became the basis of a documentary film for television, shown on Channel 4 in 1985. When I was approached by Birlinn, the publishers, to write a book about the Levels, I turned back to the transcripts of those interviews from twenty-five years ago and they, along with Chris's photographs, form the basis of this present book. I decided to try to update some of them wherever possible, to see how life had changed in the intervening years, and went back to talk to the same people, their children or successors. The result is an oral history of a way of life that reaches back from the present day to the beginning of the 1900s. One of the things that a written oral history cannot quite do is give the whole flavour of a language: the accent, tone and rhythm of speech. I have tried, without resorting to any system of phonetics or any wildly eccentric spellings, to indicate something of this, especially where it seemed absolutely intrinsic to the speakers themselves. Their stories should be heard with the inner ear as well as simply read. Their most obscure vocabulary is explained in a glossary at the end of the book.

The landscape itself, of course, attests to a far deeper history, to a time when man first started to try to shape the environment, to keep out the sea and cope with the flood waters that made much of the Somerset Levels and Moors a place of lakes and swamps. What characterises the land more than anything is water: the water that spills out over the moors; the sea water that rushes up the tidal rivers or batters at the coast; the water that has made and keeps the peat bogs alive; the water full of fish and eels; the water which man has struggled to channel, contain, control and, indeed, exploit for many centuries and which has dominated all aspects of life and activity. This book is not a history of the making of the Somerset Levels; there are already a number of excellent books on the subject, which I have indicated in my bibliography, especially Michael Williams's *The Draining of the Somerset Levels*. However, it is, perhaps, worthwhile pointing to a few essential features of this watery landscape. The Levels and Moors consist of about 250 square miles of lowland basin, open to the sea and the Bristol Channel in the west, surrounded by ridges of hills to the north, east and south. The Bristol Channel has the second highest tidal reach in the world, nearly forty feet, and the hills, the Mendips, Quantocks and Blackdowns, have some of the highest average yearly rainfalls in Britain. At high tide the sea pours up the rivers and, whenever it rains, the rivers struggle, and fail, to contain the water that runs into them, falling, as they often do, for less than a foot per mile as they wander towards the sea. The problem is obvious and further complicated by the fact that the inland moors are often much lower than the land at the coast. It is this coastal belt, formed by depositions of marine clay, that is most properly, if pedantically, called the 'Levels' with the 'Moors' inland, though most local people use the words interchangeably. It is better to imagine the moors as a series of basins, rather than just one big one, with the ridge of the Polden Hills dividing them north and south almost in two equal parts and lots of little 'islands' of higher ground, especially on the southern moors, where villages and settlements were built. This is why so many of the villages have peculiarly similar endings to their names, all derived from the Anglo-Saxon suffix for island: Atheln-ey, Thorn-ey, Mucheln-ey, Middlez-oy, Chedz-oy and so on.

The whole lowland basin was a great boggy swamp and the sensible Romans avoided it almost entirely and left it to the Britons who pottered about in boats. By the fourth century they were gathering round

Glastonbury to lead lives of solitude, contemplation and prayer. Athelney Abbey, which was founded in 878, could only be approached by boat and it was on Athelney, of course, that King Alfred hid and burnt his cakes before rallying his men and defeating the invading Danes. Nowadays, it looks the most unlikely place to try to hide but in the ninth century it was what is always described in history books as a 'fastness', a secret place, hidden within the swamps and wild waters of the Moor. The Anglo-Saxons certainly settled on the higher ground in the area and grazed their stock on the moors for a few months in summer, but there is no evidence that they actually started to try to drain or reclaim the land. This really started with the great ecclesiastical powers of the Middle Ages, especially the Bishops of Bath and Wells and the Abbots of Glastonbury who competed for lands and influence — sometimes physically in the persons of their monks and servants — and started to exploit the moors systematically for their peat, their fisheries and their pasture lands. Rivers were diverted, retaining walls were built, cuts, ditches and rhynes were dug, causeways and droves and weirs constructed. Sea walls were built and sluices, or clyses, put in place to hold back the tides. The evidence of much of this activity is still apparent today.

All this effort was confined to very limited sections of the levels and, unfortunately, much of the impetus was lost after the Black Death and the subsequent economic stagnation of the late-fourteenth century. The dissolution of the monasteries in the mid-sixteenth century further compounded the problem. Early in the seventeenth century a great sea flood provoked a flurry of work on the coastal defences: low walls, fences of stakes, hedges and brushwood were placed to trap the mud and silt deposited along the shore. Little, however, came of many schemes to do much about the moors inland. One of the major problems was that none of the local inhabitants could agree on what should be done, a characteristic, some might suggest, that persists today. Indeed, many of the commoners feared that they would lose their rights of pasturage and that opportunities for wildfowling and fishing would be curtailed. They liked the moors as they were and even beat and stoned surveyors who were sent to map out the land. Many of these arguments about drainage, water-levels and land use erupted over the years and were even echoed recently, back in the late 1970s and early '80s, when angry farmers faced representatives of the Nature Conservancy Council in village halls around the Levels, as the conservation lobby brought in the first SSSIs, Sites of Special Scientific Interest, on the Moors in an attempt to restrain drainage activity and preserve some of the Moors for wildlife. Things are much calmer now but even so there are problems ahead. Increased fears of global warming have reopened the issue of a barrage across the mouth of the River Parrett, the only river on the moors still open to the sea, and many conservationists fear the impact such a scheme might have.

It was not really until the 1770s, with new Drainage Acts passed in parliament, that more concerted efforts were made to drain the moors, and when the first steam pumps were built in the 1830s matters really started to improve. Areas such as West Sedgemoor that had remained completely under water for most of the year could, in dry years, now be pastured and harvested for hay. Much of the winter flooding now stayed on the moors for less time and, indeed, the 'thick' water, silt rich from the rivers, was welcomed as a regular enrichment of the fields. Silt was also deliberately carted onto the ground and spread to improve the pasture. The quality of the grass improved and grazing land was extended. Even so, the overall problems of flooding were not solved and there were difficulties with maintenance across the moors, especially during the agricultural depression of the late-nineteenth century when water stayed on the moors for months, people went about by boat and malaria was a real problem during the spring and summer.

Crucially, there was no real overview of the whole complex of moors and levels. The Internal Drainage Boards fought with one another and couldn't agree, and none of their officials seemed to have any engineering or hydrological experience. There was also very little money. Michael Williams writes that conditions on the moors in the 1930s had actually reverted and were, 'Worse than 100 years previously.' The great leap forward finally came in 1939 for reasons quite external to the needs of the local people. Because of the outbreak of war the Royal Ordinance factory was built at Puriton. This required 4.5 million gallons of water a day, a huge quantity, and engineers — with one eye, it is true, on sorting out the drainage on the Levels — cut new outlets through to the coast, built relief channels, improved and increased the pumping stations, the embankments, the sluices and the sea walls. Though the problem of flooding was not eliminated — nor can it ever be — at least it was possible to deal with flood water far more quickly and efficiently.

Though work to maintain and improve conditions on the moors carries on all the while, there has been a radical change in emphasis and direction over recent years. Conservation has now become an integral part of the scene and the difference this has made to the lives and activities of farmers, peat extractors and conservationists themselves, is immediately apparent when talking to them and, indeed, when travelling about the Moors and Levels. The whole system of subsidies and grants from government which seemed to threaten a bleak East Anglian future has changed and there is much more effort now to preserve and enhance the special qualities of this man-made landscape. There will always be room for discussion and argument over exactly what should be preserved and how, but it has been of great interest to me, at least, to track the evolution of opinion and practice over the last quarter century.

This book is not an attempt at a balanced survey of everyday contemporary life on the Levels. Such a work would have to spread far wider and include all the teachers and nurses and shopkeepers and bakers, bus drivers and schoolchildren — the list is endless. The moors are still evolving, responding to the modern world: there are new businesses in old barns and workshops where fodder-beet was once stored. The population is changing every day: there are Afghan refugees in the meat-packing plants, Polish workers in the pubs, Lithuanians and Ukrainians on the farms, Indian and Chinese restaurants — all of this would have astonished anyone living here even thirty years ago. An account of these lives would be fascinating! But they're not for this book. The people I interviewed are engaged in the trades and professions particular to the Somerset Levels. The emphasis is on traditional occupations such as farming, peat extraction, withy growing. Certain topics run through many parts of the book — water, cider, eels, withies — and I have felt no need to try to suppress any of them. Instead, I have tried to encourage everyone to talk freely about their lives and work. They have done so with humour, with lively intelligence and with passion.

TEXACO

The Mouth of the Parrett

Tony Brewer, Mud Horseman, Stolford, 1980

'I had my own sled about twelve... I was about fifteen, sixteen before I was allowed out on me own... If our kids've any sense, they won't do it... I like it out there...if the tide do make up his mind to come in like a bloody roaring train, you got to do the same.'

Stolford, where the mud horsemen live, is a tiny hamlet on the west coast of the Parrett estuary, facing out across the Bristol Channel and the vast, muddy expanse of the Stert Flats. It has a grey, melancholy beauty; the wind blasts in off the sea with a fierce welcome and whips about like an angry dog. Just a little further down the coast, and visible for miles around, is the great, squat shape of Hinkley Point Atomic Power Station. The Bristol Channel has the second highest tidal reach in the world, the sea rising and falling by some thirty-five feet at the highest tides. Here, a most ingenious kind of fishing has evolved over many centuries to take advantage of this rise and fall of the sea: tall stakes banged into the mud with nets strung between them, spreading over the flats for more than a mile beyond the shore. To get to their nets and to haul back their catch of fish and shrimp, the fishermen use wooden sledges, or horses, which they push over the treacherous and ever-shifting mud before the tide rushes in again. By 1980 there were only two such fishermen working in the old way, Tony Brewer and Brendon Sellick. That year I went out with Tony Brewer across the mud flats and then talked to him and his wife, Eirwen, in their cottage and fish-house, whilst they boiled and sorted the day's catch of shrimp.

Well, fishing's been in the family for generations, I just followed on from my father. I was about twelve when I started. I was cleaning fish and that when I was about eight, nine year old and when I was eleven I did go out and sell it. I had my own sled about twelve; we weren't allowed out there unless there was an adult with us. I was about fifteen, sixteen before I was allowed out on me own.

The quantities have decreased since I was a boy. If we could catch the fish, we could make a good living, but we can't catch it. It ain't there to be caught. Our catch started to fall somewhere around 1958 when Hinkley Point Power Station was built. Well, I believe the power station got something to do with it. There's twelve acres of land reclaimed, there's millions of gallons of water goin' in and there's millions of gallons of warm water coming out; plus the fact that the sea wall's been erected and altering the currents and the sound of machinery travelling through the water. I think the combination of all that lot put together is detrimental to the fishing here. And there's the chlorine in the water that's done deliberate to kill off a particular swan-necked barnacle they got trouble with. At one time I could tell when they used it within a few days but they've altered the pattern now and its more difficult. I got a big fish net right up by the power station, right on the door step. Since 'ee bin there I ain't 'ad no Dover soles, no flat fish like I used to 'ave.

Quantity has dropped drastically. When I was fishing with Father through the peak of the season — the two tides is different, you get a high spring tide around seventeen, eighteen foot, the next spring tide'll be around fourteen, fifteen foot — well, in the eighteen foot tide we used about thirty nets and on the fourteen foot tide we used somewhere around forty. Now we got nearly sixty all the year round, year in year out and possibly up to a hundred and we still ain't catching the quantities of shrimp and fish. Every mortal thing's gone down. This year I've had five skate so far, another year

Tony Brewer bringing in his nets on his mud horse. Behind him the mud flats of Bridgwater Bay at low tide stretch towards the horizon.

I've had forty or fifty and I remember when father was bringing back eighteen in one day. Shrimps is our living and that's what we do go by rather than fish. Thirty pounds of shrimp is what we do term a reasonable day now. Well, years ago we'd dismiss that as nothing and now 'tis a good catch. You ain't got much over for luxuries, you just got your basics. Flounder is here nearly all the year round. Dover soles, they be 'ere from roughly May to October and then September you get your whiting, bit of cod, then November we get our sprats come up. And then you got congers, silver eels, bass, grey mullet. Grey mullet is here about April till the end of September and then that do disappear.

If I get the chance of a job in the winter I do take it. To what I know our forefathers never did go fishing with the sled in the winter months and that was mainly over the gear side of it rather than not wanting to. They used to go winter fishing but they used to do a different type of fishing to what we do, and we know nothing about that, that was stopped before we come on the scene. That was when they used to go down on the tail of the Gore with the boats for sprats. There's nobody living now that do know anything at all about that type of fishing. Gore Lugs they were called, the boats.

I only know what my father told me, you know. They used to have a regatta down there every year, Burnham, and Grandfather used to row across the river down Steart here and row across the river to go into Burnham on this regatta. Father was working on the farm and Grandfather used to say to Father, 'If you see a bloody old gates, you know, bring 'im 'ome. I wants 'im for rollocks on the boat.' And apparently Grandfather and whoever used to row with Grandfather always used to 'ave the hardest boat of the lot to pull and they'd win. Nobody could pull this particlar boat at Burnham, not in the regatta like, but Grandfather and this other chap along wi' 'im used to pull this boat nearly every year and win nearly every year. Grandfather was over six foot and broad shouldered. They were all fishermen.

Opposite: Tony Brewer's shrimp nets. The elm stakes are flexible enough to withstand the force of a forty-foot tide.

If I got something that's too small I nearly always throw it away in the water, and if possible I be working in the tide to let the small fish and shrimps away. We've always practised throwing away the small stuff, you know, we've never brought in small stuff. Well, when I say we ain't never brought in small stuff there's times when you got to bring it in, you ain't got time to do your work out there before the tide do turn round and say 'right, you got ter be movin' and move you've got to, and you bring in a lot of rubbish then you wouldn't normally bring in, well that's what I term rubbish is small fish. I be pretty keen to let the small fish and shrimps away.

Bren down here — I'd never thought on it — but nature is one big long chain. You start off with the microscopic and then you work your way up to the whales, and it could be that one link in the chain is gone here. The bigger fish 'ave got nothing to live on and so they aren't goin' to come up round here. I've never gone into it but Bren down 'ere, the other fisherman, he seem to think that there's a lot of microscopic life getting killed off from the power station.

I've had a right royal wrangle with the people at the power station but they reckon it don't have no effect. 'Tis up to me now to prove that they be wrong. I've got some records going back to 'fifty-eight, that's somewhere round when I took over the fishing on my own, and all the rest prior to that I didn't worry about. I could have had some from the twenties and thirties, that's when they was really catching. I've got this right down to average of what per net was catching. In 1958 I got 4,000 lb of shrimp and in 1978 there was 335. In 1959 there was 5,000 lb and in 1977 there was 2,000 lb. This year it'll be a little bit higher. They figures are gone to the House of Commons. The NFU, National Farmers' Union, is involved now. This year we've 'ad a little bit better and, well, maybe an improvement. Might be just the cycle that is coincidental with the power station being there that the catch is dropped and now they be starting to climb up. 'Tis a thing we got to wait and see.

When I was a boy there was twelve fishermen fishing out of Stolford. From the First World War they started to drift away, money got easier elsewhere. You may see a drift back to this harder sort of life because of the unemployment situation, but I don't think so. We got so many restrictions now been plonked on us for various different things. You got to bring your premises to EEC, European Economic Community, hygiene standards. You got to have different nets for different fish and they got to be a specific size, you know. 'Tis harder for anyone now than it was years ago, you just bought anything and hoped for the best. Now the nets are so expensive, specially our particular net. Our net you can't buy, you got to buy the big sheets of netting and then cut it to the size you want it and how you want it and then stitch it all up together. It takes me twelve hours to make a net, and that's after I've cut the material up and I got the pieces ready to join on and that takes me twelve hours to complete and ready for sea. The nets is nylon now whereas they used to be cotton or twine. The nylon has saved us a hell of a lot of work, don't get no seagull damage. They tear the nets to get the fish out and we have to mend them. I've known a brand new net go to sea and get ripped up the first day out. I've got a hundred nets out there now, set up in twenties or thirties. Mine are set up in a fifteen, a forty, a twenty-three and a twenty. They be all around the same locality. They could be all in a line if you had the conditions to walk on but you 'ant got the conditions to walk on so they ain't in line.

Grandfather never encouraged my father and uncle to carry on, he turfed them out to the farm work. Father 'ee done farm work and helped a bit with the fishing. He was Joe Blunt and didn't give a hoot for no bugger. What he had to say you bloody got and he got a bit victimised down here and he went off to the coal pits over in Wales and he drawed his first week's pay over in Wales when he was eighteen; and then he joined the Navy for the 'Fourteen-'Eighteen War, and then in the Depression, in the early thirties 'ee was on short-time and all that, and then he came home and took over the fishing from Uncle Jack and then I carried on after I came out of the RAF in 'fifty-four.

There's very few locals here now. 'Tis all what we term foreigners. People that've come into the district. There's only seven locals. When I started fishing there was three different families fishing, actually six fishermen. Then they dwindled away. Me two cousins took on, then we 'ad a bad season and they give up and Bren's father give up and just left us two to do it. Bren's a relation. We be all related but don't do our work together. If one of us is in difficulty, well, we'll help one another out, but we don't otherwise. We be totally independent.

Eirwen: As soon as he's doing any other job he comes home with a face down to there, but as soon as 'ees back paddlin' over there 'ees different altogether. Once 'ee goes out over the mud 'ees happy.

Tony: Out there is worse than working for somebody, you got a worse boss than anybody. If 'ee do make up his mind, if the tide do make up his mind to come in like a bloody roaring train, you got to do the same. You can't say, 'Oh, well, let's plod on', you got to work twice as hard. There are a lot of nets out there, the furthest ones out are about a mile and a half. I been out there, fished the nets and brought the basket of shrimps back in on me sled, gone back — that's when were taking the nets off — and by the time I got to the last net I'm up to me chest in water. And I've only started ankle deep. That's the rate he do turn. I've been out there when I've only been able to see to some of the nets, and then I've 'ad to go back the next day, hopefully the next day, to bring 'em in, and then if you can't you've 'ad to leave 'em two or three days till the next spring tide and then bring them in that particular tide. That was bad when we was on natural fibres but don't make no difference on the nylon ones now, 'cause them be literally rot proof, they'll stand up to a fair bit of battering, they won't half take some stick.

We like elm stakes for the nets if possible, and they got to be hedgerow sticks, not cover sticks. A cover stick is grown in a copse. If you get a hedgerow one he ain't got the competition for space and therefore 'ee's that much stronger and 'ee wont bend and twist. Some of 'em out there's twelve foot. If the little insect that do serve 'em bad in't very prevalent they do last a long time, and if we don't get the rough weather they do last

Opposite: Tony Brewer at his nets.

three or four seasons. I've had to use Dutch elm and that snapped. Elm will give you warning of when it's goin' to break and the stick'll split and go over; the others won't, they'll just snap off like a carrot. We shall 'ave to possibly go onto fir or something like that. All my elms have got Dutch elm in. That's why I bought one field, so I could have the bloody hedgerow for the sticks. I've 'ad wych elm and used it in hedge-making and that but I find that the ones that I've used myself 'ave bin more twisty and odd shapes rather than a straight stick. I got a special tool I do use to knock 'em in, 'tis a maul we call him. Now where I be is yellow clay, the poles won't hold in it, the blooming stuff. Some of them stakes is five foot in the ground, others is only eighteen inches.

The sleds used to be made out of elm, but they ain't now. The old ones used to be made out of coffin board. If they wanted a new sled they'd go and ask the undertaker. Then if they was going to Bridgwater for one they'd go in timber yard and tell 'em in there they wanted a coffin board and then they knew exactly what they wanted. With a slid it do make an 'ard job easy. You can walk in the mud but it in't very easy and I don't advise nobody to do it without one or t'other of us walking beside. Your body want to go and your feet don't.

There is some days when the wind is up and we can't go. A gale'll come up, it might be quiet here and there may be a gale down Channel that we don't know anything about and it do keep the water in here, it won't go back so that we can get to our nets, on a spring tide that is. Other than that, don't matter come rain, shine, snow or blowy. If our kids 'ave any sense they won't do it. Takin' the sensible way out of it my son David, he ought to find a job. But there it might be bred into him so 'ee don't want to do anything else.

I like it out there, 'tis peace, quiet and, well, there's something there. You fish one net and perhaps you'll see the next net full up. There might be nothing or, on the other hand, there might be a nice big fish. I just like the job, been brought up to it, done very little else. When I go out to work I always come back to it. I can't keep my feet dry too long.

Tony Brewer, Stolford, 2005

Twenty-five years later, Tony Brewer is now retired but still lives with his wife, Eirwen, in their cottage in Stolford. Cogent and good-humoured as ever, he would still like to be out across the mud on his sled, fishing.

Tony: The last time I went fishing was 13 July 1991. I remember it clearly because I was out trying out a new batch and I was up so high in mud and when I come in at night I had a bad attack of Meniere's and I haven't been out since. I've had Meniere's about twenty-six years. I had to go and have a grommet put in my ears for my balance.

Eirwen: He had awful trouble with his balance. He had to go back and forth to the ear, nose, and throat specialist till they did decide it was Meniere's, so they deliberately destroyed the balance in one ear, they did an operation.

Tony: They destroyed the inner ear, the part where your balance is. If you'd have seen me when I was out and had an attack you'd swear blind I'd been in the pub all day.

Eirwen: Oh, dear me! He felt that awful. Awful! And he must be, have been, one of the fittest people, walking out so far day after day.

Tony: That's what Dr Johnson told me. He said that if it wasn't for my problem I'd be the fittest bloke in the practice. Then I've had a minor heart attack, too.

Eirwen: When he had that he was splitting logs with a fourteen pound sledge. That was three, four years back.

Tony: I've had to slow down now. I sometimes wonder at the work I used to do, how I did get through it. Perhaps I just did too much. But then all my family did it, had done it. The fishing's been in the family 500 year. There's a Brewer in the first parish records as being a fisherman. My cousin, he's dead now, he traced back the family tree. And I reckon they must have been fishing here for years before that and using the horses, the sleds, slids, that's really ancient. Because you look at it, 'tis a comical contraption, isn't it? But he does what he's intended to do. The only thing we've changed — well, Father started it — is we used to always buy a coffin board to get the bottom, and it was like pushing a bloody timber carriage along. So he said, 'bugger this for a lark', so when timber was scarce in the War he used deal and then after we went onto piranha pine. You could bend it more, if you put your foot on the back of the plank and the front would rise up, you was sure you was going to run well. Mind, the slid has got to be made to suit the person pushing it. I mean, some people are longer from foot to knee, others from knee up. So we build them ourselves to suit ourselves, different heights and proportions.

The slids actually grind out. By the end of each season the boards grind out. And there's the wear and tear. So we have to make a sledge, a new slid, roughly each year. You wouldn't think it because you think the mud is soft. But there's a high degree of sand. If you rub the mud in your hand you'll feel the sand. It's gritty. It's like pushing the board out over sandpaper continuously every day. Whether it's elm from the old coffin boards or piranha pine, they still grind right down. But the piranha pine don't seem to snap off like the elm. We very often had one bust off by the bow, where the bow do come up on the front thurt piece, he'd bust off there. But very often the legs do rot off before the bottom has gone. And the bender, which is usually made of withy so he's got a bit of give, flexible, takes all the strain so if that goes when you're out you've a devil of a job to come back in. A hell of a job if you broke one when you was out fishin'. The old fishermen years ago used to have an elm stake and split'n down the middle and that was their limmers like that, all made of elm but I favoured elm below and deals or whatever on the top. When I gave up I was still fishing full time. I just had to stop from one day to the next.

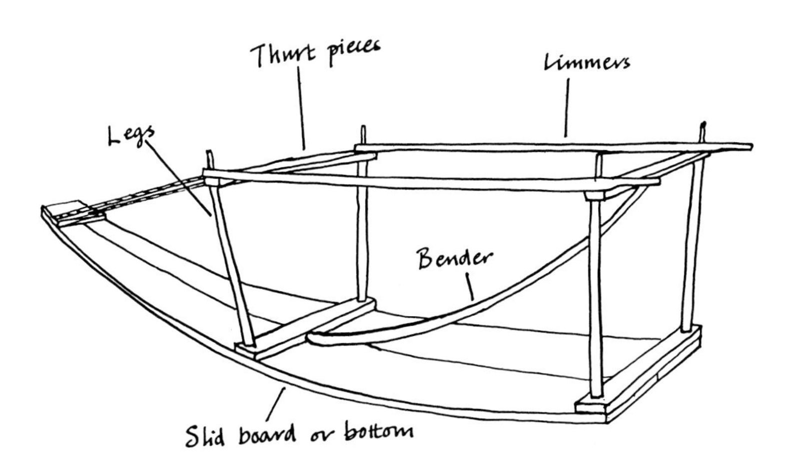

Eirwen: It had been worrying me for a long time. So I said to the doctor that when Tone goes down that path to go fishing, day and night I said, I never know if he's going to come back up the path. Because if he goes down out in the mud and before I know it he's in difficulty, it will be too late to get the helicopters out. And, I said, if he goes up under the rocks where he goes with his fish nets and he goes down, no one will know, no one will find him in the dark. So the doc said 'Right, that's it, it's time you called it a day.' And he never went out after.

Tony: It took some adjusting. I was always hoping to get back. I'd made new nets, they're out back now, brand new never been to sea. The boy was due to leave school and I thought to myself, well, I'd just as well get all the gear ready, then I haven't got to worry about getting new gear in. But it's never been used. And David, my son, he's thirty now, he likes to take the tractor and go out up under the rocks where we got nets, but he won't push the sledge out. He suffers from asthma and dodgy hips. I remember one day he was out fishing with me and I gave him the bloody job to push back in and that was the end wasn't it?

Eirwen: Yes, his feet were turning when he was walking. He's got a little girl now, she's sixteen months old. They said she's all right but she sits exactly the same way, so we've told David to keep an eye on her.

Tony: So, anyway, that was just before he left school. It was a big net that was washed up, tangled up in my stakes part way out and I said to him, 'I'll put 'ee on your sled and you can push 'n in, into the beach.' And he hasn't bothered with it since. So, I'm disappointed if you know, because I'd like for somebody to carry it on, because I'm the last of the really traditional ones. Brendon Sellick, he do do it his way which isn't the same as my way. Basically we were the same, but to me there was a big difference. My equipment is different. Same as Grandfather's. Mind you he never encouraged the boys to go fishin'. Father went to the pits over in Wales. The money was three or four times what they was getting here. Then in the War, the 'Fourteen-'Eighteen War, he was a stoker on the *Temeraire*, then he went back to coal mining after, then in 'thirty-three he come back here and he had a struggle to get going but he never went back to the mines. I met my wife over there, in Wales, she's Welsh.

Eirwen: I'm from right up in the valleys, you can't go no further. I was visiting a friend and Tone came in and he gave me a lift home. He used to keep chickens, see, all the sheds we got out back used to have poultry, and he'd take them all ready dressed, all ready for Christmas all up into Wales. This was all for family and friends up there. There's a long connection. Anyway, I never thought no more of it. But I came home Monday after work, this was after Christmas and my mother said, 'There's a letter here on the mantelpiece for you.' It was from Bridgwater. I said, 'Who's that from?' She said, 'Well, how do I know?' Well, anyway, it was from him. My friend May told him that I wanted him to write to me, and she told me that he wanted me to write to him. She was one of those friends! And I've been down here forty years now! And our daughter and our son and grandchild are all round here, not far away.

Tony: Anyway, to get back to the fishing, it was definitely getting worse before I stopped. The only way I was able to keep going longer than I should was my being able to go up to Hinkley Point and to catch the mullet that was up there. But it was bloody hard going there. I had nets laid out along the rocks there by Hinkley Point with floats on, so as when the tide come in he do lift them up, and when the tide goes out they do come down again. Of course, this wasn't walking out with the sledge, this was with the tractor. This was secondary to the shrimp and that but it turned out quite good. Mind you, we was only getting ten pence a pound for it. And two shilling a pound for bass. That's a lovely fish, though, isn't it? The mullet and the bass used to come up much more on the morning tide, 'twas noticeable that there'd be more on the first tide than on the next, so I'd go up there first thing, very early. But everything has gone down. The power station accelerated the whole thing. And the fishing out at sea. But I could tell within two days when they were chlorinating the water over there. They did that to kill off the swan-necked barnacle that clogged up the intake and I could tell straight away. That would come back out into the sea. They never admitted it so that we could claim. We could have hit 'em for six. But they changed their pattern of chlorinating and did a lower rate from April to October. I could give them the dates. But they said we didn't keep enough detailed records and they never came and said they'd offer us anything. They never said, 'look, we know this is hard for you,' or anything and they're so big and us so small. There was only me and Brendon doin' it.

I mean, I used to have a forty, fifty-pound pecker basket hangin' round my neck and one single net's worth of shrimp would fill this basket. And just before I packed it in I was fishin' between ten and twenty nets to fill this basket. That's the difference. When I started first, that was about 'forty-six, going out with father, the shrimps was running over under line, what we call it, that was from the tail of the net right the way back through, they was resting all along the net. And I always say, and so I've been told, apparently there was no shrimps anywhere like ours. The taste, I mean. Whether it was the cooking, whether 'tis the feed they're on, I don't know. Oh, they're nice when they be hot! They'd all be fresh cooked, lined up in the baskets there by the door, and our daughter'd go and pinch handfuls.

Eirwen: Yes, and Tony's father'd shout at her and she'd run in! And we used to have a cat similar to the one we have now and you'd get the odd prawn or two in with the shrimp. Anyway, that crafty devil used to go along when the baskets was leaned up against the wall and he'd find a prawn and he'd hook the prawn out.

Tony: We didn't used to get a lot of prawns. Only, for some reason, when I was away in the RAF, then they'd get ten, fifteen, twenty pound a day. But we've hardly seen them since! I don't know why. Just the odd two or three. One or t'other of us'd eat 'n. Or maybe we'd have enough to put together a quarter pound for a special customer. We used to take most of our catch up to Weston or Burnham, some to Street or Bridgwater. All the local fishmongers. We'd deliver, we'd take 'n. Only if they was goin' up to Weston, they'd go up by train, if they was goin' to Burnham they'd go on the Western National and, of course, we'd deliver the town shrimps, Bridgwater that is. There's not even a single fishmonger in Bridgwater now. There's one in Taunton, I think. We'd send the mullet up to Billingsgate on the train, but that got to a state where the carriage cost more than what the catch was worth. And then, I don't know how it come about, someone said get in contact with Lawrence and Ray from Brixham and they do deliver to London. So I'd catch it today and by tomorrow morning it'd be in Billingsgate. We'd pick up their lorry on the motorway. We'd drive it up to the motorway and meet them on the motorway. We'd phone them up the day before and say we'd something for them and they'd be there waiting for us. They were very good. They'd take everything. You'd send anything to London but not our shrimps, funnily. They didn't sell there. We'd keep them for round here. I've seen the shrimp they had up there though, on the slabs up there, and 'twasn't very nice to my way of thinking. I'd chuck the bloody lot out if they was mine! Not good enough, the colouring of them and the salt was bloody brine!

I'd always boil them in fresh water with so much salt, all measured out. There was six of us cooking shrimp here at one time and all tasted different! I didn't ought to say it but mine was the best! You got to put a proper amount of salt in, not just sprinkle it and you must boil 'em quick and hard. Not just sam-soaking them, what we call it. Cooking them up slow. I always used coal to get a good heat, some fierce heat, but others'd use logs and paper and anything as long as it'd boil eventually. But you need to get 'em in quick and out quick. When the furnace was goin' well, I've put a lot of shrimps in, stirred 'em up, gone and got another boiling, washed they off and put 'em ready and the lot that I'd put in first was ready to come out. That quick. All done in the old copper with the coal fire underneath. I never changed that. Never used electric like others, that's still too slow, that's still sam-soaking, cooking too long, overcooking and cooking too many at a time. When you wanted to do them for peeling, when you wanted to sell peeled shrimp, they was cooked a bit longer, and more at a time to make them a bit easier for pulling. They were easier then. We'd never peel all of them but we'd always do some.

Eirwen: We'd finish peeling at ten o'clock at night. He wouldn't peel no shrimps after ten o'clock. Once we'd had our evening meal we'd have a big pile on the table and we'd set to and peel. If we had only a few we might finish them off but we wouldn't have no big lots after ten.

Tony: And I didn't get in till late in the summer. I know you was sat down doin' it but after you'd been out fishing and then you'd have your meal and sit down in the warm, sometimes it was a job to keep awake. Then in the morning we'd take them into Bridgwater.

Eirwen: When I started to drive and we got our own car, I used to deliver the shrimps. I'd go round on the Tuesday, Thursday, Friday all around everywhere, Stockland, Steart, Cannington, Stogursey and they'd buy out of the car. I'd take the scales and we knew what people would want and we'd pack it up here for them all ready. And we'd sell to the fish-man that'd deliver all round about, he had shrimp off of us. Mr Powell, V.T. Powell. Now you don't get anyone coming round anymore. Only the milkman every other day. And the postman.

Tony: But I don't consider you'd make enough here now to support a family by fishing. Not full time if you didn't do anything else, had no other source of income. And it used to support six families when I started fishing. Then I had one long line of reaps, baskets, stood outside from the fish-house door to the front door, full of shrimps drying off and then possibly more baskets on top. By the time I was finished I had five baskets if I was lucky. There's just not enough out there anymore to make it worthwhile and it's hard work. I'd go out on the fish nets twice a day and shrimp nets once a day, by the time I was finished. Twice up here over the rocks and once out over the mud. I couldn't keep that up. When I was younger I was doing the shrimp nets twice a day, too. Mind you, over the rocks I'd partly have to go out because of the foxes. They'd go and chew the heads off of the fish and make them unsaleable, although they was better for it. They'd bleed and the flesh would be whiter, because a mullet is a grey colour fish. And the foxes'd only take the head. They got used to it and tried to beat me to it! Our daughter and her husband do it from time to time, they love it, they don't go out with the sled but they go over the rocks. But they put the nets out the other day and weren't quick enough and the fox did get their lunch!

We've been up the House of Commons about the fishing. Our MP was Vernon Bartlett back along, and when we was stopped by the Air Ministry, I don't know the ins and outs of it, but I know it went to the House of Commons, we won our fishing back. We had bombing ranges down here, air to ground down here and out in the sea we had bombing targets. They was worried about hitting us! So we were stopped for eighteen months. Then we got it back. They were still bombing out there, mind! But it was far enough out. They stopped after the War. But Friday 15 October 1948, between eleven and one, I'll never forget it, cannon shells all round me, some bugger using me for target practice when I was out over the mud. Couldn't resist it. Gave me the fright of my life. We don't know who done it, but we did partially hear 'twas a Polish pilot but we don't really know. The harbour master used to have the same trouble, they was always having pot shots at the buoys. Having fun!

We used to be licensed to fish from Lillstock Harbour right the way round to Combwitch Pill but now they've got the nature reserve and we be curtailed to the Stogursey parish boundary, roughly from Lillstock Harbour to old Steart Common gate. It hasn't really made much difference, though the nature conservancy did give us the right to shoot seagulls, to get them off the nets. I often took the gun out with me but they was bloody crafty, they seemed to know when 'ee was on the slid. When you went out without the gun they'd be there but when you went out with the gun they'd be disappeared! That hasn't happened once but dozens and dozens of times. They got to know when the gun was on the slid. As soon as the water'd go down they'd be out there. You had to time it to get out there quick enough. The timing was roughly two hours to low water, or leave the beach when the top line was showing, the top of the nets. But then we could be fishing the nets in near and the nets out there'd be white. White with gulls. The dog was handy then, occasionally! But you had to watch her and you didn't have time for nothing, you was lucky with the shrimps if you had time to change your clothes if you was soaking wet. You had to get 'em in and cook 'em straight away. Specially in the summer.

But I never took much notice of the weather or how cold it was, even in winter. I've been goin' out there year after year naked-legged, with short trousers, when the water's been freezing on my legs and I never noticed when I was pushin' the slid. If I wasn't pushing it, I used to wear a long raincoat over my shorts to keep the wind off. But its funny you know, people say how hard it was and I never minded. I'd love to be out there now.

Brendon Sellick, Mud Horseman, Stolford, 2005

'You could say it's a hell of a place for a nursery, the Bristol Channel and Bridgwater Bay, a real big nursery for all the adult fish that do come up and spawn and then they lie up in the mud pools when they're babes.'

Although Chris Willoughby had photographed him, I had not interviewed Brendon Sellick before. So just before Christmas 2005, I went to buy some shrimp and talked to him as we sat in his little fish shop in Stolford.

Usually we are fishing over Christmas but this year, because it's neap tides and the tides have dropped out there — and once it goes down below a certain level we can't get to the nets — we've had to stop. So we pulled the nets up yesterday and it's worked out just right. We'll have a few days off, five or six days off and then we'll start again. The first time it shoots off we'll go again. On the spring tides we're fishing for eight or nine days then it drops down and we get two or three days' neap tides which we can't get out on, the tide doesn't go back far enough to let us get to the nets. So that's how it goes all year round. The last few years we've worked over Christmas, the tides have been that we've had to go fishing but this year we've got a bit of a break.

I've not been going out myself the last couple of months. Whether I will go out again or not I don't know. I'm over seventy, see, and it is hard work.

Brendon Sellick, with Hinkley Point Atomic Power Station in the background.

I've done it up till now and I could still do it but the boy's still doing it, Adrian and the son-in-law Keiran, he does it, too, using the sledge in the summer time and that. Of course, he's working and he does it in and out, like. And Adrian does it when he can as well.

I reckon there's not so much of a change in the fish stocks now as what there was forty years back when the power station was built. That's made a great difference. By continuously working, it definitely has diluted the stocks of shrimps. Whereas we'd catch two hundredweight of shrimps in the peak, you'd be lucky to catch forty pounds now in a day's fishing in the season, from April to Christmas. But now the shrimp population has gone down steadily, it's been diluted. We aren't getting other fish like we had

Brendon Sellick checking a net.

previous years, too. The cod this year has been very poor and last year wasn't good. It looks like we're down in a dip. That's pretty general round the country. We aren't getting the cod like we had in previous years. Nothing like. If you go back ten year ago it was not so bad, but I don't reckon that's to do with the power station because they come in from the Atlantic, the cod, and they've been diluted by the big trawlers, out in the approaches where all the big trawlers are to. But here the shrimp population's been killed off by the power station because of the continuous flow of the water. They wouldn't say, of course. But the old shrimp's going up and down in the Channel maybe a dozen times, like a rabbit in a field. You got someone with a gun there, eventually he's going to get shot. And that's how I feel it is with the shrimp. They're goin' up and down, up and down. You'll never destroy the whole population but maybe three-quarters'll go over the years. On account of the water that's going through the systems, the huge intake for the power station. I don't know exactly and I don't know if it's quite right or not, but I been told that the volume of the Bristol Channel and Bridgwater Bay water goes through the power station once every four years. That's the volume of water! And every drop of water that goes through with a living thing in it, if you was waiting outside for it two minutes, it would come out dead. It wouldn't survive. It's the heat.

We get the Ministry of Fisheries here three or four times a year, they was here only this week. They check out all what we catch and they take it away for testing, of course. Ever since the nuclear power station was built at Hinkley forty years ago, they've been testing the fish we catch. You know, we've been selling it up to London or Cornwall or whatever and if there was anything detrimental in the fish they'd stop it. That's the Ministry of Agriculture and Fisheries at Lowestoft. Then there's the independent people at Taunton, the Environment Agency, they come out, exactly the same procedure and then Hinkley Point Nuclear that have got laboratories at Combwitch, they'm doing even further tests. So there's three different lots checking the fish. And over the forty years I've often asked some of them but they've all said, 'No, we can't find nothing.' So it's good for us and the fish and it's good that they're doing these tests all the time to make sure.

You could say it's a hell of a place for a nursery, the Bristol Channel and Bridgwater Bay, a real big nursery for all the adult fish that do come up and spawn and then they lie up in the mud pools when they're babes. Even little Dover soles in the spring, you get thousands of them, little baby ones, you can hardly see them and then you see them grow over a matter of weeks. Over a seven- or eight-week period you can see them grow as big as a postage stamp. And then when they get twice as big as that they disappear, they go back. And in the spring they do bide up in all these mud-pools, in these thousands of acres of mud pools, when the tide's out and the sun's playing on the mud and it's really nice for 'em, like a heated pool, the temperature must be just right. I suppose that's evolution like, they've been doing it for centuries and the shrimps the same.

But somehow the other fish have coped better than the shrimp. I suppose the shrimp do stay more in the same place, they live here all their lives, they don't go away. They just come up and down. Whereas the cod and the whiting, the sprats, the plaice, the Dover sole, they might only stay in the estuary a couple of months and then they're gone. But the shrimp, I think, lives here and that's his environment, up and down, up and down. You very often hear from the people that do work up there at the power station that there is often a basket of little flat fish, little mullet and soles, in the intakes. You'd have thought with all the money up there they could have someone who'd sling 'em back over the wall, or even put in a drain to take them back to sea. Because they die there otherwise and sometimes there is an awful lot of them. You'd have thought they'd send someone down to talk to us.

We, as a one-man-band type of thing, can make something out of it still. It wouldn't have worked like it was when I was a boy and there were four or five families doing the fishing, dependent on it. Before that there was seven or eight families. That couldn't exist today. But being as we're just here on our own and you get a good price for the fish now, we can hang on. Whereas when I was a lad you only had pennies for it, literally pennies. And if you had a good catch you had to go all round the markets selling them in the villages. Now you don't have to catch very much fish to make your wages. So there is still a living here if you're willing and capable. So hopefully my son will keep it going and maybe he'll give up his job slowly and phase in as I phase out. Once you've had a job, mind, and a good salary or wage, the fishing, like a lot of farming, is hit and miss. You might have a good three weeks and then have three weeks that are very poor and you'll say, 'Oh, bloody hell! This ain't no good!' But you have to stick with it.

And now we've got the little shop here selling fish. We've had that four or five years now and it's quite good. Before that we were in Mud Horse Cottage. The council gave us permission to convert that old fish-house into a home and me and the wife do live there. So we are selling mostly from here now and people come to us. Though we do still take stuff in and that. If we do have a nice little catch of bass or sole or whatever and the shrimp, of course, and there's somebody up Bristol or Bath or there's customers all round that do ring up, then I say, 'Yeah, I can give you a nice few fish.' They come and pick it up.

But for twenty years I went into Weston two or three times a week. We always done it years ago. There was twelve shops up there then, now I don't think there's one. There used to be four or five in Bridgwater. Now there's just the supermarkets. We'd sell a lot of shrimp and stuff up Weston, especially in the holidays. Eels, shrimps that kind of stuff. We still catch a nice lot of eels in the nets and there's a good trade in them. When I used to catch 'em, we used to throw 'em back. You couldn't sell them. You let 'em go. Now an eel is worth two or three quid, each, a nice eel. That's my favourite, eel. I eat a lot of eel. If you can catch 'em you can sell 'em. As many as you can catch. I've had orders now but I've had to say, 'Sorry, they'm gone, that's it till April.' We were catching until last week but we've stopped now. That frost come in and that's it, they'm gone wherever they'm going. It's a good job they got somewhere to go, that some can get away with so many trying to catch 'em. The elverers in the rivers, up the Parrett, they've devastated them. The price they get for elvers now is ridiculous. In the peak of the season, some years back, a couple of blokes could pick out two hundred kilos of a night. I've heard 'em say that you could sit on the banks of the river and see nothing but a black cloud of elvers as far as the eye could see. Some years ago now, mind. It used to be ten shillings a pound they'd give then, fifty pence a pound. Now it's £500 or something stupid. A hundred quid a kilo, anyway, easy.
What do they give for them when they get them out to Japan or wherever, for God's sake?

Why we're flogging them out that way, I don't know. With the elverers catching all the elvers, the stock's been going down, diluted. You can't have five hundred people sat out on the banks of the river catching everything year after year. The adults that do survive and grow, there's people like me trying to catch them on their way back! It all adds up to diluting the stocks. Especially the great big silver eels we used to get. If he can get back to the Sargasso or what have you, he can produce, you know, whatever it is, thousands and thousands of babies. But on a thundery night in eel traps, up Bristol and all different places, they can catch hundreds, a ton of eels coming down, make hundreds of pounds in a night.

We sell 'em alive. As many as we can get. A lot go to be smoked. I've sold them to a fellow in Gloucester and there's Brown and Forrest, the smokery down here. I've sold a fair few to him over the years. But shrimp is still the main thing. People get to know us from a long way off and they like their fresh shrimp. We do catch a lot of mullet, a hell of a lot of mullet. We had a hundredweight a few days ago. People keep asking for it. We've had a ton of sprats, lovely sprats, the last few weeks and we've managed to sell them but they're not so popular. It's the young people don't know what to do with them anymore.

I've done this fishing since I left school at fourteen and now I'm seventy-two, non-stop winter and summer. I think I've been extremely lucky, it must have strengthened my body, going out there till I'm blue. Sometimes, especially when I was young, I'd think to myself, 'Cor, I don't have to do this for a living, surely?' I'd be blue. But I think it has strengthened me up. I went out for a sheep that'd got stuck in a ditch the other day. I went to pull it out. He'd been there for hours with just his nose sticking out. I took a rope to lasso him and I had a bad leg and anyway, I slipped and went bang, right in under the water. And my daughter was with me and she was crying and couldn't get me out and I had a job, it was so deep there. Anyway, I got out and I didn't think too much on it at the time but, looking back, I could easily have blacked out at my age. I could have had a heart attack. If it wasn't for the fact that I was pretty fit and used to being wet and cold, I might not have made that! That's how

Brendon Sellick undoes a net to retrieve his catch of shrimp.

easy it could have happened and I'd have been dead with the sheep. If you think about pushing the sled out over the mud, day after day over the years, well, it must have made me quite strong, pushing back two or three hundred pound on a good day. Then, of course, you might get days with nothing but broken nets. But I suppose, you know, there must be a terrible lot of people who'd love to be able to have the chance of doin' it. There's a hell of a lot to be said for it. But unless you was brought up to it you'd find it difficult, you need the knowledge. It's dangerous out there and it's far from easy. But when you do get the rewards, you know, you think, 'That's some good stuff.' It sort of bucks you up.

Bob Thorne, Salmon Fisherman, Stolford, 1980

'… I'm the last of the run. Me grandfather and me great-grandfather going back generations, they did it… The butts are in the same place

Bob Thorne with his salmon butts at Black Rock.

all the time. Mine's at Black Rock, see. There's three ranks: there's the Mud Rank, the Middle Rank, the Outside Rank...'

Bob Thorne lives in the hamlet of Stretcholt. He comes from a long line of fishermen, and a thriving fishing community, that once worked all around the Parrett estuary and the lower reaches of the River Parrett. He catches all sorts of fish and shrimp though salmon are his main concern. He takes them either from rows of traps called butts or putchers, or from a flatner, a flat-bottomed rowing-boat, with a dip-net. He knows the river and its ways like no other, remembering the days when considerable traffic went up and down: barges laden with bricks and tiles from the Bridgwater brickyards, steamers sailing across to Wales for coal, goods ferried in and out all around the British Isles and beyond. His life and work is by no means confined within the muddy banks of the Parrett but connects with the land about and with the wider world around.

I'm the last of the run. Me grandfather and me great-grandfather, going back generations, they did it and then there was the other family, of course they got intermarried and that, and I carried on. I was born into it. When I was a kid goin' to school I'd fish the butts and the shrimp nets and that, but the War, I was away for six year and then as soon as I come home I started off again.

Me father 'ee didn't do much to it, he couldn't you see, there was nine of us, but me uncles and me grandfer and that, I'd be off with they all the time, line fishing. I can remember when they had the two pecker baskets, they used to have a yoke in them days to carry them to bring the fish in and I used to sit up in one of the baskets and they used to carry me. They also had part-time jobs. Like old Bucky, as well as the fishing, 'ee used to work in the brickyard and Uncle Cecil, he used to do his fishing, a bit of hedging and ditching for the farmers, thistle cutting, do a bit of griping, you know. That's where you'd see a field and there were little gutters across the field every so far, to throw the water off. At the end of every summer the sheep and cattle'd pound them in and that, so's the grass'd grow over them. So, ready for the winter, come September, you'd get them out there gripin' the fields, clearing the gutters, though they didn't do it to all the fields, only they that'd lie wet. Say you had a twelve-acre field. Well, you'd have a ditch all the way round and some of they fields is so low, covered in water, so what they used to do is dig gripes right across the field, keep 'em dry.

I used to go down Channel and do a lot of fishing with the boats. Back in the fifties I had a seven-ton lifeboat I bought. I do a bit now, but I do it with a flatner now. I use a drift net, a couple hundred fathom of net. You can catch anything, bass, mullet, whiting, the odd cod or two. We start off with some shrimp nets, say up till the beginning of June. Well, then the shrimps do clear off then for spawning. Then, come the middle of September, you start shrimping again and then we used to have nets October for whiting and then November your sprats'd come in. The butts for the salmon do go in for the season. We used to start on the second of February but years ago they altered it so we start now the first of May. You go on till the thirty-first of August. Go out twice a day to check the butts, don't matter what the weather is, never miss, four hours after high water. Say 'twas high water at half past one at night then I do go out at half past five, work in the dark because if the tide do come in, the fish'll wash back out again.

Years ago like — there's the Brue or then there's Kennington Brook, and then there's Parchey River and then there's the Tone and then there's the Parrett — well see years ago all they rivers used to have gravel beds up through 'em and salmon used to go in all them places and spawn. There's just the odd salmon goin' up them places now. But the thing is they've altered it so much that they can't get up there the same. Years ago where everything was done by a man, you know, all the weed took off with the old staff hook, cut the weed, chuck it out, now they've got these bloody great machines. Well they do rip it all to hell, see, and through doin' that they destroy the gravel beds. You go up any of they places now you can't see no gravel beds. Bloody great deep holes, or otherwise 'tis all silted up, that's where 'tis to, see, machinery can't take the place of man, machinery do destroy it. Man he don't, when he do it be hand. That's the difference.

From Oath lock up, the Parrett is fresh water. Well they used to go up Oath lock and then branch off into the fresh water for spawning. The eels they do it opposite to a salmon. The eels do come in and grow but they go off, as far as we know, to the Sargasso Sea to spawn. Salmon's opposite. They go off to the sea to grow but come back to this place to spawn. But not so much today. I think most of the salmon today — because there's very little spawn up the Parrett now — I should say the majority is brought in by the tide, because on a spring tide this tide out here runs seven to nine knots. You don't get the big fish today like you used to do and nothing like the amount. Years ago, back in the fifties, you could catch anything up to 100, 120 fish in a season. But now last year 'twas the worst year I ever had in my life, nine salmon I 'ad all year, I didn't pay me expenses. The year before that I had about seventeen. You never get anything up to forty fish now. Now I do it more or less for a pastime. I'm in me sixties, where'd I get a job now?

The butts are in the same place all the time. Mine's at Black Rock see. There's three ranks: there's the Mud Butts, the Middle Rank and the Outside Rank. There's eighty butts in the Mud Rank, there's ninety-two butts in the Middle Rank, anything up to 250 butts on the Outside Rank. 'Tis where they've always been, this is the oldest type of fishing in the world. All these butts is put where the tide do run ashore, behind a point. The Black Rock is the point of the cove. The tide do come in behind there and shoot across the river to me butts. The point of the cove, that's the name of a point in the river. You see we've got names for the reaches and the points. Well I'm set to catch them on the ebb and most of the ebb tide comes round the cove and shoots across the river to Black Rock and then back straight on down. So these butts was put there in the first place to catch most of the tide, see. But you'm only allowed to fish one-third of the river, two-thirds got to be left open for fish to run through. My butts is only about one-fifth of the watercourse, I couldn't handle anymore on my own and in any case it wouldn't pay now to do it because the fish ain't about.

The stakes that hold the butts in position are elm, they soon grow up. An elm stake you want to chop 'n when 'ee's green. Rip the bark off and then stick'n out in the salt, when 'ees green. And then the salt water do trap all the sap. Soon as I see spring of the year, soon as I see the buds, just as green start to show on the elms, I go and cut the stakes, skin 'em, take 'em out and stick 'em in the river and that do trap the sap in 'em and for some reason that do make 'em just like 'lastic. You could bend him right round and 'ee wont snap, now there's no other tree'd do that. If you use anything else it'd just snap. Got to stick the friction of the water when it's moving through the butts, got to have something that'll stick that friction three times a day. You got to stake the butts 'cause there's thousands of tons of water out there. You stake each side of the butt. You put in your tail stake, slide your butt down over your tail stake and tie him at the tail and tie him at the mouth to each stake. Your stakes must be about three to four inches in the butt, that's for the front stakes, and two and a half to three inches in the tail stakes. The butt can only be about six inches in diameter. He's got to be small enough so that when the stake is up through 'n, the salmon can't force his way out through the tail.

You make a shackle to start a butt, 'tis just a withy wove round in a ring. You've got your full-length ribs, then you got your three-quarter ribs, your half ribs and your short ribs. I do cut the full-length rib six foot. You do put on your first two bands then you add in two three-quarter ribs, then put on your third band and then you add in two half ribs and then you put on your fourth band and you add in seven short ribs. Well, then you put your head-band on. Then your butt is going from six inches up to twenty-eight, thirty inches in the mouth.

They used to make three sorts of butts, what we used to call the half butt, the three-quarter butt and the five-ring butt. Years ago, when there was a lot of sand dabs about and there was a good sale for them — there's no sale for 'em now — years ago everybody wanted sand dabs or what we call flooks, see. Well, instead of having the bands we used to put our first band where the shackle is, then we used to have a continuous coil round the butt up to the third band, which is the centre of the butt, then right up to the fourth band which was the three-quarter butt, see. That was so that you did catch all the flooks. Now all the flooks just slide out o' they butts. I did have a conger wedged in some years ago, 'ee was ninety-six pound. There's a better market now for the salmon than there was in those days because the fish ain't about. I can remember when I were a kid goin' to school, me uncle used to pay the rent on this house with one salmon a year. That's 12s 6d.

I've thought it out and I've seen it dwindle over the years and thinking about it, you get all these people blaming pollution and they'm not breeding them the same and that, but if anything there's more salmon bred today than there was in the old days, today they do breed millions in these salmon stations. But the trouble is some years ago, off the Icelandic coast, they found out where the salmon do go and live till they ready to come home to spawn. Well, someone found out, only by accident, that all the fish that the Eskimos were stashing away for the winter was salmon. So now there's two big canning fact'ries set up there and fact'ry ships there. Certain times of the year they're catching anything up to a thousand tons of salmon a week, and none of they countries got salmon of their own, they don't breed 'em. Therefore there's like we and Norway, the two biggest breeders, can't stop they and there's we breeding them and they over there catching a thousand ton. Well, the salmon don't live to come back. All your different people blame pollution but there's only one thing that's doin' it, that's over-fishing. This fishing off the Icelandic coast been goin' on for twenty-odd year, I seen my catches dwindle after a couple of year but then they steadied. Then they brought in all the monofilm nets, that's bloody transparent! They'm as strong as steel and you got these trawlers working in pairs off the Irish coast — why they ain't stopped it I don't know and some of they'll have eight mile of net between 'em just drifting there. They'm catching thousands and thousands of salmon, all round our coasts, thousands. Yet there's me, I'm licensed up to the hilt, for every fifty butts I put in I pay £29.50. I'm only netting one-fifth of the water across the river and yet they buggers can go out there with these trawlers and stick down miles of net and just drift away night and day and swaff it in. Now where's the sense? And yet all your authorities is grumbling about how the fish is dwindling.

The people that you got in power today ain't got the bloody guts to do their job. The salmon do come off the Icelandic coast and they hit the north of Ireland, well then they do split up and you get lots of salmon do come down the Irish sea, parts of it is only sixty mile wide, 'tis only a bloody ditch today. You can see the trawlers from the shore. All the salmon are making for their breeding grounds and the thing is they'm not coming scattered like a field of bloody turnips sort of business, they come in shoals, they'm all in bands. When they got them scanners going and they pick up a shoal of fish, 'taint one or two salmon, 'tis thousands. They just go ahead of them, run their nets out and the salmon come on. Bloody ridiculous. They'm out in what they call territorial waters, they don't even have to have a licence to do it. All they got is their trawling licence. I've got to have a special licence 'cause it's a game fish. There's no quota whatever. That's why, I reckon, the salmon's died out like they have. You can't do no inshore fishing without a licence, yet soon as you get out off, you can massacre 'em. That's been goin' on years.

There's always been farming and fishing here and brickyards, like years ago there was brickyards, 'cause of the clay, the blue clay. Some of the best clay in the world here in Somerset, 'tis more or less a clay bed you see. There used to be quite a few used to do boats, there's a lot of that now, and many of them's poachers. The trouble is all your magistrates. It's laid down that a man can be fined anything up to £400 for poaching salmon, they rose it now to £1,000. But you go in court and they'll fine you £15, £30 pounds if you'm unlucky. You've only got to catch one 15 lb fish and there's your fine. They'll go out poaching today, get caught tomorrow and next night they'll go out poaching again. Nowadays, especially with all the unemployed, poaching's a thing. They'm out wandering the banks in the dark with torches. There's bailiffs but they don't get about much. I could put a stop to it but it's just one of they things. I'm on the Fishery Board, I'm the representative, for the putcher and dip-net fishermen. There was illegal fishing going on at Brean Down a couple of years ago. Well, I put a stop to

Bob Thone at his salmon butts, walking out towards the Outside Rank.

that, they got fined several thousand pound but they had nearly 2,000 fathom of net. Just for the local odd ones, I think to myself, well, they take the odd fish. If I was to really go to town on it I'd be the most hated bloke in the area. If they was doin' it with nets I'd go for them. Sometimes you get the odd one and then I just go and see them personally. But if they go out with a stick, knock one down, then you know... Say there was ten salmon in the river and you was walking the banks you'd be more likely to catch one than I would in the butts. The dirty water do make them come up. I do see them. They say, 'Hello.' And I say, 'Hello, my son, you missed ee, dinée.' They say 'Huzzah!' 'Tis country life. You don't nail your countryman for the sake of one fish. They'm not a threat.

'Tis a bloody desert here now. They ripped out all the hedges all the trees is gone. All these fields down the road here was all cider orchards, they'm gone. There used to be two covers here, they'm gone. All you see round here now is bloody plough-fields, corn and that. 'Twas all small fields round here when I was a kid, the biggest field down here on the flat was about sixteen acres, that was a hell of a big field, the majority of 'em was two acres to ten. Fields here now is forty, fifty acres a field. The ditches is gone, 'tis ridiculous. What changed your farmers was your politicians and your scientists, they started bringing out this big machinery, they started wanting all this corn and that. It started with the last War and t'ain't ever stopped since. Every time a field gets bigger you've got to get rid of a ditch, you've got to get rid of a hedge, you've got to get rid of the trees and that's how it goes on. They all still got dairy but years ago a farmer had thirty cows, a biggish herd. He'd need a 150 acres, he'd have a few sheep and horses. In they days a farmer'd grow everything for his cows on that 150 acres: his hay, his roots, everything. On that same 150 acres today they'll have seventy, eighty cows and have sixty, seventy of they acres into corn as well. That's the trouble.

Before the War there wasn't anybody I didn't know in the village. Everybody knew everybody. Now, today, I suppose all I know in the village is the ones my age. The village is five times as big and 99 per cent of they is outsiders. I couldn't say if that was a bad thing or a good thing but I don't know 'em, I don't mix with them. There's a village community. I suppose 'tis a good thing in one way that it mixes people. But in the other sense…

When I was a kid there was all one community. We was all share and share and the men used to go off together and we used to go off with our fathers rabitting and that. In they days you couldn't afford a joint of meat, you'd go off rabitting or bird batting, catching birds, see, to make a pie. You had a net on two poles, and we used to have a lantern with a candle in it strapped round the waist, and one would walk along with the net one side of the hedge and someone'd be the other side of the hedge with a pole, and beat. Well the birds'd fly out of the hedge toward the light and you'd catch 'em in the net. 'Twas blackbirds, thrushes, home-screetches, pigeons, moorhens, odd pheasant. Then you used to come home see and pluck 'em and make a pie. It used to be bloody beautiful. We used to do a bit of reballing, catch a few eels just for the fun of it, because with the fishing we could always put down an eel butt or two and catch our eels. Some places, round Stathe, Athelney, they call it clatting, we used to call it reballing. Thread up a bunch of worms on some strong wool and then string 'em round your three fingers, tie 'em in a bunch and put 'em on the end of a stick plied round or else a piece of stick with a piece of string hanging down with a lead weight on the end. Then you go out where you know there was an eel and just touch the bottom with the worms and just lift, make sure your worms weren't too high off the bottom. We generally used to go out when 'twas getting dumpsy-dark, night-time, when the eels start moving. Sometimes we used to go out and catch thirty, forty pound of eels. Another time we'd only catch one, just the luck of the game. And sometimes we sat out till midnight at it. If you've got a plate with some salt on just dap your hand in and you can catch hold of the eels to skin 'em. You wouldn't wait for them to die, that were a slimy messy job when they'm dead.

The rabbits we'd get with ferrets or a gun, but you didn't do much shooting 'cause you couldn't afford the cartridges, see. They was two shillings a box. Well, two shillings! The old man used to bring home 18s 6d from the brickyard, so two shillings for a box of cartridges was a lot of money. When I left school I was thirteen and a half. I was bringing home 6s 3d a week, my first job. In British Cellophane in Bridgwater. They'd just opened up in 1936 and one of the managers there was trying to get some boys for the factory and he said to Mother about he had a good job for young Bob. Work then were scarce and so I went in but I wanted to go straight on the fishing with me uncle. The headmaster said, 'Yeah, 'ees all right up on he's education, he can leave.' So I went in early to work. There was six of us. We was put in the pulp room. This pulp was all sheets like cardboard, you had to gauge them. Twenty-two bales a day and eleven on Saturday. So after a fortnight I came home and told the old man 'twas bloody slavery over there. He says, 'Up to you, my son, I ain't goin' to interfere. You got to make your own life. You know work's scarce but you can always go on the fishing. I ain't getting tangled up with your mother,' he says, 'you sort it out for yourself.' So I done another week. 'Course, I never been used to being penned in a bloody great shed six days a week. The manager said, 'There's a job goin' in the caves, I could pay you more money there.' So they put me in the caves. That's where they did ripen all the pulp, came out like a lot of fluffy cotton wool. Then they do mix it with different chemicals and 'twas just like tomato sauce. The caves was just a building, no windows, the temperature was about eighty-six degrees. All this was put in bloody great tanks to ripen before they could make cellophane and every time they did empty a tank it did leave a thin film of like red rubber inside this tank and you had to dress up in a rubber suit with a mask on and breathing apparatus to scrape it all off. That was the job he give me. He give me 9s 3d. There was men there doing exactly the same job I was doin' getting six pounds a week, a hell of a lot of money. I stopped there exactly a fortnight and said, 'I ain't doing that, I want my cards.' He say'd, 'You can't do that.' So I stopped there another fortnight, just sat on my arse and that was the longest fortnight in me life. 'Twas two life times. Friday night he give me my cards and that was it, I went on the fishing.

A few years later I was off in the War. 'Twas April 'forty-one and they was getting together for the invasion of France. I went across on D six and got hurt bad, I lost an eye, I ended up then in the Field Ambulance. I was a volunteer, and the only reason I volunteered was three of my uncles was in the First World War and they did have a go at me, see, I oughtn't to let the family down, I had to fight in this one. I was only seventeen. As soon as I was eighteen they sent for me. After that, one morning we was put on this bloody ship. They started giving us this camouflage kit all in light denim. We knew then we was after the Japs. They loaded 8,000 of us on the *Georgic* for Ceylon. She was the sister ship to the *Mauretania*. She was several days behind us with the second wave, see. They was 35,000 tonners. Well, we was going through the Red Sea. I always mind it. 'Twas a beautiful day, like a mill pond that mornin', beautiful, and all of a sudden the tannoy's started and they said the Americans have dropped an atom bomb on Japan. Well, we didn't know what an atom bomb was. So now we'd be goin' to Bombay. And then later they said how they dropped another and the Japs'd chucked it in.

Then I ended up in Malaya as the Rodent Officer! Everything went wild there, 'twas overrun with wild dogs and rats. When I went there first I was refuelling ships. Then they said they wanted a volunteer for Rodent Officer so 'course all the lads said, 'He, sir. He's the one for that.' 'Cause they knew I was a bloody moocher back in civvy, see. So he just said, 'You!' and I was volunteered. They give me six Jap prisoners and two Indian lads, a jeep, a three-ton Dodge lorry and we just travelled from Singapore to Kuala Lumpur shooting dogs and taking them to the nearest 'cinerator. People were being bit by rats and dogs everywhere. And the dogs'd go around in gangs, thirty or forty dogs. Well, old Lieutenant Colonel Wheatley let me 'ave his sixteen bore shot-gun — cor, beautiful gun, Damascus barrels, lovely gun 'twas — and he said, 'You look after 'ee, boy, I think more of 'ee than I do of me wife!' You could knock a dog down stone dead fifty yards away. They wouldn't allow you to use a rifle 'cause of civilians about, all out here working in the rubber plantations and pineapple plantations. Working with the Japs was all right but you never had to tell 'em to do anything silly. They should have give us all training. Well, we used to all joke but you can't joke with a Jap. I don't know about today but in they days they was trained in this stupid religion and that. If I'd have told one of they, 'Go out there and knife yourself.' 'Ee'd go out there and knife heself. That was how they was. When we was goin' in these villages these chaps would walk behind I like little miniature sentries. I was sort of their idol, just how they was trained.

It was a holiday to me. We'd lived rough all our lives. We hadn't starved or nothing but we'd lived rough. We had a good home, good parents, but we had a really rough, hard life. When I went in the Army there was just a bit of training, bugger all to do, and as regards guns I was brought up with guns and was a better shot than all they was. 'Twern't very often I'd miss a rabbit or a bird. Life was easy and simple in the Army, everything done for you, just obey orders. A cissy's life. The only part that was different was when we went across to France. 'Twas just like the fifth of November, sky was covered in different coloured tracers. 'Twas pretty to watch. Yet as soon as your foot touched that soil your heart started beating! That was different. That was one time when I was... when 'tweren't no holiday. When you walked in up that sandy beach 'twas different altogether. You couldn't go back, you could only go in.

I come home 26 July 1947. Nothing had changed, only me. I found out I couldn't control myself in home life. I was like a wild animal compared to home life. Home life was like a jumbled up heap of rubbish to me. I used to walk out of the house and sit under the elm trees. There was one, there was a gurt knot on her, where we used to sit as kids — used to go out there and sit down. It took me a long time. The family realised, and then we gradually got back in together.

There's no place like this country. The thing is, see, you can't tell no one. That's the trouble with this world. If people could only know through talk, or experience what things is like through somebody telling 'em, 'twould be a lot easier. You don't experience a thing, 'tis impossible to know it. Now, very often, I do think back. I used to be a bit of a wild bugger when I were young. Things that my father used to say, I used to go, 'Bloody old fool.' But very often now I do find myself telling youngsters exactly the same as what my father used to tell me and after they'm gone I do very often have a grin to myself, I think, 'Yes! They'm out there saying "bloody old fool."' Generations don't change.

Nephews do come on holidays and they do come out wi' me an' that but I'll not encourage them, there's no life for 'em, there's no life for 'em. 'Twould be impossible for them to do it today. There ain't a living in it. I don't even attempt to get one of them to make a butt or something, or knit a net, for their sake. 'Tis just as well to bloody die out. You won't get a government that's got the guts to stop what's goin' on out at sea, therefore the fishing can only get worse. I've seen it dwindle. 'Tis better to be forgotten, what few fish you would catch, let 'em live on. For the last fifty-odd years I been doin' nothin' but fishing, therefore that's my life. You just think of old things that 'av died out, that modern technology has killed. There's just a handful in isolated places like this, because everything done in the modern way today, 'tis bound to get worse. They'm talking now about the destruction of our surroundings! Already gone too far, progress can't go backwards. They'll make odd attempts in a few places, put a few trees in, but the destruction around will go on faster.

'Tis a good thing some of the things 'ave gone. Just imagine bird-batting today, 'twould be illegal today, you just imagine it with the few birds that survive. But in they days the birds was as thick as the leaves on the trees and it was a way of living, surviving, 'twas nature. We 'ad all that food around us, we didn't kill for the sake of it. I wouldn't dream of killing anything I didn't need to eat. Yet today they'm so frustrated, the youngsters, it do make your blood curdle what they do get up to, but you only got your bloody elders to blame for it, not the kids. The kids is just the same as what we were. Mother was a school teacher, see. There was nine of us brothers and sisters, used to get up to bloody all sorts. I had an air gun, pinching apples, swabbing out the orchard. I'd see a garden with a lovely lot of cauliflowers, wait till it was dark, down the road and take 'ee home! 'Old Mrs so-and-so did give me this Mum, to take home to you.' If it was anything very serious Father used to put a stick across our arse, the old man. He only ever hit me twice in me life, gave me a real bloody good hiding and that was once when I nearly killed old Arbie lived next door. With my air gun. The second good hiding I had was for shooting young Dick Gifford wi' bow and arrow. We was playing cowboys and Indians. We didn't see no danger. We used to make arrows wi 'tin heads on, you know from the old cocoa tins, for shooting pigeons and moorhens. I see that now, the arrow goin' up and down in the cheek of his arse.

Bob Thorne, Stretcholt, 2006

Bob Thorne seemed hardly to have grown older. Vigorous as ever at eighty-one, with the same fierce independence, he was sawing wood in his yard and seemed to have stacked enough to supply the entire village.

But, like Tony Brewer, he had retired from his fishing with deep regret. He had, however, forgotten nothing.

I used to go to sea with Uncle Charlie when I were a boy. In the old *Sunshine*. He kept it in Bridgwater Docks. 'Course there was eighty, ninety boats there then, ketches, schooners, the bloody lot. Anyway, we'd go all over. Go over to Cork, in Ireland, with loads of nails — that'd take three days, there and back — then over to Barry in Wales fer the coal, all sorts. The last trip I done was in 1935. We'd gone down to Appledore in Devon with a load of tiles from Bridgwater and we were coming out of Appledore to go to Newport for a load of flour. When we came out it was blowin' westerly and we was comin' back past Ilfracombe when the wind swung round and started blowing a bloody gale, dead in our face. We was running with the tide and bloody waves were comin' over the side. We only had three crew and we battened down everything that was movable and Uncle Charlie said, 'You better go down under, young Bob.' But I said, 'I want to stop up here.' So he said, 'If I lose you, I'll never be able to speak to yer mother.' So they tied I to the mast! I always mind that! The bloody waves was comin' over and the spray was drownin' I. When I came home they knew we'd hit some rough weather and me Aunt Mary let me down! She were nearly twenty year old and I was still at school, I was about twelve. 'Course I told her and she let on. Then Mother made me tell her. Next thing I know, Uncle Charlie came down and he were going to Barry — they were short of coal in Bridgwater — and he come down to see if I wanted to come along. And Mother said, 'He ain't goin' no more! You ain't drownin' my boy! I've heard all about it.' And I never went out again. Of course, 'tweren't much more'n a year later that I went to work.

They buried Uncle Charlie at sea. He had a heart attack and died one day goin' over to Ireland and they buried him in the Irish Sea on the way back to Bridgwater. By then they'd done away with the barges 'n that and they had the steamboats, the *Crowpill*, the *Enid* and the *Parrett*. They were bigger, see and much faster. They'd carry nearly a hundred ton more and the *Crowpill* was a submarine chaser in the War. With one bloke shovelling coal on her flat out, she'd do about fourteen knots, with two blokes she'd do twenty. She'd go down the river and send in a wash like a destroyer! She was the only boat that could leave Bridgwater, against the tide, go out across to Barry, load up with coal and back down tail of the Gore, ready for the next tide in. So from the morning tide till the evening tide she'd be out, loaded up and back.

There were nine of us brothers and sisters. My mum died in 1942 of appendicitis and my dad in 1956 from his accident. He was fifty-six then, same as the century. Round here, still living now, is me and Thelma, Tony, our younger one, he was working at the Go Corner pumping station for the last thirty-odd years, in charge of that, he's in the bungalow there now. Then there's Edward, one of the twins, in Bridgwater; there's Laura, she lives over Woolavington, Gaffer, he lives in Bridgwater. Then our John, 'ee used to live here but now 'ee's retired, he moved to France! He's a Froggy now! He's the youngest, sixteen year younger than I. Then there's Joan, she was in the ATS and got posted to Singapore and when she was there she met this Aussie soldier and when she got demobbed she didn't come home. She went to Australia and married 'ee. And one sister she's dead, died of liver failure in Wells of these tablets they give her. But she 'ad a good time, she were in her seventies.

But I was the only one who went fishing. When I was a kid with nappies on they used to put I in the two-pecker willy baskets, they used to put I in 'ee, and the only thing I can remember is this bloody gurt arm in front of my nose when my dad 'ee carried me out fishing. They'd put me down on the rocks where they do fish the nets and the butts and that, then carry me back. 'Twas 'cause my mother'd had the twins then. Mother used to play hell 'cause I used to crawl about and get mud all over. Well, anyway, that was my earliest fishin'! And 'cause I was brought up like that, when I got

Bridgwater flatner lat bottomed rowing boat for fishing on the River Parrett and its estuary.

older I couldn't get out there quick enough. As soon as I could run up the road I was up there with Uncle Cecil. He was fishin' full time. Then the War come on and I went in the forces. And when I come home in 'forty-seven I went to see Pocock's in Bridgwater 'cause they was building flatners. I went to see old Pokey and he said, 'Yeah, I'll build 'ee one next year, Bob.' So he built me one next year. Then I 'ad 'er all ready for 1949.

From 1949 I got every licence I took out till I retired, and I've every tide book from 1949 up, hundreds of them. And I've written down every salmon that I caught. The first year was 1949 but I didn't start then because my father was ill from an accident and I had to run his coal business. But after that I got down every salmon that I caught, with its weight and where I caught'n. Here's the first: 5 May,1950, seven pounds, Combwitch. That was boat work, with a boat and a dip-net. Out in the boat, the flatner. Then twenty pounds, Horsey Pill; fifteen pounds, Bridgwater and so on. 'Cause I did travel the river full length, from the tail of the Gore down off Hinkley right up to Somerset Bridge. Sometimes I done that twice of a day, all with oars, rowing. In they days there was no outboard motors!

When I started, in 1949, 'twas ten shillings for a rank of fifty butts and ten shillings for a boat and net. My Uncle Cecil who lived here in this house, in 1938, paid £1 10s. There used to be around sixty dip-net licences taken out. That year I chucked out I think there was two. It was £47.40 for one dip-net! People couldn't do it. They altered it, see, when they said they wanted to preserve the fish, when we was catching half a dozen fish and trawlers was catchin' ten ton a day. That's why so much poachin' was goin' on 'ere. Blokes just couldn't afford the licence. Now there's nothing here. Not one butt being fished, not one dip-net.

I got Uncle Cecil's licence here from 1904. He wasn't fishin' at Black Rock 'cause my granfather and his father and old Thomas Thorne, my great-grandfather, was fishin' at Black Rock, that was the butcher's shop, what they called it, 'cause you could put in 450 butts where everywhere else in the river you could only put in ranks of fifty, 'cause the river was narrower. So the boys comin' on, the young uns like Uncle Cecil — 'cause the three seniors was fishin' Black Rock, that was yer limit, three, 'cause there wouldn't be enough fish there fer more — so what they did do fer the young uns comin' on, they let 'em have a rank of fifty. Well, when you had a rank of fifty — this is how stupid the law is — you couldn't put down fifty, you could only put down forty-nine. If you put down fifty you had to pay an extra ten shillings on top of the ten shillings you paid fer the forty-nine. The fishing stations on the Combwitch side were all owned by Lord Clifford, bar Windmill, and when his estate was sold up the Fisheries Board bought all his stations and closed 'em. When I started in 1949, Ed Reasons and Bucky and old Morris and all o' they, they had all the stations on our side, but there was one station left that was over on Lord Clifford's side so they let me 'ave 'ee. So, until there was a station going on this side of the river, which was Black Rock, I did fish there fer several years. Just by Cannington Brook.

There were seven or eight ranks o' butts. When I had mine in at Black Rock, I walked straight out the path here at the back of the house down to the river, or cut out across anywhere. I had my shed out on the saltings where I kept all the nets and that and the boats, the flatners tied up there. The water do cover the saltings over but when the tide's out you can walk out across the grass o' the saltings. I used to put in 350 butts in three ranks: the Mud Butts, they were nearest in, then Middle Rank out on the rock and, furthest out, Outside Rank. Because of the shape of the rock and the run of the rock, you could only make holes in seams. The Mud Butts was all right, 'cause there was enough mud to hold the stakes, but when you come to the Middle Rank you had to find a seam in the rock to make the holes for your stakes, and then you had to come up in front about twenty, thirty feet to find another seam for your Outside Rank. Every year when you did take your stakes out, see, you did put a flat stone over the hole so's he didn't fill up, 'cause if you got small stones down in there, you had to have a spoon filed down to dig 'em out. The holes in the rocks for the stakes was made hundreds of years ago by my ancestors and we still use 'em! They reckon they've been fishing like this for three hundred years. Before that they just put in rows of stakes to trap the fish as the tide went out. Anyway, when you went to set yer stakes back in, you had to find the flat stones, lift'n up, get yer bar in and wriggle it around 'cause the hole would be all full of slush, then drive the stake down to the bottom with yer mauler and then add chippings of stone — plenty on the rock — and wedge 'em in. Then yer stake'd be firm and when yer butts was tied to 'n 'twas as firm as a concrete wall. See, on spring tides, wi' thic' Middle Rank especially, I seen the water two feet higher in front than behind, there was such a weight o' water. On a spring tide the water'd rise and fall by forty feet! That's why it did run so.

In the summer we'd put the shrimp nets up behind the butts and in the winter when the butts was up, the shrimp nets was tied to the butt stakes. We used to leave in every fourth stake, which was six foot, just right fer to tie yer net. The stakes'd last fer years, that's why they was elm, see. And the butts were made of withies. They was only down fer four months, look, that's why 'twere such a lot of work. I made all the butts myself, about ninety new butts every season, every year, 'cause the withy'd rot away. And I made the mauler. 'Twere like a gurt sledgehammer that you'd bash the stakes in with, only you had to hold'n straight up high over yer 'ead fer to bring'n down on top of the stakes, they was so tall. Fer that what we used to do, see, was we had an elm tree that was about six inches in the stump and you'd cut off thic elm tree about three foot off the ground. Then, in the spring of the year, 'ee'd shoot out. Any shoots below the top of the cut you used to break off and leave only the top shoots. Three or four pr'aps. When they was about three years old and about as thick as yer wrist, you'd pick out the one that had the best knit. The best growth from the stump, a long knot to un, three or four inches down into the stump. Well then, you'd know that was a knot that'd hold. You'd cut all the others off level. When 'ee was about four, five year old, that shoot'd be six, seven foot high and a good three inches through. And at the same time the stump'd keep growin' so that stump'd be about ten inches through. Then you'd cut the stump off down at ground level and cut the shoot to about four foot, four foot six long, trim'n out and round the end off of the stump, scoop'n out a bit. Sometimes they was heavy enough like they be, but if they waren't nearly heavy enough, what you'd do, you'd scoop out a bit deeper, have a drill, drill four or five holes sideways into the stump and then fill'n with lead. You couldn't do it now very well 'cause of the elm disease.

I was still fishin' every day when I stopped. Full time. You can see in my books that the fish was gettin' less and less and smaller and smaller. There's nothing there now. There's not a single inshore fisherman working the river now. Whereas back when I were a boy, winter fishin', there was seven boats goin' out from Burnham, four from Highbridge, nine from Black Rock, four from Combwitch, I think, and three from Dunball. This was goin' to the tail of the Gore for sprat fishin'. Well then, in the summer there was Fish House, Middle Rank, Mash, Clyse, Dashoots, Marchants, Combwitch Common, Westers Point, Bonters, Black Rock, and Stone Wall. There was twelve lots of butts from the mouth to the Fish House, both sides of the river. Twelve fisherman there and all twelve did also do boat fishin' with a dip-net and I suppose there was, at a rough guess, another twenty others that just did boat fishin', not the butts. So all together there was about forty men working up and down the river for salmon. Not all of 'em did do the winter fishing, too, some of 'em just did the salmon in the summer. Just at our lot at Black Rock there was Uncle Cecil, his father Joseph, Morris, his cousin, my father, Granfer Thorne, Bert, there was Bucky, Alf Reasons, Bill Millard, Tom Reasons, Jim Reasons. Yeah, they just in my family. Bucky and Bert and Granfer Thorne, they kept their flatners up the brickyard.

Catching with a dip-net is a risky business, 'cause thic salmon can turn quick and he's gone, out over yer head, like. But when I was out in Malaya I used to watch the fishermen there with round nets and I used to think to meself, 'Cor! If I 'ad one of they in the boat, I could catch a salmon any bloody angle.' Whereas with a dip-net you could only dip or chuck over, see? They were so big, they had a six foot head on. So when I come home, see, I made a round net. I got stainless steel pipe from when they closed the Queen's Hotel in Bridgwater and I put'n in me vice and kept tappin'n and half flatnin'n and as I did he come round in a perfect circle. When I finished he was thirty-four or -five inches in diameter. Old Morris and

Bert and they, said, 'You shouldn' do that, Robert, you shouldn' do that. If Father was alive 'ee wouldn' like it. 'Ee always used a dip-net!' If Father didn' do it, you didn' do it! I said, 'They days is gone! I'll be catchin' fish when you can't.' They used to see I goin' up river and catchin' the fish and they came round and, by the end, they'd say, 'Bob, can you make I a round net?'

I made smaller ones, too, two foot, what we used to run the banks with. If we seed a salmon out there hit the butts and go back up the bank, we'd run up the bank and catch'n. You'd be held in by the bank with the tide rushin' up, say, and all of a sudden you'd see a set of fins come up and you'd be away! And then 'ee'd die away and you'd be out there. And 'ee'd come up again and you'd gradually creep in on'n and 'ee'd be up there and you'd drop your oars and you'd get'n. You'd follow in the boat, see. Do you know, when there's been some hard rain, June, July and there'd be some fresh water comin' down — fresh water'd always travel on top of salt — you'd have six or seven inches of fresh. Well, that's enough for the salmon to come up and have some good oxygenated water and go down again. When 'tis like that the bastards won't stop up long enough. I've chased 'em fer three mile and not catch'd 'em. I've chased 'em from Powder House to Gaunts and then chucked in on 'em, given up. You're drifting in the flatner with the tide, but they do turn round, they do swim everywhere. You might see 'em back up above 'ee come up. Well, then you've got to stem tide. Then the bugger might turn and you'd see'n a hundred yards below 'ee and you'd go like buggery to catch'n up!

But when there's no fresh water about, see, the water do get dead of oxygen with all the mud'n that and sand, then you'll see fish jumping out the river, dying, suffocatin'. Well, that's the ones you do pick up on the ebb tide on the sand banks, they get left there. You might see'n go down and not come up and you'd think to yerself, 'Well, ee's half way down Marchant's Reach.' Now, there's a big slack just round the back of Windmill and there's a big slack down off the point at Bonter's. 'Ee got a good chance of ebbin' up in one of they slacks. So you'd travel around and hang on ther for half an hour and nine times out o' ten you'd see'n ebbing or you'd go on down Powder House and 'ee'd be already ebbed there and there'd be a couple o' gurt salmon-gulls pecking into'n.

There could be five or six boats at a time, held in one behind t'other, lookin'. And we'd all be chasin' the same fish! Up Dunball I've seen as many as ten boats goin' fer the same fish, all their oars in on another. They'd cuss and get tangled up. But I never did, I wouldn't barge in, I'd hold back. And they never done it to Thorney! You'd 'ave to get there first! That's where I used to gain so much, I was that much faster then they 'cause they were all older men than I, I was in me prime then! I could heave a boat on! When we was all out there 'twas a chance who'd get to'n first. But the buggers used to keep their eyes on I. I'd see a fish out there and nobody else'd seen 'n, perhaps a hundred yards out. So I'd just wash me crook off, put'n in the boat, sit down and, 'I think I'll get on early today.' And I'd push the boat off and drift. And all the time I'm looking round and you'd hear 'em say, "Ee an't seen nothin', 'ee an't seen nothin'.' Then I'd be gone past the last boat, see, and p'raps over on the point, just a hundred yards away, I'd see'n tip up and I'd slew the boat and ease out a bit. And then, all of a sudden, p'raps one or t'other of the back boats'd push off, 'cause they'd 'ave seen the tip over there as well. All you'd see is the tip of the fin. Well, of course, by then I had a hundred yards start on them. Well, providing 'ee did show, I 'ad that fish in the boat before they got half way there! And they used to say, 'Crafty bugger's 'ad us again!'

'Course, then I used to have fun wi' 'em. I'd find a dead fish, gone stale and I'd put this twine through 'ees belly and just behind his fin and tie 'n to a couple of holey bricks. And he'd sink and put up and there was his fin, just like that. The tide'd work 'ees tail. When I was past the point they could see me and I'd pull on behind the rest of 'n. Then all of a sudden the first boat'd spot'n, then t'others and p'raps all four boats'd come on. Then half a mile down they'd catch'n. Then there'd be a stink! They used to cuss like hell! I used to do that fer a pastime.

By the time I retired in 1994, over the last years, the fishin' was steadily getting less and less all the time. What killed it was modern techniques. One of the most deadly o' the lot, what's destroying everything, is drift nets.

Because you got yer sharks, all yer types of sharks, yer dolphins, yer porpoises and all they type o' fish is what we used to call the doctors. They'm the doctors of the sea. 'Tis like a fox or a badger or a stoat, all that, they're the doctors of the land. If you've got an animal that's bad, the fox'll take'n out. The badger'll take 'n out. So, all that type of fish is doctors, you know. That's why the seas are kept clean. Now what they'm doin'? Now they've got this drift netting which is the most stupid thing they ever done, because drift nets'll take everything that comes against'n. Right well, even long before I finished I'd get dead dolphins and porpoises come in the river and when you did look at'n there was the marks of the net. You could easily tell what mesh nets they were using by the size of the squares on their skin. Oh yeah, the bastards, see! And then they say, 'Oh dear, our living!' and all this. I'd shoot the bloody lot, these deep sea fishermen! They'm nothing but selfish bastards! There's we you see: we never 'ad no modern techniques, we'd study the weather and that and go out fishin' and we could earn a living. And then after the War all the modern techniques come in. And all they do is sit on a heated seat and study a screen and shout out, 'Run the nets!' And then you see 'em bring 'em in! They got so much in there they can't even lift the nets out of the water! They got like bloody gurt vacuum cleaners, pipe over the side, sucking 'em up! And there 'tis comin' in like coal out of a mine. And the thing is a fish lays, roughly, 1,700 eggs every pound of weight. Roughly. I'm takin' it on the species of salmon and trout. Well now out of thic 1,700 you'll get, say, 500 come into fish. Well, in my day, we'd go out and we could earn a good living if we came back with five or six hundredweight of fish. We was doin' well and that was that. But they'm fishin' fish at such a rate and the fish is only laying the same number of eggs as what they always did. What you want is fish to advance with technology to keep up with these bastards, produce thousands more eggs! Well, 'tis impossible. Yet you can't tell yer politicians or yer fishing people.

See, I was on the Fisheries Board fer ten years and then I chucked in in disgust. 'Twould 'ave been easier fer I to walk into thic wall and hit me fuckin' head off than talk to they! 'Twas useless. I was the representative for the inshore fishermen and, o' course, there was twenty-six of us on the Board, farmers, landowners and the rest! And what did'm know? Nothing! 'Twas useless. And then when you did say anything to 'em about the trawlers they'd say, 'Oh, we can't handle that.' And they were piling it on we all the time, while they that were doin' all the destruction were roaming free. 'Tis a case of squash the little man, 'tis worse today than what it was fifty year ago! I walked out. I told'n they was a lot of useless bastards and walked out the door.

Well, the salmon licence kept goin' up year be year, and the fish was getting less and less all the time and they wouldn't take any notice in Bridgwater, the Fisheries Board. Well, the last year that I done the fishin', I done a whole season's salmon fishin', a whole winter restoring me butts, 'cause every winter I had to make between eighty and ninety butts to keep me stock up, me 350 butts. They do rot out see, they'd last two years, three years absolute limit. Every year I did tackle the Board about reducing the fee fer me licence to correspond to what little I was catchin'. But oh no! They couldn't do that and they couldn't do that. So in that last year, after I paid me licence, I made sixty-four pounds profit. That's for a season's salmon fishin'. That's ridiculous. The licence was more'n £400. But they wouldn't listen, so I said, 'Right, you bastards, that's it!' So I come home and took 'em up, took up all me butts and made a big bonfire and burnt the lot.

So, anyway, the next year I didn't take out a licence, did I, and after so many years they wanted to know why, the Board. I was the oldest one, see, my licence was number one. So I told 'em straight. Well, the next thing I know is I had a letter saying that we'd come to an agreement, that they would reduce the licence down to whatever I wanted. So you can just imagine what I told 'em! I went in there and told 'em to stick the lot right up their bloody arses! You see, it would have took me four years to build up again, I could only have made about ninety a year, that was the amount of withies I had each year and to make that amount was a full winter's work. I was seventy then so I could have been dead before I'd done! So August 1994 I chucked it all in, 29 August, and I caught a six-pound salmon, that was my last fish from the butts.

The Peat Moors

Albert Bush, Peat Worker, Westhay, 1981

'When they dig with the machines like that now, I do go out and I do turn them over spit-spat, turn over the blocks of peat, like. Open the ranks out so that the air do get to them quicker.'

Strictly speaking, many of the moors are open peat moors, but this chapter is about the moors to the north of the Polden Hills where peat is actually dug. To the south, moors like West Sedgemoor have peat that lies just as deep but there is no historical or physical evidence of peat ever having been dug in these southern areas. The precise reasons for this are a little obscure but may have had something to do with differences in the structure and consistency of the peat itself. More probably, though, it was because the southern moors stayed wetter far longer into the summer and it was simply never dry enough for the peat to be dug, dried out and carted before the moors flooded once again. However, in the areas that peat was dug the tradition goes back many centuries, far back beyond the first recorded rights of turbary, peat extraction, in the early medieval period. The peat moors have an extraordinary atmosphere: ancient, primeval yet strangely temporary, as though they might all gradually dissolve into the mist. There are the great holes where the peat has been dug, colonised by reed, full of water. Then the roads wobble and ripple like waves in a choppy sea. The buildings list over into the soft ground and the farms seem ramshackle, half-ready to move on. But because of the extraordinary qualities of the peat, its ability to keep and preserve structures and artifacts over thousands of years, it is here that we have evidence of some of the earliest of man's activities in this country: the lake villages of Meare and Glastonbury and the ancient trackways, some 5,000 years old, that have been exposed as the layers of peat have been removed.

The whole question of peat extraction over the last twenty-five years has led to some intense debates between the extractors, the farmers and the conservationists: how should the land be properly used? How far should the permitted zone of extraction extend? What do the conservationists want to conserve and how should they best do it? How do all these activities support or undermine the local communities? Since the war, peat has no longer been dug for fuel but, of course, for horticulture, and some have questioned the value of using such a non-renewable resource in this way at all. However, over the years a compromise seems to have been reached which keeps most involved here reasonably content. But, though the flora and fauna have their champions and

Opposite: Old peat diggings, Westhay.
Above: Digging peat by hand. (Photograph courtesy of Godwin's Peat)

are doing well now, the one group certainly doomed to extinction are the old peat diggers, those who worked the peat on the moors and dug it and stacked it by hand in the days, quite recent days, before complete mechanization. There are still those around who remember that life vividly.

When I started digging peat, that there was all the trade there was in the village. Pretty near all the village used to work on the peat at that time, for Alexander's and everybody else, and there could have been up to fifty pair of diggers working here. The diggers would work as pairs. But, of course, now you got the machinery you don't need the hand diggers only the odd digger now and then to dig the heads out where the machines can't finish off to. To start your head off you've got to put your line down and mark out your head which is normally about four feet wide, and then you chuck your unridding in the pit which used to vary from a foot to eighteen inches. And once you've got all that cleared off, you start marking up your head and you start digging your peat. You generally take off about four layers which is a matter of about three foot six inches deep. Before the hay knife come about they used to use what we call the turf scythe, they used to mark and dig wi' he, the same tool. But now they use the hay knife and the spade, but the spade must be pulled up a bit for your own comfort and easy working. Of course, then you got your shovel, mowing scythe, got your marking stick, got your chopper and by the time you've finished you've got about eight tools you would use on digging peat.

Well, years ago before the machines came in it was all dug by hand, then it was a job for anybody who wanted one, who didn't mind working hard. 'Twas all the work there was in the village at one time and people wanted a job and that's what they used to do, dig turves, which later come on for digging spits. It was done on a piecework basis, the more you dig the more you earn.

When they dig with the machines like that now, I do go out and I do turn them over spit-spat, turn over the blocks of peat, like. Open the ranks out so that the air do get to them quicker. I do that night times meself. That's the only way to dry 'em, they got to be opened up. They got a machine now in Germany that will dig 'em and they all dry automatically.

Well, when you start to dig your head of peat, 'course you got your water problem to start wi' which you have to get a pump and put goin' for a day before you can start diggin' your peat. But before the pumps and that came about they used to 'ave what they call the lathe-bowl. You used to have three sticks put up over the edge of the pit and a chap used to work a swinging action with like a bucket on the end, and used to scoop the water up over the bay, and then he'd go on and dig his head of turf and if there was any water come in over night he had to do the same thing in the morning to start off again. But as the years gone by the land is drained better, there isn't so much trouble to contend wi' pumps, not now.

I started off for Mr Godwin back in 1949. I used to dig turves and then I went on spits and then I went into the factory. I'm in the factory now. I haven't been here all the time – I s'pose I've had a couple of year off – but I been here twenty five years.

Richard Roland, Godwin's Peat, Meare, 1981

'... we used to grind peat down at the old factory. I went to work there. Then we had shortages at the peat diggings and I said, "Right, I'll go out there and dig peat with old Freddie Baker and Bob Rogers." They put me through my paces. I learnt to dig peat with them in the old-fashioned way... Then Grandpa Godwin said, "Well what do you want to do? I don't want to carry on the business, will you take it over?" I said, "OK, I'll have a go."...'

Richard Roland was in the forefront of the modernisation of the peat industry. He came into it at the time when peat was still being dug for fuel and there was hardly such a thing as a conservationist. He adapted to all the changes thrust upon him and was himself responsible for much innovation. He was also deeply engaged in the debate over the future of the peat industry and the evolution of the alliance with nature conservation bodies active in the area.

I married into the Godwin family in 1950. I met my wife during the War, I came out of the army in 'forty-seven, then went abroad and came back in 'forty-eight and just by chance I got talking to the old boy — that's Mr E.J. Godwin — and he said, 'Why don't you stay around and work for me?' So that's what happened. At the time it was a very small company turning over about £12,000 a year, mostly in fuel. We had a small business of horticultural peat, we used to grind peat down at the old factory. I went to work there and then we had shortages at the peat diggings and I said, 'Right, I'll go out and dig peat with old Freddie Baker and Bob Rogers.' They put me through my paces. I learnt to dig peat with them in the old-fashioned way. I did that for about three years; I didn't want to do it for the rest of my life. Then Grandpa Godwin said, 'Well, what do you want to do? I don't want to carry on the business, will you take it over?' I said, 'OK, I'll have a go.'

I gradually cut down on the peat fuel, it was very labour-intensive and very cut-price, and I concentrated on the horticulture side. That gradually grew over the years and we got to a point where I thought, 'Well, the best thing to do is go and sell this myself.' We were selling through agents, that was very low price. I got a very good response. In those days I sold mostly to professional nurserymen, professional growers. There was quite a lot of peat in those days, there was a market.

Then I went back into the factory and things began to develop, the retail market began to start. I decided to sell in shops as opposed to the nursery trade. That was a more lucrative market. I got some plastic sacks, a PVC type of sack. I thought those were fantastic. I bought 10,000 bags at 2s 8d each. At that time I was paying about nine pence for a paper sack or a hessian sack. I came back and thought, 'I'm just going to put the price on and see what happens.' We never looked back from that day. Within six months the Metal Box Company produced polythene sacks and I got my name printed on them. I was the first in Europe with peat in polythene bags, now everybody in the world's using polythene packing. It completely revolutionised our industry.

It did take a good twenty years to build up to size, it was a slow grind. Also buying land. When I joined the governor here, we had twelve acres of land, the rest he rented. It was the old-fashioned way of renting, never buying. You could buy at £150, £200 an acre. Now we pay up to £10,000 an acre. The peat varies according to what was done to it before. Most of the land in the Somerset Levels round this area was all hand dug over many, many years. If you take a line from Westhay to Burtle, that moor over there was hand dug, the whole of Shapwick had been hand dug. Now in the old days they went down approximately four mumps, that's four of those square blocks of peat, and then they got down to the water-level and they weren't able to control the water, and then they left it and went away somewhere else. And the land was reconstituted into agricultural land or was just left for trees to grow over. With the advent of the modern digging machine and modern drainage, we were able to go down to the clay beneath. A virgin piece of ground in the area could be up to fifteen feet of peat, especially in the Sharpham area. In the area around Burtle, Westhay, virgin ground was about nine to ten feet and, depending on how the water-table was when they cut it by hand, the peat could have been down to about six feet. Some of the land we have bought had only six feet of peat, sometimes five if they managed to get down deep.

Carting peat turves for fuel. (Photograph courtesy of Godwin's Peat)

The family tradition on peat goes back through five generations. In the early days it was all fuel, peat fuel. They used to dig pockets of it in those days, instead of digging like they do now in straight lines. There used to be sixty or seventy carts leaving the area every day selling peat in a radius of forty, fifty miles. At the advent of the railway, the Somerset Railway, Cornelius Godwin used to load these trucks with peat and send them of to Swanage, Gillingham. He used to go down with the horse and trap and stay down there till he'd sold all the peat. It was quite an adventure every summer. Nobody else had thought of it in those days, to sell right out of the area.

They would hire these chaps to dig and pay them fifty pounds to fill an acre. That wasn't very much money. That constitutes between seven or eight weeks' hard work. Then the peat had to be dried, it had to be either winrowed or hyled and then after that put up into ruckles. Then if they wanted to keep them for winter they either put them up into big ricks or they would put up ruckles, full, and kept them dry like that. The digging machines revolutionised it. We were the second company in Somerset to buy a digging machine and that machine would do the work of twenty men. We got them

Ruckles of peat stacked to dry.

from Germany, we'd seen them working there on sphagnum peat and that's a much lighter type of bog than ours. It cost about £8,000 in the early sixties. Till then it was all done by hand. I myself introduced milling peat on the ground, open-cast milling instead of digging the peat up in blocks. I would take off the topsoil, the unridding, and mill the peat on the ground and scrape it off as it dried. This is a very economical way of digging peat but we needed the soft peat to go with it as well. We needed the machine-cut peat to mix with the milled peat because the milled peat was inclined to break down very quickly and you needed the soft peat to keep the structure open.

Another idea of ours was stacking peat. I'd seen it stacked by hand all over Europe and England into ricks and I thought that if we could get some hardstanding and bring this peat in and bulldoze it up into heaps we wouldn't have the problem of trying to get peat off the ground in the winter months. The problem was the water. We would have all our workings under water, any peat left on the ground could be under water through the winter. I can remember the days when we were using light railways and we had railways under feet of water going down and taking just the dry tops off the winter ruckles. It was virtually impossible to keep production going, and this is the reason that I had to stockpile. Once it was bulldozed up into heaps it was harder and firmer than it ever was in the ground, it shed water.

The drainage has improved tremendously, mostly by the Somerset Drainage Boards. All the various drains, the River Brue, and the pumping stations have been improved so much. Nowadays, we get a flood and in a few days it's gone. And the river banks are so high now that we never get over-spillage into the peat fields like we used to. That means we can virtually guarantee to go on digging peat now right through the season. We usually start about March and go right through, as long as the weather holds, and as long as we can clear ground. We work in a circle and go round and round. The quicker we dry it, the quicker we dig it again. Also, our own pumping systems mean it's very seldom we get flooded nowadays. They never had an integrated system where they could drain a whole moor before. Now, the pump is there all the time, working continuously.

We can lower the land and leave it drained at the lower level. We can even leave it in a condition to be re-farmed. If you want to reclaim the land, you want to leave a certain amount of peat there, or subsoil, and take up about six inches of clay and mix it with this subsoil and re-seed it. We are doing this now. This was all the plan before the milk quotas came in. Now the price of agricultural land is dropping but we still think in the long term it is worth reclaiming land for agriculture. Another way is to empty the land completely and sell it for water amenities or lakes. The Wessex Water Board are quite interested in this, there's the Avalon Lake Scheme. At the moment there's four experimental lakes in operation in the Shapwick area, though I don't think the scheme will happen on the scale they thought, it's too expensive.

I don't think there is any necessity to have any of this land round here spoilt. We work closely with the conservationists. I'm very keen on conservation. I object to licences being given outside the zoned area, which came in in 1967. A good plan, it did control the digging, stopped this ad-lib digging going on, making eyesores of the countryside. At the moment our livelihood is curtailed by the amount of land that we can purchase, because of the zoned areas. What happened prior to the early sixties was that you applied for planning permission to extract peat and you'd get it. You had to apply for a licence and you would get it. It wasn't zoned. Anywhere in the Somerset Levels you could get a licence. The authorities, the County Council, decided they had to regulate this, they couldn't have people just digging Somerset away, so they decided to zone the area where people could dig. So many acres in the zoned areas and any area outside that zone they would not consider granting a licence. Now we are hoping that they are going to release some more land. The Council claim there's another thirty years worth of peat in the zoned area but we don't. We have an Association of Peat Producers and we have submitted our reserves. We consider that our life is more like fifteen to twenty years. Frankly, I think they don't really want peat digging in Somerset now, I think their object is to see it out. I don't know why. This is my personal opinion. It's the oldest industry in Somerset, but I don't think they will extend it more than at the outside thirty years. There's plenty of peat here, enough for fifty years at least at present production rates. Where we have got existing planning permission to dig peat and the conservationists've put an SSSI, a Site of Special Scientific Interest, on that land we can still go on. Well, we think we can. But they ask us how we intend to leave that area afterwards.

We co-operate with them, we discuss it. There is a block out on Eddington Moor, very poor third-grade farm land. An ideal situation for a natural lake. They are very interested in that and coming up with ideas about leaving islands in the area which I shall do, and when it's dug up in twenty years time you will have a lake with islands, not a blot on the landscape. There's a great deal of negotiation that's done about all this.

Unless we get more land, the industry over the next twenty years will slowly grind to a halt. We shouldn't have to extend into SSSIs, there's plenty of areas without SSSIs that have peat beneath them. They are farmed and a lot of farmers who have peat around here don't want to give up their livelihood, they don't want to sell their land. You've got to respect that, even if they can get a good price for it.

Now we are diversifying into composts and different types of high-class peat products rather than more peat. We are horticulturalists. We have a nursery out here and we are quite experienced in growing. We are producing composts now for all sorts of plants. It gives us a better financial return and less volume. We would rather go along those lines. Peat is like oil: once it's gone, it's finished. If we can still get a healthy return for our capital and sell less peat we are quite happy.

What we have in the Somerset Levels is a highly decomposed sphagnum moss together with sedge reeds. When this land was all marshland the Neolithic people that lived here, the lake village people, adopted methods for getting from one high point to another high point. The best illustration to give is to get from the village of Westhay to the village of Burtle. They cut silver birch and elder and oak, though not very much oak because that grew far away, and they laid trackways with this brush and trees and shrubs across the top of the marshes from A to B. And the marshes were still rising, the peat was still growing and rotting, and eventually grew over the trackways and the nature of the acidity of the peat kept them, preserved them in virtually their original state. You can actually take a trackway up and find the original axe marks and you can identify every tree. The silver birch has even got the original bark on it. This is going back, the oldest track dates from 2,800 BC. Every year the Exeter and Cambridge archaeologists come down to excavate and we have a person constantly working here and looking and following the peat machines around to find the trackways. They have mapped every trackway, there are lots of them. As soon as we find a trackway, or they find one, we stop digging that area. They come along and excavate it and record it and after that its gone. But what we did a few years ago, one the original trackways we found, the Abbots Way, we've given about a hundred metres of it to the Somerset Levels Project and it's there underneath the ground for ever more. And above the ground we've made an artificial trackway; a replica, to show what it's like. We wanted to see it kept. They found axe heads, beads too, things like that. Canoes have been dug up.

The cottages here were once all full of peat workers. We used to get the wives working, stacking the peat in the summer. It was a hard life. When I came here a peat digger would earn five pounds a week, that's working from half past seven till half past four. That was really hard, digging turf. We used to give each man a gallon of cider a day, he'd sweat it out. As the hand digging finished, it phased out. Cider's all right if you work it off, but nobody otherwise could drink a gallon a day. They'd sup at it, it was like a drug, a stimulant, keep them going and numb the pain.

The only hand operation that's left in the industry now is the hand stacking. Although we cut the sods by machine we've never yet developed a satisfactory machine to dry and stack them. The very big peat companies in Southern Ireland and so on have never yet found a way other than by hand. Even the Germans with all their mechanisation. It's the turning of them. When you dig a head by machine the blocks of peat are laid down with air spaces through them, consequently the top ones will dry very quickly, the ones on the bottom will remain wet. So they've got to be turned over, the bottom ones turned to the top.

When I first came, I was a complete outsider, I had to prove myself their equal, kept pace with them. I got on with them very well. They could be a little bit anti. The son-in-law! It's an image I never wanted. It was non-com-

Open water and reeds on reclaimed peat workings, Westhay.

munication if anything. It was being able to get into conversation. They didn't want to communicate to start with, I had to tread carefully but I had a lot of respect for them, I learnt from them, I worked with them, especially with turfing. When you're on turf you've got to walk with webbed feet, and some of the old boys there when I was working and dug my heels into the turf they'd go, 'Tut, tut, tut.' They took pride in their work. You mustn't knock the edge off a piece of turf, you'd spoil it. They didn't want to see their work done badly. For five pounds a week they were very proud of what they did. You had to get to know them, you could never boss them, they were so independent. Still are. We don't even have a time clock in the factory now.

In those days the peat diggers only got paid when they worked. These were very hard-working people, a breed unto themselves. There's not so many of the original villagers left, there's been such an infill. But the old Somerset villager through here was a very strong and independent character. They still are. They might be poor but they were very proud. And very industrious.

Andrew Roland, Godwin's Peat, Meare, 2005

'There's a lot of peat here in Somerset on the moors. We only harvest a fraction of it, say 2 per cent... there's less than 1,500 acres that's available, that has an extraction licence on it. Out of the 50 to 60,000 acres of peat land. It doesn't seem very much.'

Andrew Roland took over from his father Richard and has carried on the process of modernisation within the bounds of the peat extraction zones. In order to extend the life of an industry that exploits a finite resource, he has had to find new ways to refine his product, to become more of a horticulturalist than just a peat producer. There is, now, a more general consensus than there was twenty-five years ago over the future of the worked-out diggings and a greater degree of commitment to conservation issues. The idea of returning old peat workings to agriculture has been abandoned in favour of open waterways and great reed beds that support a growing population of birds and other wildlife. The area now also teems with conservation bodies like English Nature, the RSPB and the Somerset Trust for Nature Conservation. In fact, this alliance between the conservationists and the peat industry has produced a fascinating landscape that is still evolving and attracts many visitors. Andrew Roland reckons there is enough peat left within the zone of permitted peat extraction to last another twenty or thirty years. After that it seems probable that all the old workings and some of the surrounding moors will form one great nature reserve.

Well, we're here on the moors north of the Poldens and there is a difference between these moors and the moors to the south like West Sedgemoor. Those moors are peat moors, too, but they've never been dug, I don't think. It's partly because of the sphagnum moss content. The moors on this side started to become a raised mire so it has a higher content of sphagnum moss building on top of the fen reed peats, whereas the

Above: A new lake on old peat diggings, Westhay.
Opposite: Mountains of peat at Godwin's.

EX120

West Sedgemoor is far more oxidised, deep reed peats, fen peats, and so the peat in this area around Glastonbury is a better quality for horticultural use. And they never dug it for burning on the southern moors either because, I suppose, traditionally the peats here were near the centres of population, Glastonbury and Wells. It was traditionally dug by the churches — we had the conflict between the Bishops of Bath and Wells and the Abbots of Glastonbury fighting over rights to the peat for fuel. Also the moors are higher here, we have these raised mires, and they are more accessible to turbary rights. Because we are higher we are drier, whereas the constant flooding and the accessibility on West Sedgemoor probably made it much more difficult to get to the peat, dig it, dry it.

There are no turbary plots that I know of south of the Poldens, they're all in the Brue Valley basin. Turbary rights, the right to go out and cut peat on the moors, was assigned to properties or estates by the Church and by the Crown initially, though in the last two centuries there were assignments via the land registry. So certain houses had rights to go and dig peat on certain plots, which were often two or three miles away from the village. If you owned a piece of land, say, in the village of Meare or Westhay, there would be a plot of land in maybe Godney Moor area that was your half-acre plot that you could cut turf on. Because a lot of the moors were not fenced — or rather ditched — at that time, they were common land, and areas were assigned to landowners for cutting their own personal turf to burn on their own fires. It's not the right to go and dig peat for horticulture or anything like that. It's an ancient tradition that is part of your own personal fuel allocation that pertains here in Somerset. The laws of turbary pertained also in East Anglia, and do in Ireland even now where they are still very relevant and are still on the statute, whereas I think they've almost run out of statute here. The earliest records of turbary rights go back to Henry VIII's time and beyond, they are mentioned in all the disputes between the Abbots of Glastonbury and the Bishops of Wells, quite ancient really. Of course, people have been digging turf to burn since agriculture commenced, since they found out it was an ignitable fuel and could keep them warm in winter.

Cutting turf has always been a summer occupation, it's like a harvest: as the winter flood waters recede in the summer months, the peats would become available to harvest. They were dug in early summer and dried by mid-summer and taken off by the autumn before everything flooded again in the winter. But because of the raised mire here you would have had areas of peat here above the water, because a raised mire works by capillary action rather than by flooding: that's the difference between a fen peat and a raised mire. All the moors here — Godney, Shapwick Heath and Westhay Heath — all had sphagnum tops on them, but the raised mire actually ceased to grow about AD 400 because the climate changed. We are probably the most southerly of the Atlantic mire and bog systems. Somerset is quite close to the southern tip of England and the rainfall conditions and the drying out actually stopped the continuous growth of the raised mire. As soon as the rainfall drops below a certain level the sphagnum outgrows its capillary suction area and dries out. And then probably reverts back to grass and cotton grasses and things like that. The sphagnum is diminished and more invasive plants take over because they can then re-establish on the drying peats.

The peat industry is still very relevant here in Somerset, there are still reserves probably until 2042, that's when our current planning consents are due to end, so looking ahead I would say that the industry probably has twenty years of peat extraction ahead of it with the Somerset black peats and sphagnum-type peats, but I suppose it has changed in that there is a lot more dilution of the peat than there was about twenty-five years ago. Most now are blends with up to 40 per cent mixture of peat-free additives such as wood-barks and manures going into the current mixes. Also, because we are going down in level, we are going down into more of the reed peats and we are importing sphagnum peats either from Ireland or the Baltic nations in order to keep the quality of the growing medium up. This is a direct result of the fact that we have been constrained so much by planning regulations in terms of the area of peat that we can dig now. That could change, I suppose, but one has to look carefully at the reserves and see what we can legitimately add to the peat as buffers. Also government recommendations on environmental issues are saying 40 per cent inclusion of peat into the horticultural product, we are even looking at a 90 per cent inclusion by 2010. That is an aspiration that I do not think will be met. That means that you will have only 10 per cent actual peat in a growing compost. That's what they want but it will be very difficult to achieve in that timescale. One of the targets that we were set was a 40 per cent inclusion by 2004 which I think most of the producers are reasonably happy with. It's been pressure from environmentalists both directly and indirectly to government that has brought about this change but it's a commonsensical change in that all of us are happy to use recycled materials in order to prolong the life of a resource that is not sustainable. These are materials like bark from the timber industry that have a valuable part to play in air porosity in composts, so rather than using coarser peats for that we use bark. You are tailoring your compost for a specific use — a potting compost, a general purpose compost, a hanging-basket compost — we do all those. We manufacture John Innes compost and sub-contract for one of the major growing-media specialists in America and Europe. We manufacture part of their range here in Somerset for the southern area of England.

Obviously the area we are digging has contracted in the last twenty-five years though we are probably actually extracting the same or slightly more and our volume has almost doubled because of this inclusion of other materials, this diluting of the neat peat. We are also selling other products as well such as chipped bark, so we are now more of a horticultural company than a straight peat company. That seems to be the way to go and obviously we are looking into the future. We have to use the cost advantage of being on the doorstep of a natural resource, but to prolong it by bringing in other materials of a recycled nature certainly makes sense. Beyond that, beyond the next twenty years of peat extraction for which we have permission, we shall probably import the peat here. The difficulties of getting planning consent, to move this factory off the Somerset Levels, would be extreme. It's dusty, there is a lot of traffic generated and noise, so the logistics of upping and moving would be horrendous. I mean otherwise, if we did not have our own source of peat here, why not relocate to an area that is maybe on a motorway hub or something like that? But we are such a low-priced product at the bottom end of the market that the costs of obtaining twelve or fifteen acres — the sort of area we need for storing peat and pallets and so on — would be terrible and at this juncture it would be extremely difficult to get an economic return if we moved from where we are. It would also have a huge economic impact on the area. We have always employed from the local community, grandfather, father and son. I mean I am the fifth generation myself. On the peat side we are employing thirty people which is quite a substantial economy in mid-Somerset, especially in a rural area like we are.

Obviously, the problem with peat is the cost of transport. If you try and bring it across from Canada where there is a lot of peat, it would be uneconomic. But from Ireland and the Baltic States at the moment it still seems reasonably economic.

Peat land is still roughly the same price as it was years ago, £10,000 to £14,000 an acre. And the supermarket effect, with major players there, has kept the price of growbags and compost pretty much the same. B&Q, Homebase, Focus take the bulk of the volume, dictate the market price. They are the leading companies that sell peat and compost in the market place and to a certain extent they can dictate the price they pay producers. So we are all working on very tight margins. It's difficult for a small-to-medium-sized company like ours to remain competitive in a market place that is dominated by such large players.

Of course, the planning constraints are fairly onerous now. Since you interviewed my father we've had a thing called a ROMP! It's a Review of Old Mineral Planning and that's given us quite a lot of environmental targets to reach on the after-use of our dug-out land, so that's added an extra burden. That's probably the reason that the price of peat land has gone down, or not gone up, because you have to restore it to a wetlands after-use. One of the ideas twenty-five years ago was that before you dug for peat you'd scrape off the topsoil and then when you had dug out your area and got down to the clay you'd plough it up, mix the topsoil with the clay and return it to agricultural land. Of course, it would be much lower and would need to be pumped out. Now, though, it's more looking at reed harvesting and conservation after-use and fishing and, in certain parts of the moors, leisure use, boating activity and so on. With a consortium we own half of a major lake in the Glastonbury area, the Rock's Drove area, which will go to boating activity of the quieter sort, rowing, sailing and so on.

At the moment we have about fifty acres we've already restored. If you imagine that we are below sea level on most of our plots, so that once the peat's been dug out, the natural water-table would be about one and a half metres, two metres from the base clays we've dug down to, we use those base clays to actually make banks around the enclosure and then determine what after-use we want to put it to. So we can build islands, we've built a three-lake system for fishing, we've got a reed bed, we've got an open-water area for nature conservation and so on. So we have met quite a broad section of the targets laid down for after-use in this area. So once the peat has been dug out we scoop the clay up the sides and the unriddings that have been left, the old topsoil, is used to cap the banks so that we can get regeneration of wetland-type plants within the more sterile clay areas. You can see the slightly raised banks around the tops of the old diggings and most of those now use the blue lias clays from the base below the peat and we actually make physical barriers to hold in the water so that we've got a hydrologically secure area where we can adjust the water-table in order to meet whatever regime we need in it. If you want a low-water regime for sedges we can do that, if you want a slightly higher regime for reed we can do that, if you want an even higher one for open waterways where reed won't grow we can create that, too, so that all of our planning consents now have got determination as to what the after-use is to be: sedge bed, reed bed, open water or even leisure activity. In the last case you have to have over two metres of clear water depth so that reed doesn't grow up through it. Now, you see, we are growing reed for thatching material, same as the Norfolk reed. There is a possibility now that we shall have all our own home-grown Somerset reed for thatching houses here which has never really been a thing here because we've not had the consistent depth of water to be able to do it, unlike in the east of the country. Now with a commercial reed bed we can control it hydrologically, we can flood it, grow the reed and then drain it down for harvesting, get harvesting equipment in there. On the Norfolk Broads they have difficulty controlling the water-table for harvest and that's probably one of the reasons why it's quite an exclusive product. We can probably do it more mechanically here in Somerset. That's part and parcel of the wetlands after-use and we are going to be doing this ourselves. We have some trial plots at the moment and we'll probably be involved in this in some way.

There's always an argument about costs and benefits. We have to build the bunds, the clay lips around the dug-out works, we have to have a plan for after-use. English Nature's involvement has been strong, they are a consultee of the planning process, and the environmental lobby has certainly got its points across but we also have to think about what we want to achieve as a company so it's been a marriage of the two sides. Obviously, we want to have some commercial after-use of our lands, so it's a meeting of minds, really. We are on good terms with English Nature, though naturally we'd like to dig a bit more and the opportunity to have the peat extraction zone extended would be of benefit to us. That is always under review. Certainly, we have gone through the odd planning process and have won at appeal an extension to the zone, probably not as much as we wanted, but we did get our points across and the director at the enquiry has accepted a lot of the case that we put forward. At the next review we've got a further opportunity to take it to appeal again if we disagree with what the County Council proposes. We have to go through the process. A part of our aims has been achieved though we haven't got them all, but at the moment we are not uncomfortable with the position.

We have had to accommodate the scientific interest in the area, of course. It is interesting, though, that there are accommodations that can be made by all parties. For example, if we have an SSSI applied to an existing planning consent, English Nature — which used to be the Nature Conservancy Council and is about to change its name again, I think — have the right to stop you extracting peat but, in so doing, they have to compensate you for loss of profits. So we still have some small quantities of land that we are digging peat on that are SSSIs, because English Nature have approved the after-use of that SSSI and are quite happy for us to extract the peat rather than pay us the compensation.

The administration of all this, from our point of view, has been quite costly. Like a lot of businesses now, compared to twenty years ago, we have been faced with a lot of interference from government. That's part of our society — we are becoming ever more regulated. Conservation issues and restoration plans are an additional expense that we have had to absorb and try to pass on into our product range in order to achieve and comply with the regulations.

Most of our operation now is open-cast milling. We still have a Steba machine that's sort of like mechanised hand-digging, taking out the mumps of peat just like they used to do by hand, but we don't really use it now. So that's changed — it's all much faster and more efficient. We rotovate the peat and then dig it up with Hymacs. We still have to unrid, to take off the top, the oxidised peats on the top. That peat is highly oxidised and has no structure to it, it hasn't remained wet and is not a good horticultural product. That's the unridding and it has to go back into the pit and is used in the restoration. So after that we take a great big tractor and rotovate only about an inch and a half at a time. Then we leave that there to dry, the sun's the only thing that can do that. In a sunny week we can take it off in a few days, if there is a storm of rain we have to wait and maybe even rotovate again to free it up. What we are trying to do is have an area of open peat that is above the capillary action of the bog. If you rotovate too deep it never dries quickly enough, you want little and often. We dig back in heads. If you go and look at an open-caste system you'll find that half of the ground is down to the clay and you are keeping the peat up at high level because you are digging back and placing that peat out on the top again to use for rotovating. Also keeping the peat up at a high level gives greater opportunity for the wind to evaporate the water off in the summer. So once we've rotovated, then scraped it off, we cart it off and pile it up into these great mountains of peat that you see around here and leave it there to be harvested by the autumn. All these eternal peat piles that you see are not eternal at all but constantly changing and moving, being eaten away and refilled again. We get about 20 or 30,000 tons of peat a year, about 40 to 60,000 cubic metres. Then we stuff it into sacks.

It was really in the War that all this horticultural use of peat started. It was the introduction of the John Innes formula that was used for 'Grow for Britain' and this was the first formulated growing medium that was standard so that we could raise consistent vegetables to a consistent standard. And it was the location of peat near to the Home Counties that Somerset responded to. My grandfather was certainly one of the first people here in Somerset to mill peat, granulate it down to a fine particle to be used in the John Innes formula. Peat, sand and loam in the right proportions. So Somerset peat was being used in the John Innes formula right from the beginning. Up until the War, peat was still being burned, being used as a fuel. Then the price got better for horticultural use and it was very hard work, cutting turf by hand which was really the only way to get it out in the blocks needed for burning. Then they had to be stacked, again by hand, for drying. Then loaded and transported! I don't really see a revival! I can't see us becoming a fuel company! Of course, it's still being burned in Ireland.

There's a lot of peat here in Somerset on the moors. We only harvest a fraction of it, say 2 per cent. We're minuscule: the whole area is only about 2,500 acres. A lot of that now has been bought for nature conservation. What was the Fisons Company gave a lot of peat land to English Nature. So there's less than 1,500 acres that's available, that has an extraction licence on it. Out of the 50 to 60,00 acres of peat land. It doesn't seem very much. Not all of it, though, is good horticultural peat. But we always felt that it was a bit odd to be stopped from extracting peat in such a small area. It's a bit hard for small companies in a propaganda war to get our points across when dealing with highly organised conservation bodies who are very anti-peat. I suppose Somerset is probably the least contentious of all the areas of peat extraction compared with what is happening in Scotland and Yorkshire but if you are anti-peat you are anti-peat everywhere including Somerset. Although we are working on small agricultural plots down here in Somerset pro rata to the larger bogs, for a conservation campaign they can't make exceptions. Though, certainly, the peat diggings are seen as better, in many respects, for nature conservation than the unworked land ever was and English Nature has put on record that they prefer the after-use, the dug-out workings, to the grade two or three agricultural land it was at the start. We are creating more conservation possibilities than what was there before. I think that, again, that is a very difficult story for us to get across and for conservationists to admit to. You know, if you are starting with a grade two agricultural field that has been growing monoculture maize and then you dig the field for peat and when that's finished you create a wetland reed bed there where you have marsh harriers, Cetti's warblers, silver-backed diving beetles, certainly it's a better environment for nature in its end-use. OK, one has maybe twenty-five years of extraction to put up with and I admit that it's not of any great conservation value whilst you are extracting peat, but in my opinion the end justifies the means. In fact it seems rather odd that if you have a dug-out peat working that is instantly declared an SSSI, quite such restrictions should be put on peat extraction in the first place. But to give English Nature their due, their involvement in the process has helped us to achieve these conservation aims and I think they are far more relaxed about the situation in Somerset and that's why we don't have so much of a controversy with them here, because between us producers and the local representatives of English Nature we are achieving those aims.

Years ago there was a bit more controversy, too, between farming and peat extraction but farming has been on the decline. The problem initially was really where you had a peat extraction site next to farm land, you had the drain-down, the draw-down of water from the farm land as the peat was dug. But as farms have shrunk now and we have very definite areas, zones of peat extraction, most of the farmers have sold their land within those areas for peat extraction at a good price and so the dilemma has almost solved itself. Obviously, there are peripheries and boundaries where you can get difficulties but with the restoration lands and bunding, the clay banks that we make, that addresses the problem of water draw-down. The old idea that you could intensively crop the land, pump the water out, lower the water-table, that doesn't fit within the aims of the conservation bodies any more. That doesn't accord with the recommendations for after-use within the PPZ, the Peat Production Zone. You get the oxidisation process and the land starts to shrink and gets lower and lower. It's very short term. We think that with the care we have taken over restoring the old peat diggings for nature conservation, with the work we have done, it should last for a long, long time.

Minnie and Matthew Wall, Farmers and Peat Producers, Atlasta, Westhay, 2005

'It's all done by the machines, now. It'd be a rare sight to see anyone out working on the peat now. Years ago everyone would be out, the women and children too, the women used to work a lot on the peat. Not digging the peat, that was hard, but stacking and drying and that.'

Minnie and Matthew Wall, born in 1913 and 1919 respectively, live along the soft, sinking road from Shapwick to Westhay, in the heart of the peat moors. They were still working until well into their eighties, and their lives — like many here — revolved around farming and peat extraction, both on a small, family scale. The sheds where they milled their peat and bagged it up are now all empty, though for years they resounded to the rattle and roar of the milling machine. Much of the twenty-five acres which they dug for peat is now an SSSI, a Site of Special Scientific Interest, often called the 'jewel of the moors' because of the careful, attentive way in which it was worked. (Sadly Matthew Wall died just two months after this interview.)

Minnie Wall, Atlasta, Westhay.

Minnie: Atlasta, the farm's called. The people who built the bungalow went bankrupt and we had to wait two years before we got it built. So it's called Atlasta. We always hated it. We moved here in 1953. And before that I lived in Station Farm, just down the road, that's where I was born, lived there for my first twenty years, something like that. My husband was born not far away, on the peat. He was born into peat.

Matthew: My family worked the peat. Well, we done a part of both, you know, like so many round here, do a bit of peat and keep a few cattle. There were dozens of farmers round here, everyone had nine or ten cattle, did a bit of peat work, through the summer anyway, and a bit of milking.

Minnie: My family wasn't like that, we didn't do peat, just the farming. Just the milk. We never did anything else, I never moved away. I went to school at Westhay, about a mile from here, walked there every morning and back again after. We didn't have the water-supply or the electric, didn't have the electric till 1970. The water we had before. There was another farm about half a mile up the road that belonged to the same man as our farm did, and we had to go up there to fetch the water with the pony and cart, four or five churns, every day. My uncle lived across the fields here, he was the same. We used to bring his water back. We had a well at home but the water was salty. All salt water, down on the salt rock.

Matthew: About 300 feet down, I think your father used to say, didn't he? The salt rock. You could taste it. It's all salt rock down under here, an enormous amount, all through this area. So you couldn't give it to the cattle.

Minnie: Oh no! We'd just use it for cleaning and that, couldn't use it for growing or for drinking. But where we got the water from, it was up on the hill about half a mile off, on the corner of Burtle Road. It's higher up.

Matthew: Lovely and clear water here, mind, but it is salty.

Minnie: I always worked on the farm. My mum and my two sisters would never go near a cow or a horse, never look at one. That was my life. I loved it, still do. They would do the housework and that. We had a man to work for us and I had a brother and I joined in with them, with the rolling, the haymaking and everything. Milking by hand. I did that when we got married and started farming, milking by hand. We were up by half past four. A different life than now. Then we got the machine, the milking bail out in the fields. Then my husband had, well, he used to get up in the morning and be perfectly all right and by dinner time he'd have a temperature of 103.

Matthew: It was the dust out of the hay. It was what they called 'farmer's lung'.

Minnie: He had the 'farmer's lung'. It was cutting the hay with the hay-knife, so we had to give up farming. But we had plenty of peat land and the peat was just beginning to sell. So we started on the peat.

Matthew: Yes, if you had nice clean hay it was all right but you had to shake it out in the stalls and the dusty hay had fungus stuff in it, that's why you get the dust. It was poisonous really.

Minnie: Yes, every day he had this temperature coming and I thought it was funny that he was well the rest of the time, so I watched and saw that it was as soon as he'd been out and cut the hay with the hay knife. We had ricks then and you had to go out and cut the hay off with a knife, off the hay ricks, take the top off, cut a foot and a half or so off every morning to give to the cattle. You'd take so much off every morning and you'd go right round the rick in time. Carry it on your head and take it down to the cattle in the field. Put it down on a nice dry place, if you could find one. Everybody did that. Nobody made silage then. When we started farming my dad gave me a cow and we had about twenty cows in the end that we had to feed and then we had to give it up. While we were doing the farming we didn't work any of the peat. But he was never very keen on the farming anyway. His family had always done the peat.

Matthew: So when we finished the farming we turned over to the garden peat, the horticultural peat. We were cutting peat for burning right up till the end of the Second World War, weren't we? Using the horse and cart. Then the tractors gradually came in and everyone went over to all this gardening peat. You see no burning peat now, nobody cuts by hand now. I used to do it, a bit of digging, but my elder brothers did most of that, so I'd drive the horse and cart, different things. It's all done by the machines, now. It'd be a rare sight to see anyone out working on the peat now. Years ago everyone would be out, the women and children too, the women used to work a lot on the peat. Not digging the peat, that was hard, but stacking and drying and that. I did a lot of that.

Minnie: I never did that. But I worked all the time on the gardening peat when we'd stopped farming. I used to bag it all up at the machine, one bag on each side, keep two bags going.

Matthew: We did that right up till our eldest son died about six years ago. Nothing else but garden peat, potting compost, mixtures, growbags, that sort of stuff. My son went off selling it.

Minnie: We had two sons, you see. The younger was a schoolteacher and the the older learnt his trade as a carpenter but he weren't too keen on that, though he did it for ten years. But then, when we started doing the

Above: Minnie Wall outside her peat milling shed.
Opposite: Corrugated chapel, Blakeway. The chapel was originally on Tealham Moor and was moved some sixty years ago to Blakeway. It has not been used as a chapel for some decades.

SWEET'S
PEAT
COMPOST
PLANTS
LOGS HAY
PEAT BLOCKS

peat, he bought a lorry and he used to go all around, quite a lot of places, Torquay and that, and we did our own selling. We had a rotovator behind the tractor, rotovate the peat, scrape it off with a bucket on a tractor or a Hymac and we were still doing it when my husband was eighty-four and I was nearly eighty. Then my son had a heart attack.

Matthew: He had quite a good business, though the competition was very keen.

Minnie: We've still got quite a bit of peat left, though we don't do anything with it now. But everyone here who had any peat would cut it and sell it. When people stopped burning peat and the machines for cutting came in there weren't so many needed to work here, so they went to the factories in Street, to Clarks shoes and Morlands and that. But that's all going now.

Matthew: Of course, the peat working has changed so much. In the days when we were cutting peat for burning you'd never see the deep pits. They take it all now, right from the top right down to the clay and make these deep pits, but you couldn't do that with burning peat. After three or four mumps deep it was no good at all, wouldn't hold together, it would fall to pieces, no good at all. They're using it all now for the horticultural peat, right down to the clay. In the old days you'd never see these deep pits, never see the clay. All the time I was peat working when I was young I never seen any clay, though I was out there every day.

Minnie: We worked the peat for years but I liked having the cattle. My mother said that when I was three or so if the door was open I'd be off out with the cows. I loved it. I'd be out there now! Always liked outside, never inside. I'd leave the housework, just leave it. Of course, I had to cook and bring up the children, but I always preferred out to in. I never wanted to go to town and get a job. And there was enough with the twenty or so cows we had to keep us going.

Matthew: You had to make sure you didn't get in debt!

Minnie: When the milk cheque came in, once a month, I paid out all the bills. Paid everything and what was left we had to live on. We owned our own land, most of it was ours, my dad gave it to us. We brought up two children on the milk from twenty cows, well, we started on the peat by the time we had our youngest, Trevor. I had seven pounds a week left after I'd paid the bills. Never borrowed a penny but we managed. Then things got a bit better when we did the horticultural peat and our eldest came in with a lorry and the machinery.

Matthew: We worked about ten acres or so down at Pool's Heath, that was our main peat, but we had several places where we did cut it, probably about twenty acres all together. In about forty years. Got right down to the clay and then it was finished. If you go up through the old railway, right the other side of Ashcott and before that, all the way up there on both sides, is reed as far as you can see. Comes right into the drove, all reed. As soon as you dig down to the clay, the next year it's full of reed. They'll spread out and shoot on. That's the start of the peat again, they do say, though I fancy we'll have to wait a few years!

Opposite: Olive Hardwick and family, Blakeway. Olive was the last of the few women who dug peat on the moors.

Farming

Ray Darby, Traditional Dairy Farmer, Chapel Farm, Middlezoy, 1981

'King's Sedgemoor is a good sort of place in a hot summer... it doesn't dry out at all. But in the winter everything has to clear out of here, back to the village, Middlezoy. You can only get out on the peat at the end of May, it gets very, very paunchy...'

Though agriculture now represents only about 3 per cent of the economy of the Levels and Moors, it was the effort over many centuries to bring this waterlogged land into pasturage that has marked and shaped it. The first real efforts to bring more land under cultivation, to drain and enclose the Moors, were undertaken by the great ecclesiastical powers in the area, but it was not until the Enclosure Acts in the eighteenth century, much later here than elsewhere in the country, that the patterns of rhynes, drainage ditches, and droves that we see today really got going. This was especially true on the southern part of the Levels where a series of relatively isolated moorland 'basins' presented particular difficulties. What had been open areas of common land — when not under water — were parcelled out amongst those who formerly had rights on the commons, with a bit of high ground around the home village, a bit of middle ground and a bit of the lowest lying ground allocated to each. This resulted in a pattern of extremely fragmented holdings which still persists today, with farmers sometimes having to move their cattle over considerable distances to get from one of their fields to the next. Any field which comes up for sale usually goes for a high price as farmers compete to fill in the gaps in their land. Ray Darby is typical of such farmers, with fields spread over five miles from his farmhouse in Middlezoy. His farming practice is also firmly, defiantly, traditional and he has never been tempted to under-drain his land. The one great innovation that he brought in was the mobile milking bail or parlour, which can be hauled by tractor from field to field so that the cows do not have to be moved all the way back to the farmyard to be milked. Of course, when he was a boy all the milking was done by hand and the milk had to be put into churns and brought back to the farm by horse and cart.

Above: Drinking from a rhyne on the moors.
Opposite: Ray Darby.

King's Sedgemoor is a good sort of place in a hot summer, being on peat — and it's a great, big, spongy, marshy peat — it doesn't dry out at all. In the winter everything has to clear out from here back to the village. You can only get out on the peat at the end of May. You've got great problems when you've got lots of mud and rain, it's very, very paunchy. In one summer a while back, when it was very, very wet and we were using the old-fashioned heavier bailers, we had four tractors and a crane to retrieve a bailer from the middle of a ten-acre field.

A big problem is when the water-levels go up and down, for the cattle. All their drinking is done from the rhynes and ditches and to mind, one day, we've had as many as six cattle in the ditch to be pulled out! That's the biggest trouble we get on this moor, cattle getting in a ditch or a rhyne, and once they get in they don't get out themself. It's quite frightening to see cattle in a ditch when there's only just about their head showing. We pull out quite a lot. This year it hasn't been quite so bad but we've pulled out ten or twelve in the last eight weeks. Otherwise, the peat fields, we get along fine, without any modern drainage. We work quite well changing the bail from field to field which means the cows don't have to walk very far and consequently, I reckon, we get a milk raise because of that.

We have sixty-seven cows at the moment. When we run out of grass on Sedgemoor to get to the next acreage, about fifty acres, we have to go right through the centre of the village and we always use four or five people on bicycles to make sure to travel through the villages. The family consists of five people: the wife, daughter and two sons and we all come out to get them through. But this only happens about every eight or nine weeks when we move from one block to another. We try to keep them off the roads as much as possible because cars and cattle don't mix. Our fields are scattered about in four parishes! From one end to the other that's about five and a half miles. That's the longest distance we travel, but not too often.

When we leave King's Sedgemoor and the surrounding area just before Christmas, the middle of December, the cattle come into the yard and they stay there till they go out about the last week in May. They don't get out in any field for about four months.

No one's done any drainage here, nor do I want to, because I feel by draining peat moors you're going to shrink the peat and therefore lower the surface and then in future generations someone's going to have to pay to pump out all that water because you won't get gravity drainage as you have at the moment. When I was a boy, King's Sedgemoor would be under four of five feet of water in the winter. Nowadays we keep just about awash at a bad time, which is probably bad for the soil, neither dry nor wet. I would like to see it flood for a week or so every winter. That'd kill the vermin and refresh the soil.

Ray Darby, Chapel Farm, Middlezoy, 2005

Ray Darby is farming in much the same way as he was twenty-five years ago. He has a few more milking cows, more fields, but the historic pattern of the farm is much the same, fields scattered about the moors and on the higher ground round the village of Middlezoy. He still takes his milking bail to his cows down on King's Sedgemoor, then hauls the milk back to the bulk tank in Chapel Farm. Perhaps the greatest difference in his farming practice lies in the administration of the farm. He is much concerned now with ESAs, Environmentally Sensitive Areas, SSSIs, the Environment Agency and all the new government schemes for helping a farmer like him to stay farming on the Levels.

We got seventy-three milking cows now, not a lot of difference to what we had twenty years ago. We'll bring them in off the moors up here to Chapel Farm just before Christmas. They're out there on the stubble turnips now. It's nice and warm so we put up with the mud and they get on with eating the turnips. You can grow either stubble turnips or swede rape. With stubble turnip it's a double crop on the acreage. I mean when we put in ten acres of wheat, after the wheat's gone, so long as they're planted about 15 August and we got reasonable weather conditions, you can get a tremendous crop. The cows walk out on the turnips and strip 'em, pull 'em up and crunch 'em up, they just love 'em. They milk well on them, too. Most farms, the cows have finished eating green stuff in October, but my cows are eating green stuff right up to a day or so before Christmas. They need some concentrate too, but it's a lovely healthy feed.

I'm trying to make it dog and stick farming. Land you can go out onto with your dog and throw a stick for him. Stay off of sprays and artificial. We do use some artificial but very little. We also got 100 acres of cereals. The wheat, well we don't plant all that much because we got set-aside. Eight per cent, so about eight acres. You can't use it at all, just mow it to keep the weeds down. The only thing that's kept us going making a reasonable amount of profit is the ESA payment and the IACS, Integrated Administration and Control System, payment. The whole farm, virtually, has got a payment on it if I want to get it. IACS is what you get for growing cereals — you have to do the set-aside to get the payment. Or the SSSI, I got that too. I got a whole lot of them. And the ESA payment, I banked it the other day, nearly £12,000, so you see without that... There's lots of conditions, mind. It's my land and they come along and tell me, 'You can do this with it.' But the thing is, it's a bit like I like to farm it anyway. There's not much difference between what I do now and what I'd do if I didn't have the payment. So it's a good thing.

I haven't done any drainage systems, I decided it had to stay like it was. Most fields are like a saucer and that's bad. You can dig a trench out on the surface to let the water run off but you can't put any drains in under. We bought another field not long back and it was a mass of rushes and they said those rushes had to be cut, took away, and then weed-wiped, sprayed, because the rushes were crowding out all the grass and I done that the last two years and the field's coming back to normal pasture and good. If you work with them, these people, I haven't found them too bad. One girl, a bit new, told me that some ditches needed cleaning. I'd only cleaned them two years earlier. Trouble was there's more nitrogen in the water now, and there was duckweed and all that. It looked worse than it was.

We're farming the three of us, my two sons and I, and it's about five and a half miles from one end to the other of all the farm. I bought three or four fields just lately, trying to put any spare money I got into land so that when my time comes they won't take away the money that we worked so hard for. So it's grown over the years. I only started out from Father with twenty-six acres and I turned that into over 300 all paid for. Grandfather bought this farm but it wasn't called Chapel Farm then, it was called Taunton's, I don't know why. About 116 years ago he bought the house and then Father had it for all his life and then it's passed on to me and now at seventy-three I can't expect to be around here for more than another twenty years! My two sons'll have it, though, sadly, they won't farm together and it'll be split up. Definitely. I can have a big stick and hold it up high, I don't need to hit them with it but it's got to be there. When I'm gone… Just the three of us work the farm. I'd like to get in some more help at times. Grain hauling, I asked a couple of chaps, 'Would you be prepared to do a bit of grain hauling into Bridgwater?' But oh no, it couldn't be done. I hauled tractors and trailers, four loads a day approximate, 259 tons and a few kilos all by myself this year. At seventy-three I consider that not bad going.

One of the great things when you make silage is moles. You don't want not even one mole hill in your silage because that's spread around tons and tons of silage, the dirt gets in, goes in the trailer, it's literally spread over the whole clamp of silage. It lowers the grade of the silage everywhere. So if it flooded for a few weeks, moles can't swim very well, they'd be all gone. That's my feeling on it. What they do now is they push the water on to us, they don't want it in the Tone, in Taunton and so on, so they flood us for three or four days, five or six inches deep, leave us all soggy, then drain it out again. In other words we're just used as a dumping ground, a drain, and that happens two or three times a year, virtually every year. It didn't so much last year but I think it will now, soon. Once already this year the River Sowy came over the banks when the tide was high because it's a gravity feed, no pumping. King's Sedgemoor is not pumped at all. No, no it just has to run out and if it coincides with a lot of rain with a high tide, there's three or four hours a day not a drop of water runs out, so it builds up and then it runs out when the tide goes down, out at Dunball. As a boy, for about six weeks or more we could just about see the tops of the gates on the moor when it flooded. I remember when I was about nine or ten and another boy and me tried to make a boat out of canvas but Father spotted it and ripped it up, worried we'd be drowned.

Now it's the Environment Agency mainly decides on the water-level because it's all just been changed. I used to be vice-chairman of our IDB, Internal Drainage Board — Othery, Middlezoy, Westonzoyland — along with chairman Mervyn Winslade. They only allow us two members now when we used to have about twenty. I voted myself out of it because I decided that we wouldn't have any say with the Environment Agency anyway. They keep the whole thing going now. Like everything else it's all got so big and we are all

Paul and Chris Darby at the milking bail.

told what you can have and what you can get. It's not any fun anymore. No.

Let me tell you one little thing happened to me last August when I was busy hauling corn with number one son. They changed our collection of milk. It comes at the most awkward time ever, so our tank was never empty, we're waiting to put new milk in because it's full from milkings before. And so a couple of times we didn't wash the tank. So what do we do? Leave the milk stood out in the yard? Because we bring it home in one big lump, the milk, we don't milk into the stationary tank, like other farmers, we milk out on the moors in the milking bails. So we left it like that and my bacter-scan went up awfully high, I admit, higher than it ought to, so we eventually got this cured but we had three readings which incurred a penalty of six pence a litre, knocked off of my milk cheque — that's £2,300. I had a lousy milk cheque. We'd never had any trouble for fifteen years but all these things coupled together, mainly instigated by the haulier picking up our milk at a crazy time, and my grouse was that milk went in the lorry and it was not real bad and it was sold all in the line, so I gave them £2,300. It was sold anyway, of course it was. It went in with everything else, it didn't contaminate the lorry, but because on a line of bacter-scan they said it was too high — and I admit it did go too high but they should have come along and helped sort out the problem but no — 'twas all left to us in August. I asked if they could pick up a different time — oh no, that couldn't be done. So that's money I gave them on top of the usual profit they make on selling. It always falls back on the producer. That's just a grouse, I know it was my fault, but they said we always had had exemplary keeping quality, the bacter-scan was perfect.

My feelings about the farm haven't changed but, of course, a lot has. For Father, when I was thirteen, fourteen, I was sat on a milking-stool and pouring it in a churn. Then when I started farming in 1958 we bought a milking bail and the milk went into a machine, this wonderful new machine, and we stayed on like that for about fifteen years. Then we were told we had to go bulk. All these things progressed on and then went alternate days, the lorry only comes alternate days, which is all for cheapness. Everything has got to be done so cheap, so that the supermarkets can make their high profits.

If we here can make a profit and keep going, everyone ought to be able to. But, having said that, I do have the advantage of all this ESA money, take out the IACS payments which is a good number of thousands, take out the ESA payments, the SSI payments, English Nature, all them, and couple that with that little blip I had in August, I'd be bankrupt twice over. That's with seventy milking cattle. So many times I've heard that without 200 head, 300 you can't survive but I say you can. It's not easy. You can spend so much so easy. We've toyed with the idea of giving up milking and we ought to. It's not economic the way we do it. But then what? Do beef. Then we're into buying in calves, keeping twice as many, so instead of keeping what we got now, about 180 head of stock — seventy milking with followers to replace the dairy and some beef — we'd be up 350 head of stock. My policy is dictated by the ESA. You've got to eat the grass. You can't do anything else with the grass down on King's Sedgemoor. You're not allowed to plough it. And you can't drain it. So this is what we get the payment for. You're not allowed to use much artificial and I'm happy with that system. It's not easy money but work with them and it's good money.

I got cattle right down on the moor now, in December, the grass has been so nice. And I've got free grass, too. There's three or four who've bought up fields down on the moor just for the investment. Not farmers. They've been made redundant or what-have-you and had £30,000 or £40,000 and they've bought land and get all the payments from English Nature or the others but they don't want the grass. But they've got to do something with it, got to have it eaten, so they ask me if I want it. They can do a bit of duck shooting there, for themselves, though they can't let anyone else go down with them. This morning I went down to see the cattle there and I put up three, four lots of ducks, some deer, it's a haven, just what the English Nature people want.

It's so different from when I started, when my father was here. There was none of that conservation money. Just pony and cart, milking cows, and that's all you did. I was not the first but nearly the first with the milking bails. I bought my first in 'fifty-eight. Before you milked by hand out on the moors, brought it back with the pony and cart. Things have changed one hell of a lot when I look back on it. Now it's gone the other way. We were making a real profit about sixteen, seventeen years ago. In 'seventy-six with the terrible dry summer we had beautiful grass down on the moor. It stayed green there when everywhere else in the country was parched. We had about sixty cows that we were milking. Every other high ground farmer was feeding their cattle barley straw to keep them alive and my milk fetched then £10,294 in one month. A little farmer like me! Now, with a few more cows, twenty years and more on, we are lucky with £6,000 in a month. Simply because the price per litre was higher. That was exceptionally high because of supply and demand, we had the good milk then and other people didn't but let's say £8,000 would have been about it normally.

My fields are still just as fragmented, nearly, as they were twenty years ago, though I have bought some more fields and I've got five or six in a row now which makes it a bit better. They don't come up very often, mainly to do with tradition. 'Oh, no,' they say, 'that was Mother's field and I wouldn't sell that one.' Even when I've suggested we do a swap so that both of us could get our fields sorted. Oh no! That's sentiment. Right down on the moor the fields will fetch £1,600, but on the nice high ground where you've got the IACS payments too, you are talking £3,000. And you can't make that money out of it. Well, to be quite honest, I have made up my mind already that now the single payment's in, whether we use it for growing grain or we don't we still get the payment on the single payment thing, so I'm going to give several fields a rest next year and just not plant them, because the cost of planting and spraying and combining, for wheat cereal, the cost of doing all that work, if you get a good crop, just about pays you out, if you don't get a good crop you're going to be in debt on it. It's scaling down, the payment. For the next ten years it's going to go down, down, down and then farming'll be on it's own, we shan't be getting anything from them. Well, not for the grain. The single payment takes over from IACS but not the ESA, that's separate, the environmental payment, so I'll still get that, I'm sitting pretty as regards that. This is why I don't mind buying extra fields so long as I can find a few cows to eat them off and keep within the rules. They're paying us just about a hundred pounds an acre. It's good business to buy at £1,400 or £1,500 an acre and get £100 an acre hopefully for ever. But you have to eat off the grass, you see. They check up and come round — some nice young lady, hopefully. I was down there, I'd mowed some thistles off a day before I should have done, end of July and she came along and said, 'You're not supposed to cut them till August.' And I said, 'But I'm only a day early!' 'Oh, that doesn't matter,' she said, 'I've walked the whole moor all day long and this is the last place and I've found you.' She loved it! She was from DEFRA, the Ministry of Agriculture, I'm talking a few years back now, and she was so happy to have found one field where I'd done something a day too early! It made her day.

It's not really difficult to keep within the guidelines. I'm farming now slightly better than what Father used to. We do make sure to dig out trenches and things and get rid of this surface water because I know it causes trouble if you don't. But I'm farming more or less how I want to and I couldn't improve, I couldn't go mad about it. The cattle are still drinking from the rhynes. But this year I've had to complain three or four times because the water-level will suddenly drop and the cattle can't reach down to drink. We've had cattle getting in the ditch. It suddenly goes down one foot six, the ditch is empty. This is from the Environment Agency. That lazy torment what should be looking after things properly needs my boot up his backside! If I want to talk about anything down King's Sedgemoor, I've got to ring up Bristol now. Everything's gone big. With the Internal Drainage Boards the local farmers used to look after everything, not any more.

We're more tied down now, there's lots more stress now, mainly the fault of all the paperwork. There's forms to be filled, all my cattle have passports. It's a good thing but there's so much paperwork. All sorts of rules have to be adhered to. It's probably good, what with foot and mouth like we had and everything, but it's more work. It's so difficult on our place, even if I got more help. The fields are all scattered about. If I were to say, 'go and fetch the cows from the moor', you've got to find the field first. It's all intermixed with others. This is the way it is.

David Henry Durnam

David was born at Crossways Farm near Moorland in 1924. His grandfather bought the farm in 1920 and remarkably little has changed over the years, despite 'the electric' coming and the mechanical muck-spreaders and the tractors that replaced the horses. Life may have got a bit easier but it has never been a rich living. In 1982 when these photographs were taken, the farm had seventy sheep and twenty-five head of beef cattle. David Durnam had an enormous bull that he could ride and a ram which followed him everywhere, the flock trailing after. He had an orchard of cider apples and made his own cider, to which he was partial. Now in 2005, the orchard has all blown down and the cattle and sheep have gone. His farm is strangely quiet though he has a new dog and a few ducks. With no children and no family he lets out his fields for pasture. He is seen here (opposite and above) sheep shearing at Crossways Farm and with his dog (right).

Above: George David's farmyard, Burrowbridge.

Opposite: George David milking by hand. 'At the moment I'm milking 12 cows. There's 14 followers, so that's 31 head altogether. I found that 12, with milking by hand all the time is about right. They give about 40, 45 gallons a day. That's enough in my opinion. And I enjoy milking them by hand, you know. Time doesn't matter, it's my own, it doesn't bother me. With a nice quiet cow you can relax and you've only got the cow you're milking to think about.'

Ralph Baker, Progressive Farmer, Stileways Farm, Meare, 1981

'... I was born on the Moors... in the village of Meare... When I left school I came to work on my father's farm... I've added two extra farms... I've got thirty years of diaries sitting on the shelf and in 1955... with the same farming system, the tasks we were doing then hardly compare with anything we are doing today...'

Ralph Baker gained a national reputation as a pioneer of drainage schemes on the Levels and Moors. This brought him into some conflict with conservationists and, to a certain degree, with traditional farmers on the moors who wanted a higher water-table and a more traditional approach to farming. This interview took place just after the publication of Marion Shoard's great polemic The Theft of the Countryside, *which acted as a clarion call to conservationists and all those opposed to the system of farm subsidies which were drastically transforming the English landscape. Ralph Baker featured strongly in Shoard's book as one of the villains of the piece. However, in all his proselytising for improved drainage he was only expressing what a great many local farmers felt: the need to prevent too much water coming on to the fields in the first place and then to get it off as quickly as possible, in order to make profitable and productive a farming system that was threatened by contemporary economic reality. He also had a real love for the wildlife and the natural beauty of the Levels and thought that modern farming and wildlife should be able to find a way to coexist. He would refer to himself, along with the marsh orchids and the snipe, as one of the threatened indigenous species.*

I was born on the Moors. I was born in the village of Meare and my father was a farmer. Our playground was the Levels. When I left school I came to work on my father's farm, and that's the farm I have today, I've added two extra farms so it's now 400 acres that I'm farming. It's a very big farm by moorland standards. It's still conventional in the sense that it's still a Somerset moorland permanent pasture with dairy cows, as it was in 1955, the only difference is the production's gone up. I keep a diary of what we do every day, I've got thirty years of diaries sitting on the shelf, and in 1955 on the same farm with the same farming system, the tasks we were doing then hardly compare with anything we're doing today. For instance, in those days we were cutting hay and baling hay loose and putting it in stacks, ricks, in the field; cutting reed from the ditches to thatch the ricks; cutting spars from the willow trees, pollarding them for the spars. We would feed the livestock in the winter from the stack in the field by cutting it with a hay knife into squares and carrying it out on the top of our heads and slicing it up. You would cut it into flats, we called them, and bring it into the yard where the milking cows were housed. We would buy mangolds, because we couldn't grow them, and feed them to the animals in the stalls. We couldn't grow them because it was too wet and you had the danger of flooding. It was pretty severe and you would expect that most of the winter you would loose the farm to flooding.

The fifty acres that I under-drained in 1973 was a reed bed. This is the fifty acres which has been of such interest in recent years, it was the first piece that was under-drained in the Somerset Levels. I've had thousands of visitors to the farm in the last few years, there's hardly a conservationist in the land that hasn't come and looked at it, a lot of them were farmers, too, wanting to see.

When I took over the farm in 1963, I called in ADAS, the Agricultural Development and Advisory Service, to advise me how to drain it. The ADAS officer came out with me and drove around the fields. He said, 'Quite honestly get out while you're still young and get a decent farm.' Because it was that type of swamp. But it wasn't easy to get farms. I was very glad that I got a tenancy. In 1966, '67 I was coming home one night from a Round Table meeting and it was pouring with rain and I was worried by where to put the cows because it was obviously going to be a flood. None of those people from the Round Table, from all walks of life, would be affected by the flood, they may have to drive through a bit of flood water in the road, but it wouldn't cost them anything. I thought, 'Something must be done!' I thought

Duck punting on the flooded moors in winter.

the only way I could drain the farm would be to launch a big drainage scheme to drain the whole of the Brue Valley but I realised the difficulties of convincing politicians and government that it was the thing to do so I applied to the Nuffield Foundation for a scholarship in 1969, to study arterial drainage, not just the engineering of drainage but the social, economical and political implications to farmers of largescale land drainage.

I went to Holland, Germany, Denmark, Finland, Ireland and I saw schemes with private pumps that I decided I could adapt to my own farm. I decided to drain my own cabbage patch independently of the rest. So in 1972 I put in the first under-drains and private pumps in the Somerset Lowlands. And in 1973 I invited the Somerset Trust for Nature Conservation to look at what I had done. The conservation movement was just emerging and I thought we could all go on together. There is something very special about the Somerset Levels, it's special to me, I'm an indigenous species of the Somerset Lowlands as much as the flora and fauna, and I would hate to see species destroyed, but at the same time it is also my workplace and I had to make a living. If farming is not prosperous you go back to the reed bed syndrome which isn't that exciting for conservation anyway. What is so good for conservation is the land as it has developed through the years.

I was driven by the pressure of lying in bed at night, the fear of seeing your business destroyed by someone else's water coming down from the highlands, the fear of flooding. I had to do something about it. It wasn't a grand vision, just the need to do something. All the 150,000 acres of the Somerset Lowlands, or all the 5,000 acres of the Brue Valley could have benefited from a drainage scheme, but conservation ruled the day with Sites of Scientific Interest and that. It's been done in the Fens and there's no reason why it shouldn't be done in the Somerset Lowlands. I asked the question why in the Fens and why not in Somerset and I expected to find more progressive farmers, more prosperous farmers, better drainage engineers. But, in fact, what I discovered was that because we are sure of rain in June and July we were quite safe in dairy farming, but in the Fens they were very unsure of rain in June and July, and there's nothing worse than being in dairy farming and being short of grass. It's very important to have rain in June and July and we had that, so our grassland in Somerset is used for dairying. On the Fens they tended to go away from grass and towards cereals and, having started growing cereals, the last thing you can afford is a flood at any time of year: the crop is spoilt and your whole year's income is gone. So we stayed with grass and dairying and although we had floods occasionally it was difficult to tell what was lost. We did not have the overall pressure to under-drain here that they had in the East of England.

The Fenman who had learnt to farm cereals was stopped from coming into Somerset because he could never buy a big enough patch of land to make it worthwhile. He moved to Romney Marsh. I isolated my first fifty acres by building a polder round the outside, you have to keep the flood waters out, but for the second scheme I joined forces with my neighbours, a nine-farmer scheme and we used roads and natural features for the polder. In the next scheme that I did I had a 150-acre scheme. The polder doesn't keep the flood water out entirely but up to a certain limit. We do occasionally have summer floods. In 1979 for the whole of the month of June the farm was under water.

Having under-drained it there's a big plus to plough the land and level it because one of the big problems we had here was the open gripe ditches, the old field drains. You then re-seed it so you get better quality grasses, that's a short cut, you could get there by better fertiliser use, better management over a ten-year span. The way I try to put it in words is that previously it was taking forty acres to fill a silage clamp and now I can fill it with twenty-five acres. That's the economic advantage. The other big advantage is that I can get the cows out almost a month earlier than previously and to get the cows out to grass in March, rather than April — and many didn't till May — is a real plus. Particularly with the March grass because the milk price is still high. Of course, the other advantage which you can't really put figures on is being able to adopt timeliness on operations in the field. You can get out there to put on your fertiliser in the spring, you can spray slurry at the best time of year to get the utilisation of the nutriments in the slurry. The limiting factor is the water-table.

If I'd not been one of a family of six, if I'd had a father who had had a farm and my father had left me the farm and the stock on it and I was not needing to raise capital then, probably, I could have been one of the farmers content with old ways, though each generation has problems. But my

Saltmoor Pumping Station on the River Parrett.

problem was particularly acute because I started farming in 1963 with an investment of £200. I was immediately borrowing money from the bank to farm so I had to get a higher return than those who had the capital base already. So having started farming faster, you then found pressures so you looked for ways to ease those pressures which admittedly involved spending capital on improvement. You needed a little bit more capital to finance the return on the investment, which meant, in the dairy case, that you had more cows. And you'd need more equipment. These were all the things that farmers were striving to do at the behest of government through the 1960s, '70s and early '80s even.

Back in the early 1970s the Somerset Lowlands were already thought of as something special in flora and fauna and I fully supported that that must be preserved. Where I parted company with the conservationists was that the flora and fauna was fairly small, you didn't have elephants needing thousands of acres, the biggest possibly being an otter. You need perhaps islands of a minimum of 100 acres, although the conservationists need to tell us how many land features we need to go around that to make sure it is preserved in perpetuity. But I'm certain you can preserve the flora and fauna in the SSSIs now proposed — island sites of several thousand acres altogether – so I see that the rest of the land could go ahead with progressive farming. But the other thing that I recognise is that the Somerset Lowlands are an individual landscape with unique features and that is not so easy to preserve.

We could have progressive grassland farming always, provided we've got the island sites, several thousand acres, to preserve the flora and fauna. Then, if the marsh marigold becomes the saviour of mankind in the future and brings everlasting life, as long as the land is there we can plant the whole of the Somerset Lowlands with marsh marigolds. The island sites – wrong term island, because they're depressions, just the opposite to an island – the SSSIs are havens for birds. I'm not sure that you need necessarily preserve ten million of the species to preserve the species. You need to make a judgement on what birds are important and what is necessary to the nature of their survival.

Of course, the reason that land is designated as an SSSI is because it was farmed in that traditional way, because it was difficult to get to down on the moors. I've always believed there is plenty of room for everyone and regretted the controversy that has taken place. I was a member of the NCC, Nature Conservancy Council, Wetlands Project and what distressed me in the early 1970s was that there was a group of people that were throwing up their hands in horror at change. Any change. The farmers and conservationists are now much closer together than they were fifteen years ago. So often those who throw up their hands at change are trying to regain something they remember from their youth, the hens clucking in the farmyard syndrome. The true conservationists, the true scientists that applied themselves to it, turned up with some good answers. I do believe there will be a continuing evolution.

But from now on the SSSIs will be museum sites. That's fine. I would be worried about them choosing 16,000 acres in one site. I believe that the great advantage of what we've got a the moment is that we've got about ten sites of varying sizes — that gives a much better cover. I think that's OK and I think it's important to the farming community that they can get on with farming the rest, perhaps with landscape restrictions. But I think it's very important to the flora and fauna, particularly the birds, that they have feeding grounds around. Because although they do come into the SSSIs I've got many more birds coming out to graze the good quality grass than I had previously.

The traditional farming here dates from the Enclosure Acts. You were given a bit of land around your farm which was built above the flood level, and then you were usually given a little bit of silt land and a little bit of peat land so you were already travelling in different directions, that's what started the fragmentation. It has been increased through the years because whereas in most places only two farmers on either side of a piece of land would be interested in it, in the Somerset Levels the whole village is interested! So you have high land prices if you sell it in small lots and you get not only fragmentation of occupiers of land but very quickly fragmentation of owners. Under the Enclosure Acts the farm base was in the village with some down in the lowland and it was balanced in such a way that you could afford to have low production on that which was down in the lowland. So you are still in that position and having an SSSI designated in your low moorland the hardship is not that great, particularly with dairy where you can rear your livestock down on the lowland. The ones I feel sorry for are those within SSSIs who have a very high proportion of their farm within an SSSI. Where you can carry, say, 25 per cent of your farm at low production as long as you can produce well on the rest, if you've got 75 per cent at low production then you are in difficulty. In an ideal world then you probably should be looking for high land for those farmers who have a high proportion of their land within SSSIs, to keep them in business. It's very important that they do stay in business in the SSSIs because if it isn't farmed it will swiftly degenerate and certainly, on some of the land that the RSPB owns, the quality of the grass that is made into hay that comes off that is lower than barley straw. And if you've got 25 per cent of your farm doing that perhaps you can carry it but there comes a time perhaps when you think why bother with that? Why not give it up completely and buy in barley straw? It would be an easier life. Then that means that you walk out and leave. If that starts happening on any scale, if there were 16,000 acres, for instance, that no one wanted because the quality of the grazing had been allowed to deteriorate — and restrictions on mowing till July are likely to move that way — the conservation bodies, either the Nature Conservancy Council, or the Somerset Trust, or the RSPB, whoever's responsible for maintaining them, could be faced with making 16,000 acres of hay in July. The logistics of that are quite frightening. They won't sell it after they've made it because it would be worth less than barley straw, so you get the ludicrous position of organising that operation. It's just not real. But if they do not do it, it will revert to scrub, and once it reverts to scrub then it isn't going to be the Somerset Lowland which everyone is saying is so wonderful.

There is a real danger of that happening, particularly if farm pressures get tighter and you look at ways of contracting your business; what you contract out of is the SSSI land. So I worry quite a lot about what's going to happen over the next fifty years. I believe the conservation bodies have not faced up to the real problems that are looming if it becomes uneconomical to farm.

To me the reasonable thing is a patchwork. If you could enter into a management agreement for a shorter period, or you could get out of that management agreement, you could get farmers over fifty whose expenses were lower and needs were lower who would be happy to revert to a lower standard of farming, the son could then improve the land from the conservation status, but others would be coming into that status. The whole of the Somerset Lowlands would be a patchwork of different standards of farming, it's only a matter of management of two-thirds of the grasslands.

On West Sedgemoor and on Tealham Moor there are areas that have been heavily drained by the pumps side by side with RSPB land that's been preserved. Where one farmer can use resources to pump out land economically then the community — and it's the wider community that wants conservation — can just as easily afford to pump water back into some of these sites to maintain a high water-table. You can have a whole patchwork of varying water-levels, as there is at the moment and always has been. It's not anything new. We always say different farmers' cows have different length necks! Every one of them wants the water in the rhynes to be at a different level. So when there's Internal Drainage Board meetings all the farmers argue over it. But these days there's the pasture pump, they're very successful. I've never believed that you need a high water-table for wet fences, the low water-table gives a much better fence. And I've never believed that you need a high water-table for the cows to drink, you can either have a path to come down to the water in the ditches and rhynes or, if you've got a pump scheme you can use that. I've never believed you need a high water-table to grow grass, most certainly not, because the lower the water-table the lower the roots can grow, so the more nutrients they can pick up.

There is a real danger if you are cultivating frequently on peat and growing crops, moving the soil, that you are going to have a lot of oxidisation, and it's the removal of the water and the oxidisation that causes shrinkage. As long as you stay with grassland I believe that the shrinkage is going to be very minimal.

I've got fourteen feet of peat with eighteen inches of silt on the top. I've only got five or six acres with peat on top. I've farmed land with peat on the top but I've got out of it because it's difficult to farm. At the beginning I'd take anything anywhere but I've slowly been offered more choice land. The peat is difficult to farm as grassland because it's very acid so you can't get the better quality grasses to grow and if they grow they're not very productive. If it is productive it's usually cocksfoot and Yorkshire fog, which isn't very palatable. If you're going for cropping, then peat would be very much better, but if you're going for grassland then you have great difficulty in some places to get anything to grow.

Had we not had surpluses in Europe, or if we at some time in the future become short of food again in Europe or even in Britain, then I believe that the Somerset Lowlands have so much potential to produce more food, they are ideal. And that was the way that I saw us going forward in the seventies. I firmly believed that. But we now have, thanks to Europe's farmers, self-sufficiency in food and so we start from a different position; and it is likely that we will remain self-sufficient in food in the future. If we do, then it is sensible that we should take land out of production. And rather than take vast areas out of production, it could well be much more attractive to farm less intensively in other areas. So you have perhaps the SSSIs in the Somerset Lowlands being taken out of production and letting the rest of the Somerset Lowlands be very much less productive than their potential. The advantage of doing that is that if land goes for development it is lost for ever, but if it goes for an SSSI or an ESA, an environmentally sensitive area, it can always be reclaimed for food production in time of need. And who knows what the future holds? If, for instance, we had had a rye grass disease instead of a Dutch elm disease the effects on the economy of Britain, and being able to feed the nation, would have been quite dramatic. The reservoir of potential is still there. I believe that over the next twenty-five years conservation is going to be a very good way of storing land.

There's a real danger that if farmers haven't got enough income the countryside would degenerate. A certain amount of degeneration could be useful for conservation, but a massive degeneration would be bad. If the way to manage the landscape is to keep farmers' incomes sufficient, then that is the way to go. Certainly there'll be fewer farmers. There is every point in keeping the small traditional farms going from the conservation point of view, from the rural community point of view, from the countryside point of view. But I do believe they will not survive without help. If that is what the community wants then it will be very important to support the family farm, and even support them so that they can lower outputs dramatically by doing more handwork on that small farm, going back to your ancient type of farming. It's quite possible. We would find it difficult because we've been brought up to a different way now, but our grandchildren perhaps would want to go back. They could enjoy the good life!

We have this standard of living and its very difficult to give it up. I would find it very difficult to go back to the horizon of the village. I did not even leave Somerset till I was sixteen years old. I'd never been out of the county, we didn't spend money, we didn't have motorcars. I would find it difficult to go back to that and the next generation after me would find it difficult, too. But their children might be able to ease back. I see that as a reality that might have to happen and it is much preferable to a collapse in the rural economy, such as happened in the 1920s. It will have to be managed slowly down to a lower intensity. Modern technology today is able to farm vast areas and if the thing gets really depressed it is the small farmer who will go. We need to guard against that. So I cannot see how you can avoid more control in the future. Planning over the rural economy, planning control over what could be called change in the physical features of the landscape.

In the 1930s we had a lower standard of living than the rest of the community. We survived, we ate because we grew food so we didn't have the starvation of the Jarrow marchers. But the privations were quite real, we had no money in the farming community in those days. Then the 1948 Act gave security to the farmer which had not been seen since the Middle Ages, probably. That meant that we progressed at the expense of a lot of fellow farmers leaving the land. We contracted from 880,000 to 200,000; the sort of shedding that industry has been exhorted to do recently. That is the cost we have paid for feeding the nation. We must remember that we were not feeding ourselves before that.

David Baker, Organic Farmer, Stileways Farm, Meare, 2006

'It's changed so much. Now we are farming with the environment rather than against it. We still flood here, that's one of our biggest problems here on the Levels, you can't stop that.'

Ralph Baker died in 1994. By this time, his son David had already taken over the day-to-day running of the farm. David's story is a very different one to his father's and the plot has changed in a way that Ralph could never have imagined. David's answer to the problems of farming on the Levels is to farm organically, helped and supported by the premium price paid for organic milk and by a quite different system of grants and subsidies which have raised the concerns of conservation above those of productivity. Further drainage and the 'improvement' of marginal lands are no longer an issue in this new climate — as long as the milk price holds steady and the grants are paid.

I went to agricultural college in Cirencester from 1976 to 1979 and did a diploma in agriculture and advanced farm management. Not many farmers' sons in this area went away to college, they usually went to Brymore School and then went to Cannington. So in 'seventy-nine I came back from Cirencester and because my father was a tenant on most of the farms, I had to work for at least two years on the farm to qualify for the successional tenancy, because it's five years out of seven, you have to be on the farm for five out of seven years, but the three years' education counts as part of it, so I had to work for two years. So I started working at home. Then in 1984 milk quotas came in and that was one of the biggest effects ever on the dairy farming industry. This meant you could not expand. At the time we had 100 cows at the Turnbridge unit at Meare and 100 cows at the Abbey Farm unit at Glastonbury four miles away. We had two cowmen, one other general farm worker and a farm manager. Dad didn't really do much physical work at the time, he was mainly doing NFU work and full-time management. I came back as an extra. But when the milk quotas came in it had a drastic effect. It meant that you couldn't expand any more without leasing or buying milk quota. Now, because we had a lot of rented land, most of the land was rented, we always had a lot of rent to pay and didn't have a lot of surplus capital to go out and purchase milk quota to expand, whereas a lot of farmers who had a lot of money, who were owner-occupiers, could afford to borrow money to expand their milk quotas.

So that continued for a few years, trying to make money under a system which restricted the amount of milk you were allowed to produce. The only way you could actually increase your profits was to get a better milk price. The whole idea with the controlled quota was that there would be no surplus produced so the milk price in theory should have gone up. And it did a bit but not to the extent that you needed. We operated a low-input, low-output system which meant that we got most of our production from grass and silage and we had low levels of purchase of concentrate feed, so we operated that system and a 100 per cent spring calving system. This meant that all the cows calved within three months of the year in the spring.

Now, in 1987 we weren't making any money because we couldn't expand and we couldn't get higher milk prices, so we decided to make our two cowmen redundant, close down the Abbey Farm unit, sell fifty cows and bring fifty cows back to the Turnbridge unit to make a 150-cow unit there, using the money from the sale of the fifty cows to put up extra cubicle buildings and a silage pit. The farm manager chap left and got another

David Baker at his farm on the moor road between Meare and Glastonbury, with Glastonbury Tor in the background.

farm on a council farm. So it was left with myself and the general farm worker running the farm. I did the afternoon milking and the other chap, who was the same age as me, did the morning milking, all on the same acreage of land. So we operated that system and then we got in relief milkers if we needed time off. So we just cut our costs, we tried to get better by cutting costs rather than expand.

Then the chap who worked for me, the same age as me, died of cancer on his forty-first birthday. He had throat cancer. Jenny, my wife, who was a legal executive, gave up her work and took a ten-week computer course and she took over the running of the office so that I could milk full time. My dad had divorced from my mother, he left here back in the early 'eighties and he was doing NFU work and consultancy work. He did some of the office work and was still getting a salary here but he was in London a lot. He wasn't here on the day-to-day running of the farm. My mum and dad were still partners in the farm up until he died, and I became a partner in 1984. My dad actually died in 1994 at the age of sixty-three. He had a brain tumour. But I was actually running the farm on a day-to-day basis from the age of twenty-three. I went and saw the bank manager and things like that. My dad was doing lots of other things and getting a salary from that: he worked for Wessex Water — or the NRA as it was then, the National Rivers Authority — which was to do with the land drainage on the moors, he was on the Drainage Board. He was heavily involved in the NFU. He was chairman of the Animal Health and Welfare Committee in London. It was when BSE hit the headlines, he was one of the main men there and was often on television in the early 'nineties. He was advising the government and things on what to do about BSE. He could afford to do that because I was back home working on the farm!

So while Graham, my farm worker, was sick, until he died, my wife was doing the office work and feeding the calves and things like that — we had no kids at the time — then Graham died. I'd been to an NFU meeting about the Somerset Levels and farming and it seemed that the Somerset Levels was going all conservation, they didn't really want farming, everything was going to ESAs, Environmentally Sensitive Areas. We had some ESA land, tier one, but a lot round here was going ESA tier three. So a lot of farmers had given up dairying and had taken the ESA money and gone into beef, things like that. You see tier one ESA means that you are not allowed to put fertilisers on the land, you are not allowed to spray. Well, you could put low levels of fertiliser and low levels of top-wiping for the weeds, weed-wiping, but you couldn't blanket spray the weeds. There were various other restrictions. That was the least protected land, the lowest level. You were really being paid to farm traditionally as you did fifty years ago. Tier three was you couldn't put any fertiliser on at all, the land was semi-flooded, the water-table was kept very high, trying to attract birds and so on. This wasn't quite at the level of SSSIs. It was a bit below that. You were paid even more money for that but we didn't have any of those sites on our farm. We were ESA level one. We farmed 440 acres at that time and had 100 acres ESA, so nearly a quarter of our land was under restrictions. But we used to get about £5,000 a year for that, to farm in a very traditional way. It was mainly on land where we couldn't drain. Dad had drained most of the farm but this was land where it wasn't feasible to drain, it was rented land anyway. So that gave us a bit of an income on land which we used for silage and young stock mainly. So it was quite good and worked quite well on that small proportion of the land.

It also became clear at that time — I went to another NFU meeting — that milk quotas were going to stay. So I couldn't really expand milk production without spending a lot of money on milk quotas, at that time they were expensive. I'd have had to buy someone else's quota, increase my overdraft to do so. And then I went to the Royal Show in July 1997 and came across the organic stand and started talking and they said that I seemed an ideal candidate to look at organic. They told me that I could get more for my milk than I was getting at the time without the need to increase production, and that as I was farming in an environmentally sensitive way anyway I could convert quite easily to organic. So someone was sent out and did a half-day survey, then a full-day survey, and it worked out that I needed a premium of 0.8 pence per litre to make it pay. And at that time people were getting three to four pence per litre for conversion. So it made sense. So in 1997 we started converting. The Soil Association that regulate the organic thing were very interested in getting people to farm organically and because we were farming in such a way and had management agreements with the government for ESAs, they let us have a shortened period of conversion of fourteen months rather than twenty-four months. Because we were sort of half way there already. So we actually sold our first organic milk to Milk Mark in July 1999. Then we resigned from them and joined the Organic Milk Suppliers Co-operative in October 'ninety-nine.

At that time I was getting 29.5 pence per litre for my organic milk. We got that for two years when ordinary milk went down to about 16 pence per litre. It was a considerable advantage. Yields dropped by about 700 litres per cow each year because we had set limits of what feed we could use and I couldn't put on any fertiliser. The first year I nearly ran out of silage and that's one thing you can not do when you are organic because you can't buy it. There just isn't any around or it's very expensive. When I joined there were only thirty-five organic dairy farmers in the whole of the United Kingdom. So I was panicking a bit but it just so happened that next door was a beef and sheep farmer who asked me if I was interested in taking on his land on a grass-keep basis. So I said yes, as long as I can convert it to organic. So he checked with his landlord and that was OK, so I took on another 120 acres which was right next door to my farm. This meant I could expand cow numbers and had an assurance of feed. In fact, I made more feed than I really needed, though because you can't put sprays and fertilisers on your production, actual output from your fields is a lot lower.

So I achieved a lot of what the conservation people wanted by lowering inputs and farming more traditionally. We border a 2,000 acre nature reserve, Ham Wall Lake, which is owned by the RSPB and they were very, very happy with me going organic. It meant that there was no spin-off of water, contaminated water going into their fields. We used to grow conventional maize and I tried continuing growing organic maize but the first year the birds ate the whole lot, forty acres, because it's not treated seed and the second year the floods had it and the third year the weeds smothered it! So I gave up! I now grow forty acres of whole-crop, that's peas and barley. The birds don't fancy it and it doesn't mind the floods. We grow it along with Italian ryegrass and red clover. There are different ways of growing them. We plant it in the spring and harvest in July, so it's a shorter period of growth. We used to put up canes and whistling wires to stop the birds eating the maize seeds but we don't have to do that. We just put it in and roll it and the birds don't seem to get it so much. All that goes for silage, about forty-five acres now. Also, when we went organic we started with the red clover and they reckon a lot of the goodness of the organic milk comes from the red clover producing omega-3 oils. That's been proven at Newcastle University, that's what makes organic milk healthier, they did a big study there. And it is a legume so it is a very high-protein crop and it fixates nitrogen and puts natural fertiliser back into the soil. We do a rotation — only on the land that was drained can we do this, because we can plough it up — we do three years Italian ryegrass and red clover, followed by one year whole-crop, peas and barley.

Of course we are not allowed to spray so weeds are a big problem, so we increase the seed rate and get lots of seed into the ground. It's very quick to establish and comes up quick and that suppresses a lot of the weeds. We use all that for silage for the cows in the winter, we don't graze it. Red clover has a problem that if cows graze it they can get bloat, they blow up, so it's quite a dangerous crop to graze but it's good in silage.

So we've been producing organic milk now since July 'ninety-nine. But what happened was that by April 2001 a lot of people saw that people like us were making good money out of organic milk and getting high prices. So they came in on the game. We got a five-year conversion grant from the government to help us convert as well, which was quite a good lot of money, and people saw that, too, and so they came in. So it got to the point that by April 2001 there was a surplus of organic milk, they couldn't sell it all, and the price dived. It had gone from thirty-five organic dairy farms

David Baker's farm by the River Brue at Turnbridge.

to 350 in a few years. It just snowballed. And the price kept on diving. It went from 29.5p a litre to 20.5p, so you can see the effect it has on income. We have been losing money since then, we just can't produce our milk at that price organically. So we've been increasing the overdraft. Having had two years of very good profits we went down and last year we actually made a physical loss on the accounts. But now we've got to the situation this year when there is a surplus of demand again! Sales of organic milk have been going up about 20 per cent a year, there's been a really good marketing job, a lot of people are now buying organic. Fifty per cent of our co-operative's milk goes to Yeo Valley Organics and they produce a fantastic yoghurt and they've gone into cheese. And the supermarkets have been plugging the organic side — 80 per cent of all organic produce is sold through supermarkets. But it's still a niche market and we couldn't sell all our organic milk as organic milk. About a third was being sold as organic and the rest as ordinary milk, so we've been getting the lower price for that. It was just being thrown in with the rest.

But now it's completely changed again and since October 2005 the demand's gone up and they've been actually importing organic milk from the continent! We've been asked to produce as much as we can and the price has gone up. The last milk cheque we had was 25p per litre. So it's going up, not to 29.5p which it was, though. There's still a big difference for us. You can work it out: my milk quota is 750,000 litres a year and I lease a bit on top of that, so I've been producing between 750,000 to 800,000 litres a year. So if the difference is 4p per litre on 800,000 litres that is a huge amount of money. Even huger when the price went down to 20p per litre from 29.5p per litre. That's 9.5 x 800,000p which is £76,000 I was losing! So what do you do? You just try and cut costs, there's no re-investment, no maintenance. And you increase borrowing, hoping that the market will come back. And now it seems to be coming back but I've got a lot of back years to pay off, high borrowings, high overdraft and long-term loans. They say there's going to be a shortage of organic milk for two years so we should have good prices for two years. They are trying to encourage us to produce more now and are actually thinking of getting more farmers into it. Because, since the days when there were 350 organic dairy farmers in the UK, about fifty have just packed up and left because they couldn't weather the storms.

I have really enjoyed farming organically. I like the system. It's a challenge, something new. We use homeopathic medicine. We are allowed to use some antibiotics but the routine use of antibiotics is not allowed and I haven't done that since 1998. So we use different homeopathic treatments to control diseases. We put preventative nosodes into the water. One of the reasons I had confidence in converting to organic was that my local vet was homoeopathically trained, so he worked alongside me in the early stages. He's actually retired now but he still makes up homeopathic treatments for me. You can't use the routine medicines so homeopathy is normal for organic farmers. What it means is that if you administer, say, a mastitis antibiotic tube into the quarter, the teat, of a cow, you have to throw the milk away, legally, for about three days, you're not allowed to put that into the food chain, that's with ordinary milk. With the organic Soil Association standards that would be for a minimum of two weeks, after treating with conventional antibiotics, so you can see the financial impact of throwing that milk away. So it discourages you from using antibiotics!

The cows are still surviving! The cows look good. Here on the Somerset Levels we are on a high molybdenum area. That locks up copper, so we have to administer copper to our cows. I get a derogation from the Soil Association to do that because the cows really need it so I can use injections or boluses, but I also use a copper homeopathic nosode which I put into the water. The homeopathic medicines are administered through the water or through sprays on their noses or vulvas. You have different treatments, different remedies. If you take mastitis, for instance, if it looks yellow you use one treatment, another if it looks watery or white, another if it's hard and so on. One that really convinced me that it worked was we had a cow that had silage eye, like New Forest eye, an eye that goes all cloudy. The usual remedy is an injection into the eye, a small amount of antibiotic.

Using the homeopathic remedy *merc. cor*. it cleared up. You put it on the nose, on the membrane, not into the eye. That proved to me that something happened. The vet said that it wouldn't have cleared up, very rarely, without some sort of treatment. Mastitis I have been treating homoeopathically. The vets say that sometimes this clears up without any treatment, which means that there is a great over-use of antibiotics which is given automatically, but I have had good results with homeopathy. There is a sealant now that you can get, a lot of organic farmers are using it. I haven't used it yet but I will do. When a cow dries up — it's in milk for ten months then dry for two months — before it goes dry you insert this sealant and then no bacteria can get up into the udder.

In fact, now we use the homeopathy on ourselves. We use arnica, I had a bad hand and I used arnica on it and that was good and I also used it for jet lag. We went to Australia a few years ago and took arnica tablets every two hours and had no jet lag. I have a kit with lots of remedies which my vet made up for me and I speak to him every now and again.

So this move to organic has been a solution to our problems farming here on the Levels. The RSPB love us, we are producing clear, non-polluting water, the birds themselves love coming here for the red clover: I had fifty swans grazing here and a swan grazes as much as a sheep! I am an RSPB volunteer farm and they've just done a survey of all the birds, which is quite interesting. They've plotted all the birds on a map and they're thriving. The ESA people, the environment people, like me farming organically. My problem with it is weeds, as I said. The only way I can combat weeds is by topping, regularly cutting the tops off, or ploughing up. Now on an Environmentally Sensitive Area you aren't allowed to plough. So I am becoming very weedy in certain areas. The only answer seems to be continual topping. So with grazing grass the cows go in, graze the field and when it's down to a certain level you go in with a topper and that tops off all the weeds. Then you let the grass grow up again. So during the summer months you are constantly topping. My problem is doing it, doing the physical work. It's lack of labour and lack of money. I've got one person working for me now who came on in 1997, so we operate a two-man system where I do all the milking and he does the general farm work. And we can get a relief person in if we have to. And Jenny, my wife, does the office work. So with the weeds we get docks in the fields where we cut for silage and thistles in the fields we graze. A lot of organic farmers control docks by pulling them out but we've got too big a farm and too few people and it's physically impossible for us to do it. But I've got a lot of acres I farm and I make up for the bits that are weedy. The cows eat the silage OK. It's not the most productive farm but we are not looking for high productivity on an organic farm. It's not intensive.

We've changed our calving pattern from a 100 per cent spring calving to all-the-year-round calving, which means I can keep more cows, because I can milk 150 cows all the year round in the buildings I've got. I can keep dry cows away from the farm because I've got surplus land in the summer and I take them to the old dairy unit I used to have at Abbey Farm, four miles away. So I've now got about 180 cows with a total stock of about 300. Thirty will be dry, I'll milk 150 and the rest will be young ones. We rear all our own replacements and sell our calves on to market. The females we keep for breeding and for the future. We don't buy in any animals. We feed them all ourselves except for the concentrate which we buy in and as that's organic it's quite expensive. But there's more being grown now nationally.

It would be so interesting to know what my dad's thoughts would have been about all this. Back in the seventies it was all increase and intensive, that was the way to go. He did a programme for television for Horizon called *Butterflies or Butter* on BBC2. They filmed the drainage, the ploughing up of fields, the sowing of the more productive grass, all that. It's changed so much. Now we are farming with the environment rather than against it. We still flood here, that's one of our biggest problems here on the Levels, you can't stop that. About three-quarters of our fields flood in winter. So we have to farm within the constraints of winter flooding. I mean a lot of farmers are going into extended grazing, which means they are trying to graze their animals out more, like all the year round if they can. We can't do that. We could have a flood anytime from October to March so the animals have to be housed. So we can't go along that really cheap option where they are all out so you don't have to produce as much silage, you don't have to straw them down.

We try to operate a simple system but now they're telling us to produce more milk we are trying to find ways to increase production. It's economic now to feed more but we have certain restraints on what we can feed. We have an inspection once a year by the Soil Association where they check all through the books. And they are really thorough! Pretty stringent. One year they came down and said, 'Mr Baker, we've found steroids in your vet invoices.' I said, 'I haven't used any steroids, have you got a number for the animal?' And they said, 'Yes, we've got a name here. It's Kinty.' Well, that's my cat! She had asthma and the vet gave her steroids and they found the invoice. They are that keen. They go through every invoice and check it. So you can be reassured, if you buy organic they come and check that you are doing everything correctly.

There are also all sorts of things that we have to do differently from ordinary farmers in how we rear animals and that. For instance, we've got to feed calves for twelve weeks on whole milk. Conventionally you normally feed them on purchased milk powder for five weeks only, then on concentrate. But we have to feed our own milk, whole milk for twelve weeks. So that's an extra expense. An extra seven weeks of whole milk, especially when it was over twenty-nine pence a litre, is a lot of money. You feed them twice a day and they take, say, five litres a day in a controlled fashion. Well, the cow might produce twenty, twenty-five litres a day so, obviously, you don't want the calf suckling all day, it's not economic. There's also lots of regulations about feeding the cows, how much of their ration has to be from forage, grass and silage, and how much can be from concentrate — 60 per cent has to be from forage. Also you can't keep your animals in too long.

A cow will eat ten tons of silage a year, during the winter months. A lot of silage. Five tons for a young cow. So just for the cows you are talking 1,800 tons, 2,500 tons all together. A normal, conventional field with fertiliser will produce about eight tons of silage an acre in its first cut, then you have another cut which would be about five tons. Organic you are looking at five tons for the first cut. If it's Italian ryegrass and red clover it probably might even be eight tons, because it is so good. That's without fertiliser. You cut it every seven weeks and you can get three cuts, eight tons the first, five the second, three the third. So that's sixteen tons. That's about a cow and a half an acre per year in silage. Also on the grazing side you can't put fertiliser so you need a bigger area. On intensive farms that's about one cow per acre. So with our 180 cows we'd use 180 acres. You've got young stock as well so you'd probably need 250 acres for your milking herd of 180. Well, we farm 550 acres. That's the difference. That's mainly because of ESA land which is not highly productive and because we are organic and can't use fertilisers or sprays.

My mother owns about 120 acres and I pay her rent. There are cousins as well who own some. And I rent another 130 acres here to make a block for grazing and then we've got other fields further away where I keep young stock and the land for growing silage. So 550 all together. That's a big farm on the Levels. More land than I need but it gives me a bit of leeway. Potentially, things could be good. It's all down to the milk price. That's fundamental. With the price down at twenty pence I can't do it and I only survive by increasing my overdraft. Twenty-nine pence would be fantastic but I don't know if it would get there again. Between twenty-five and twenty-nine I can make a go of it. If I owned the farm outright and didn't have to pay the rent, that would be great. That would be different.

Now, of course, we have the Single Farm Payment coming along. That is the new subsidy. The IACS, Integrated Administration and Control System, subsidies which were based on production are being phased out, well they are now finished, and the Single Farm Payment is coming in and that is based on the acreage you farm irrespective of what you produce. With the IACS, the subsidies were for production. So if I grew an acre of wheat, I would get so much money as a subsidy for that wheat. I never received any IACS subsidies because I didn't grow any arable crops. It was mainly for arable and then there was beef subsidies. The only thing dairy got was the Dairy Premium which we got every now and again, a very small amount of money paid for through the government to help dairy farmers. But when you hear of the 'Barley barons' and so on, that's money from IACS where they got paid money for so-called lower barley and wheat prices, though in fact the prices stayed high, so they scored highly on that, they got good prices and their subsidies for growing as much as they could. All that was through the Common Market, the EU. So they were being paid for production. Now that's finished and it's completely changed round, now they are paying for the environment. That's the Single Farm Payment which came in last year — we had to fill in tons of forms — and you get paid for how you farm, environmentally. In fact you don't have to produce anything at all to get these subsidies, you've just got to make sure your hedgerows are nice and that sort of thing. The EU says what they are going to pay you. You have to claim entitlements and it's done on a per hectare basis. Now, to claim those entitlements you have to fulfil certain 'cross compliance conditions!' Like you aren't allowed to cut hedges between certain months of the year — which I did anyway — or dig ditches or plough up certain areas of land. In fact, a lot of the stuff which I have to do for the 'cross compliance' I was doing organically anyway.

So I've applied for a 170 hectare entitlement, and it's a sliding scale between now and the year 2015, a certain amount of payment per hectare. It's a split system, quite complicated but by the end of the period, after seven years, I should get £200 per hectare. That should be my subsidy payment. No matter how I farm. I could stop farming completely and just make sure that the farm was in a good general condition and get the subsidy, that's the system they've decided on. And they've defined what a good environment or condition is and they'll check it. They've got satellites in the sky and inspectors on the ground. So that's the change. They are saying that the tax payer will pay for a nice environment but they don't want to be paying subsidies for food production. So, in theory, if the payments are what they say, in the year 2015 I could get 170 x £200, that's £34,000, as a yearly subsidy for doing nothing. Or very little. What this means is that if you are a barley baron or a very intensive farmer your income will gradually, over the next seven years, be going down, getting worse, but if you are like me you'll be getting better. Your subsidies will be going up.

There are going to be other schemes as well. There's what is called an Environmental Level Stewardship Scheme. The ESA schemes have worked very well here on the Somerset Levels but they want to make it work throughout the UK or EU. So they'll be paying farmers to farm like that. There's also an organic scheme and I've got the forms for that but I haven't applied for it yet, though I will do, and that will be about sixty pounds per hectare. Though you can't claim for anything you've already claimed as an Environmentally Sensitive Area. So I'd only be able to claim about £8,500 a year and you enter into a five-year agreement. So I've got the forms. I just haven't had time to do it. The admin for all this is a nightmare. I haven't got the labour, the time to sort it all out. We took ages to sort out the Single Farm Payment forms back in May. You have to get it right and if you don't you get penalised. Of course, I will do well out of it. My subsidies, my entitlements will pay for my rent, that's how I look at it. If I owned it all I could give up farming and live off them. If I didn't have to pay rent I could just keep the farm in a nice condition and live off the subsidy, get another job, too, perhaps. It's crazy! It might be good for the environment but it's mad. But this country wants cheap food and until they are willing to pay the proper going rate for food, like in organic they are paying a premium for good quality food, that's what they are going to get. We bring in beef from Argentina, beef from Brazil with all the foot and mouth and all those problems, they don't care. Half the butter is Anchor butter from New Zealand. Unless the British consumer in the supermarkets wakes up to the fact that there soon won't be any British food it will be too late. It'll all be imported. That is the result of a cheap food policy. And with the Single Farm Payment now that'll get worse because farmers just haven't got to produce the food to get the money. So if the markets aren't there, if the returns aren't there, farmers won't farm, they'll just manage their farms to claim the subsidies. Go in, top your grass, trim your hedges. You can't just leave it but you could do a part-time job. Just do that in the evenings and keep your farm and not produce any food.

I think you have to have farmers farming not just to produce the food but to produce the countryside. It hasn't evolved because of subsidies! It's the cheap food policy that really has to change. The amount we spend on our food is very, very small now. If you want high quality, disease-free food, you have to pay for it. I mean where did foot and mouth come from? Then there's bird flue in chickens and all those scares. The controls on food coming into this country are just not good enough. Then there's food miles as well, all the energy and the costs of transporting all this food. We have to take it all into account. It would never happen in France! You go to a French supermarket and it's full of French food. If the general public want good quality food, British farmers can produce it as well as and better than anywhere else. It's all down to what the government and the consumer wants. The organic market is going up now and that's good, though we have to control it. Mustn't overproduce and then go bust.

There are other ways for farming to go. I know farmers who've gone into bio-mass, growing elephant grass for fuel. There's some round here. But you harvest it in the winter so on our farm, with the floods, we couldn't do it. You can get subsidies to grow it. I'm waiting for global warming to get going and then, with the floods, I can grow organic rice! A lot of farmers have diversified. We looked into converting some of our buildings into flats or for B&Bs. But they're not giving grants any more. We have a link in with the RSPB who wrote a lovely letter saying there was a need for places with disabled facilities, for tourism here and people to come and see the birds, which we could do, but no grants any more so we can't afford it. It would have helped. We've already sold off the old farmyard for a barn conversion to a friend, that was when Mother retired. There's not much else we can do, really. There are a lot of redundant buildings around but it seems that the planners want them for small businesses or light industries but not for accommodation. We just wouldn't get the return.

The next five years could go in two ways. If the milk price stays up we'll continue in organic dairy farming. I can't see a future in going out of organics, if I'm going to stay in dairy farming it'll be as an organic farmer. We've got the system and the land and I enjoy the system, I enjoy farming like this. I'm forty-nine and I have a daughter of three, so no early retirement! I'll be working till I'm sixty-five. All the signs are that organic produce is catching on. But if the milk price dies or there is over-production I don't think the bank will carry on supporting me, they've supported me for the last few years and so we'd have to stop milk production. What on earth I'd do then I don't know. My wife could go out and earn as a legal executive. I suppose I could go into beef, perhaps, but with the flooding I couldn't grow a lot of crops, just spring crops. Right now I'm one of the very few dairy farmers left as it is. There are only two dairy farmers left in the village. In my grandfather's day there were twenty-five.

My great-grandfather came here in 1895 and started the farm. My grandfather was born here, my mum was born here and I was born here. It's all on my mother's side, the Mapstone side. My great-grandfather, George Mapstone, originally lived in what is now the Rural Life Museum in Glastonbury, that was the Abbey Farm and that's the farm that I still farm. My great-aunt gave the house to the nation and that's now the Rural Life Museum. But my father kept the tenancy of the farm. But I've got nobody to carry on after me, well, I don't expect my three-year-old daughter will want to, and the other dairy farmer in the parish of Meare, his son is working away and the farm's right in the village so it could probably be sold off for building land.

So who is going to farm the land? What is going to happen? That's a big question. Land is easy to get here. There are a lot of beef farmers around but they are getting older and there's no youngsters wanting to carry on. They've all gone off the farms. I've got a cousin down in the village who went from milk to beef, but the son is an architect and the daughter's a paramedic. Nobody will continue. None of the next generation want to carry on. The farmer I rent the land from, his son's a building contractor. It's just not seen as attractive enough now, though it could still be a good life. If I could, I'd like enough profit to employ more people, more labour, to release me from actually physically working so I could do more management. Like it was in my dad's day. If I had an extra, say, £30,000 I could employ a herdsman and step back a bit and not actually physically milk and manage, as it was when I came back from college. You need a two-man system to work the farm but as I get older, that's the sort of thing I could do. I could probably produce more income like that.

So the family farm is dying out. That's why you are getting a lot of Polish workers coming over. A lot of my farming friends are seriously considering employing them, or have already done so. They house them in a mobile home, pay them the minimum wage which is a hell of a lot more than they get in Poland. So farmers are seriously looking into it because they simply can't get the labour. They can't get the skilled labour. I'm costed by Exeter University, they produce statistics about the farm, and also my farm is used as an exam case study by Cannington College. They come here every two years, have done so for years. Last year they came and out of twenty students, seventeen were French, three were English. That just shows what is happening. There are no sons and daughters going into agriculture in this country. I went to the Royal Agricultural College from 'seventy-six until 'seventy-nine and there were 600 students there. All boys, all going farming! Now, of course, a lot of it is equine, business management, the actual agricultural side is very, very small. It's gone right down. Cannington College is a classic: they've got golf course management, equine stuff, food technology. Actually training to be a farmer is right down on the list. But when twenty kids turned up at the farm and seventeen were French! In the past they would all have been English. So that is a sign of the times. So there won't be a problem getting land, it's just going to be whether you can make money out of it and whether there's actually going to be anybody there to farm it.

Conservation

John Humphrey, RSPB Warden, West Sedgemoor, 1981

'The progressive agriculturalist would see a traditional meadow here as really not being worth farming and would want to under-drain it, dry it out, plough it up and re-seed it... West Sedgemoor is a great mass of waterlogged peat which is... about fifteen feet deep. And you're supported by a skin of vegetation — that's all that's stopping you from sinking into this morass...'

West Sedgemoor is home to some 80 per cent of all wildlife species found on the Levels and Moors and has been a focal point for much of the conservation debate that has sometimes raged over the area. It is a rather isolated, long stretch of uneven lowland basin, running for about five miles from the River Parrett at its eastern edge, towards Taunton, bounded to the south and north by ridges of hills and higher ground and covering some 2,500 acres. On the map, at least, it has a pleasingly ordered appearance, bisected along its length by the Middle Rhyne, bounded by long droves to the north and south with regularly spaced, straight droves and rhynes running into the moor from either side. These rhynes and droves were laid out in 1816 and it was fully expected that this reclamation would turn this patch of sodden wasteland — which, apparently, was in such a hopeless state that it injured rather than benefited any stock kept there — into profitable and productive fields. Unfortunately, the scheme hardly improved matters at all because, despite the drainage ditches, whenever the River Parrett had any water in it there was just not sufficient fall to allow much of the water on the moor to escape. Even after steam pumps had been introduced across the moors it was still, in 1850, in a very bad state and only suitable for grazing for a few months in the driest of summers. In 1944 a new diesel pumping station was built for West Sedgemoor and that did make a difference but, even so, the moor remained, and still remains, extremely boggy and prone to winter floods. Because of this, the lack of 'improvements', and its isolation, West Sedgemoor came to be seen as one of the country's most important locations for wetland wildlife and when, in 1978, farmers started to apply for grants to the Ministry of Agriculture to finance individual pumping schemes to lower the water-table over about a third of the area of the moor, the Royal Society for the Protection of Birds stepped in and bought, after some initial resistance, 500 acres on the wettest part of the moor. Over the years their holdings have grown, but in 1981 John Humphrey, the RSPB warden on West Sedgemoor, was beginning the task of scientifically monitoring the moor, quietly observing its changes through the seasons and under many different kinds of farming practice, and trying to maintain the peace between the farmers and the conservationists who seemed, at times, to be in open conflict.

Above: A rhyne across the moor.
Opposite: West Sedgemoor, winter.

Altogether, what you can say about these meadows on West Sedgemoor is that they're very rich in species. You've got this wide mosaic: all the different flowers coming into bloom one after the other throughout the season. Most of the flowers here are characteristic of this wet habitat, they thrive with their feet in water, even the grasses are species which thrive in wet conditions: spike rush, ladies smock, marsh ragwort, marsh marigold, meadow thistle, marsh orchid, lesser spearwort and so on. Your very good high quality grasses which your agriculturalists like — because you get more food value from them, as with ryegrass, for instance — don't like their feet in water. Even if you re-seed a field with ryegrass here, you have to accept that its going to be more or less an annual because of the floods.

Another characteristic of West Sedgemoor is you rarely see two fields alike. One field might be a mass of marsh marigolds in the spring and

another has just a scattering of them. The field that's full of marsh marigolds mightn't have any marsh orchids and the field that doesn't have marsh marigolds might be full of marsh orchids. It's full of variations and it makes you wonder just how it came about. It must really be from the way the fields have been treated in the past. Most of them are cut for hay and grazed afterwards, but you can have lots of variation in that. Some of the drier fields might have a dose of manure from time to time, some have been treated with artificial. The grazing regime can vary in that you might have ten cows in a five-acre field all summer or you might have twenty cows in that field for a fortnight and then out for a fortnight and so on. All these things seem to add up to a tremendous variety in the fields. I've been making a list of all the plants in the field and their abundance; when you check you find there are no two fields alike.

The progressive agriculturalist would see a traditional meadow here as really not being worth farming and would want to under-drain it, dry it out, plough it up and re-seed it, so you can grow more grass, support more cows and so on. On the other hand there are people like us who say these fields are getting very scarce, surely something ought to be done to save a few? The RSPB has bought some and this is all right but it's the fields we don't own which cause most concern and have been causing all the political aggravation in the past. It does seem, really, that we should be able to sort out some way of saving some more of them.

West Sedgemoor is a great mass of waterlogged peat which in the middle of the moor is said to be about fifteen- to twenty-feet deep. And you're supported by a skin of vegetation — that's all that's stopping you from sinking down into this morass. One of the problems that a farmer has out here is that if the wheel of a tractor goes through this crust you're straight down onto the belly of the tractor. You'll never climb out, you have to be pulled out. So you have to wait till the top surface layer has dried out till you can come down here and carry out any farming operations. Often, every time you step water comes up over your boots.

Opposite: Winter waders in flight over West Sedgemoor.

West Sedgemoor is quite a special place nowadays, so many of these sorts of places have been drained all over the country. You could probably count on the fingers of your hands the amount of good wetland areas left in Britain now. The RSPB is buying the central part of the moor because we think it's well worth it. There is any amount of good grassy fields but we've just got these few left which are good for the nesting birds, the wintering birds and the flowers. It's costing us a lot of money, we've already spent over half a million pounds on our 500 acres. On the moor now we're half drained, not fully drained. The pumps are capable of draining the land completely but the rivers are not capable of taking the water away in sufficient quantity — there's always the threat of flooding. We're also in a position here where we've got quite a number of separate farmers on this moor; some are the progressive types and some are quite happy to see the moor as it is. In between you've got everybody else on the scale. So we've got a mosaic at the moment: improved land at both ends of the moor and to a certain extent round the edges. In the centre we tend to have the less well drained areas which, in a way, agriculturally have been neglected for quite a number of years. In the centre we tend to get the interesting meadow flora and the birds. We in the RSPB are concentrating on the central area, buying what we can, and as we buy it we offer it back to the people we have bought it from and most of them are content to go on farming it traditionally, the way we like it and the way most of it has, in fact, always been farmed in the past. Having said that we must accept, I think, that the number of birds here is not as great as it would have been twenty years ago. Some of the old stagers tell me that every field then had four or five pair of snipe breeding in it, thousands of ducks every winter. Wildfowling was quite an industry. We've passed that stage, we don't have anything like those numbers nowadays, and I think it's the RSPB's duty, really, to get what we can and if possible try and improve the situation for the wildlife generally. This is standard RSPB practice. We buy a reserve, look round for a few years, find out how everything works, find out what we've got and then try and think of ways of improving the situation.

I know there's been a lot of controversy over this moor and I've sometimes felt rather outnumbered, but I'm quite sure that given goodwill we can work together for the benefit both of agriculture and the wildlife. And that really depends on being given the right direction from government as to how we resolve these problems.

Since I've been here I've spent a lot of time looking and listening, trying to find out how the moor works, what the wildlife likes and what it dislikes, and I've come to a few conclusions. The main one really is that the breeding birds, which are the most important part of the wildlife here, do require a fairly high water-table in the breeding season, that is from March till the end of June, possibly into July. Now, if the water-table could be at about nine inches below the surface this should suit them very well. It would also help them very much if we could have one or two comparatively small areas where we could have a higher water-table, so that there were a few pools and puddles left throughout the breeding season. Now, this is where we find most conflict. These are the very months when the farmers would prefer the moor to be drying out so that they can get on with haymaking and, if you're a progressive man, so that you can get on with silage at the beginning of June. It seems to me that our main areas of difference concentrate in the month of May when we would like some of our land to remain fairly damp. As far as the wintering birds go they are quite happy with things as they are. In fact the water-table in the winter generally rises to the surface all through the winter month, whether it's under-drained or not in present circumstances.

The reason why the wading birds, the snipe, the redshank and so on, like these wet meadows is because they have these long bills which they probe into the soft soil to get their food. The soil has to be soft for them and the high water-table, of course, means that a lot of their food is up near the surface of the soil, exactly where these birds can get hold of it. If the water-table drops the food goes down with it, they're no longer able to reach it and the surface crust, if we have a dry season, becomes too hard for their bills to penetrate. That is why a fairly high water-table in the spring is important for these birds. In fact these large flat expanses of meadow don't at first look particularly good for wild life. It takes a bit of finding. I remember the first time I came here looking for the wildlife on the moors. I drove around for a day and went home wondering where it was. But once you get into it, get into the right areas, then you find that there are these pockets left which are very good indeed.

The bulk of the Somerset Levels is now good agricultural land, I've no argument with that, but we do have these few remaining areas which have always been much more difficult to drain which are good wildlife land. We do have to preserve these few wetland areas, we should save some of them.

Harry Paget-Wilkes, RSPB Warden, West Sedgemoor, 2005

'So when this all started twenty years or more ago, you had the ridiculous situation of the two elements of land management here fighting with each other and both government funded. One funded for drainage and the other funded to maintain the wetlands... The Somerset Levels and Moors was the classic place where these two elements hit head-on.'

In 2005, the situation has changed considerably on West Sedgemoor but not in the way the conservationists once feared. The whole moor is now an SSSI, so the drainage schemes which once threatened its wildlife have come to a halt as the emphasis in the government's attitude to agriculture has moved away from productivity and towards conservation. The RSPB now owns about 1,500 out of the total 2,500 acres and its aims have broadened considerably. Harry Paget-Wilkes, the present warden, can now look towards finding a way to manage the whole moor in partnership with the farmers, the Drainage Boards and the Environment Agency, especially in controlling the water and the flooding, in a comprehensive scheme rather than in the isolated patches and pockets that the RSPB had twenty-five years ago.

Opposite: Winter floods, West Sedgemoor.

Pollarded willows in winter.

In the last twenty years we've grown a lot here. We have two reserves here now in this part of the Somerset Levels and Moors. One on West Sedgemoor and one on Greylake. The total acreage is just under 700 hectares, about 1,700, 1,800 acres. We also have another reserve at Ham Wall near Glastonbury. West Sedgemoor is 580 hectares, and the new site on Greylake is 110 hectares. There's 2.47 acres to the hectare so here on West Sedgemoor we are talking about nearly 1,500 acres and on Greylake nearly 250 acres which we've had for nearly two years now. It was arable farm land and we are slowly developing it and we are reverting it back to wet grassland with some wetter swampy areas. Most of the ecological interest has been lost here over the past twenty years, it's been improved, under-drained, but it's worth bringing it back, in fact it's actually a really good block of land for us because it's got its own hydrological unit, it's a very well defined bit of land, and it's very low-lying now because of peat wastage from the previous arable operations. So it's got a lot of potential for hydrological management for wetland habitats, grassland, swamp, reed beds, the whole range of habitat types.

Greylake benefits some species more than others. There won't really be a different make-up of bird community, it'll be rather a similar bird community. But it's because of the peat, the destruction of the peat structure from the drainage in the past. That changes the nature of the peat and there are certain bird species that will struggle, may struggle, because of that. So things like snipe, things that need to probe into soft soils that support high densities of invertebrate prey, may not do so well on Greylake because the peat has lost its fibrous structure and so its ability to hold and retain water well. What happens is that during the spring and summer, when it starts getting warm and drier, the peat actually dries out and becomes a lot harder if it has been drained in the past. When you remove water from the ground, from the peat, that allows it to start rotting again, because, essentially, peat is semi-preserved vegetation and when you remove — it's formed in an atmosphere of lack of oxygen so that things aren't rotting — so when you remove the water you allow the oxygen to get back in, it oxidises, and starts to break down, starts its rotting process again and breaks down so that the peat virtually disintegrates into a granular soil instead of peat. And the granular soil can't retain water nearly as well as peat, so out here on West Sedgemoor, in the summer, it actually retains its moisture content much more and stays softer, and the added moisture in the soil means the invertebrates tend to be closer to the surface because they like moisture as well, they can be closer to the surface if it's moist, and it stays softer so that birds with long bills that probe the soil can probe and feed. But on Greylake that's going to be more difficult because of the destruction of the peat structure. So, as a result of that, what we have done in our work out there to recreate the wet grassland is actually to create a lot of surface water features that you would not get out on West Sedgemoor in spring and summer. With all the large hay meadows there we can't and don't really want to go and dig and create permanent wet features out in nice hay meadows, but on Greylake we can. We've dug shallow scrapes and linear shallow ditches and gutters, so we've tried to imitate some historical landscape features. There were a lot of these straight line old gutters, you can still see a few but most disappeared when the land was ploughed and drained and was made arable. They all became flat level fields. We've recreated that. We've perhaps recreated more than there would have been historically and they are a little deeper than they would have been because our objectives are slightly different, so previously they would have been there to assist drainage but we are using them to assist the opposite, irrigation, and create wet habitats for the birds for the summer.

So it's going to be a slightly different mix to West Sedgemoor and, obviously, it hasn't got the botanical community interest that West Sedgemoor has. It may never come back because of the change in the soil structure. It's not just a matter of making it wet again. Where you get compaction and breaking down of the peat structure it actually then benefits different plant species to those that are recognised as being part of the diverse and rich plant communities on the Somerset Levels and Moors. So you tend to get a lot more dominance of low-growing, creeping grasses on these compacted and granular peat soils, low-growing grasses and rushes, which are much better able to cope with the soil structure. Whereas on West Sedgemoor you get a much more diverse, richer plant community, flowering plants, sedges and so on. So, quite often when you get man messing around with the vegetation communities in fields, rather than it just reverting, going back to what it was before if you leave it alone, you have actually changed the balance and you now have a micro-ecology that benefits different species than it would have done before, because you have made some fairly significant changes.

Of course, when the farmers were implementing relatively intensive farming systems, they needed to be able to get on to the ground early in the season and late in the season, spring and autumn. Traditionally the ground is pretty wet here at that time of year and you wouldn't put cattle out or put machines out on land in April and May. But they need to do that if they are trying to grow arable crops and so on and high protein leys, they need to be preparing the ground. So under-soil drainage is put in to actually dry the ground out earlier. But what that does as a consequence is to really dry the peat out as I described, to allow it to dry out and start rotting and oxidising again. A lot of the volume in the peat is its ability to hold water and so when it starts oxidising and losing that ability it reduces in volume, it shrinks. And also the breakdown of the vegetative matter causes it to shrink as well, like in any compost heap. As vegetation rots the volume reduces. So peat has shrunk and the land has sunk, sunk even lower than it was before. What was once barely at sea level has gone down by some feet and become even lower, even more prone to flooding, needing pumping out. The other way peat is lost after it has been drained and has dried out is from surface erosion, it is simply blown away by the wind. So, much of the land dropped by two feet or so after these arable operations, mostly in the first few years after it had been drained and ploughed. The person that we bought the land on Greylake from was at a stage when he had to decide if he was going to invest an awful lot more money again in redoing all the land drainage to dry it out even more, putting in more drains and pumps and so on, which would cause even more shrinkage. Then in a few years time he would have had the same problem again, have had to redo the drainage again, because it would get lower and therefore wetter and more difficult. And so he realised that it would all have probably stopped working anyway, because the land height would have become so different between the fields that were being ploughed and drained and those owned by others on the moor that were not, that it would become terribly difficult to keep the water out. Intensive agricultural systems are expensive to run, there are a lot of man-hours needed, a lot of inputs when you compare them with permanent grasslands: soil preparation, applications of fertiliser and so on. It's very short-term thinking here on the Levels and Moors.

In a way it seems extraordinary that any of the farmers ever bothered to do any drainage here but, of course, it was all grant funded. The infrastructure was. So when this all started twenty years or more ago, you had the ridiculous situation of the two elements of land management here fighting with each other and both government funded. One funded for drainage and the other funded to maintain the wetlands, agricultural production and nature conservation. So at the same time as trying to designate and protect areas like this from improvements in agriculture, government was handing out massive grants to do exactly the opposite. The Somerset Levels and Moors was the classic place where these two elements hit head-on.

Now, the agricultural climate has changed an awful lot since then. It's been quite a slow process but, I think, nearly everybody realises now that intensive food production on the moors is not a viable system for these peat lands. And I think the public in general, at the moment, seems to want to support, to want public funds to be spent on, protecting the wildlife and the environment. That's where most of the money appears to be now for individual farmers and land managers. Here, there's an awful lot of money now being focused, even more so than in the early days of the ESAs, on managing land for nature conservation, still farming it, still within farming systems. This is the really difficult thing we all need to grapple with over the next few years. Ensuring that we still have farmers and farming systems that can manage the land in the sensitive way that will conserve and promote the wildlife interest. The habitats we are trying to protect and the species we are trying to look after are part of a farmed landscape, a non-intensive, extensive farmed landscape.

The RSPB is a charity, so we rely entirely on donations and gifts. The only area where there is government money is where we own land and we manage the land and get the grants, the same grants that are available to

Opposite: A drove across West Sedgemoor.

all farmers and landowners, to manage the land. When we buy land we do it out of our funds, though we can apply to the Heritage Lottery Fund. We got a part-grant from them to manage and develop our land on Greylake so that we could put in access for the public, an oak boardwalk suitable for wheelchair access, a hide, a raised viewing area, that sort of thing. Other than that it's a question of us raising money from the general public. We've got over a million members all of whom pay their annual subscription fee and then we get additional donations on top of that. We have to run six full-time staff here on West Sedgemoor, but we get a lot of volunteers to come and help. We offer six-month placements here and a training programme for students who want to get involved eventually in working for environmental issues. But we do employ over 1,500 people all over the country.

Much of our work here is land management. We have 700 hectares here and on Greylake. It's all let out to local farmers who graze and cut for hay, but there is a lot more to managing land than that, there's all the infrastructure of 'the estate' as we call it. So droves, gateways, fencing, ditches, all the buildings, all those things that need maintaining and keeping in good order. We also undertake some of the field management alongside the tenant farmers. So we undertake cutting operations and we manage some of the stock during the summer. We get about 250 head of cattle left with us and we look after them, manage them, move them around, pull them out of ditches. We've also got a lot of woodland and fields with hedgerows around the edges of the moor, so during the winter there is a lot of traditional woodland and hedgerow management, hedge-laying, coppicing and so on. Some of the woodland is designated as an SSSI, it's semi-ancient, natural woodland with very nice plant communities, here on Red Hill and on the whole escarpment for three or four miles down to Fivehead, and we have some more bits down at Fivehead. So we have forty or fifty hectares of woodland. This supports some important bird communities, the largest heron colony in South West Britain, that's up in Swell Wood. It's got a good range of woodland species that are in national decline elsewhere: green woodpeckers, marsh tits, song thrush, bullfinch, spotted flycatcher, nightingale, all sorts of things. One of the most westerly populations of nightingales left in England now is in the scrubby woods down at Fivehead. Then there's dormice as well and a lot of our management is targeted at them. It's not all about birds. Birds are our focus but we take all the other wildlife interests extremely seriously. We are trying to create a rich and diverse wildlife habitat, or maintain one, so it's never just about birds in isolation.

We've had little egrets starting to nest in Swell Woods, we've had four pairs up there this year. They're a heron species so they're fine, heron species are well known for having mixed colonies, and the little egrets probably benefit from having the grey herons around as a sort of protection. The little egrets tend to be a bit more specialist in their feeding habits. They tend to feed entirely in shallow water, occasionally you'll see them feeding around cattle, though that's not so common. Whereas the grey heron will feed in deep water, on the edges of ditches and also out in the fields on mammals, insects. But the little egret eats mostly small fish and amphibians and large invertebrates in shallow water. Eels are probably a bit big but eels were the herons' favourite food though there aren't so many of them around these days. Herons are a pretty good indicator that the wetland environment is in not bad condition. They feed mainly out on the moors, in the ditches and water bodies, but they'll eat all sorts, other birds, people's goldfish! There are over a hundred breeding pairs here in the colony and the population is increasing. This tells us that the wetland environment, which is their main feeding area, is probably improving and not declining. There are other indicators for this: otters are doing well, much better, and they were once terribly reduced. Obviously, they are very dependent on the water environment. One of the reasons they declined across the UK was the pollution of rivers. And they are coming back.

There are always pollution issues in a modern environment. Man has an awful lot of by-products in everything he does and in a farming landscape there are still issues. Here on West Sedgemoor there is still a slight problem, less than elsewhere on the whole, of pollution, though it is likely that most of the pollution issues are from water coming onto the moor from the catchment area, run-off from agricultural land from fertiliser and point sources of pollution from effluent run-off that get into the river systems and maintain a high nutrient level in the rivers. All the water for West Sedgemoor comes from these rivers in the summer, so that's the real issue rather than what is happening on West Sedgemoor itself, though fertiliser is still used in a few places. But it's mainly the water coming in. We have a large catchment area, with the Rivers Parrett, Yeo and Isle, so we get a range of pollutants, mostly agricultural run-off from artificials, but some sewage and slurry sometimes.

Things have changed a lot from twenty years ago. I think a lot of what we have been doing in the last twenty years we were doing partly in isolation — trying to work with everybody but in order to achieve the results for wildlife we were finding ourselves having to actually work alone for much of the time. And I think that has changed a lot. Now our focus over the next few years is really to be working with as many of our neighbours and as many of the government agencies as possible, because there is a really different climate out there in terms of farming and wildlife and we have a major opportunity to do things on a large scale which will develop a sustainable livelihood and income for the farmers and land managers on the Levels and Moors and, at the same time, dramatically enhance the wildlife, the wildlife interests. So that's our real focus: getting involved, helping where we can the development of big schemes, if you like, for actually improving the wildlife and managing a sustainable farming system.

We are working with the Drainage Board at the moment and with all the neighbouring landowners. It's being driven mainly by the Internal Drainage Board. We are looking again at the hydrology of West Sedgemoor. There has been a history in the last twenty, twenty-five years of isolation, of bits of the moor being drained in various ways, bits being conserved. So you end up with a very fragmented system which hydrologically doesn't work that well, there's lots of blockages in it where everybody is doing something individually. We did that because it was the only way in those days to achieve the results for nature conservation. Similarly the farmers drained in the ways they could. But we are hopeful that in a couple of years there will be a unified hydrological system which takes advantage of the new high-level scheme payments, as they are called, the new agri-environment stewardship payments that are available, to actually develop, with all the landowners on West Sedgemoor, high-level schemes for their land and our land which work on a single hydrological unit. So it's going to be quite exciting and there will be some fairly significant changes.

New structures will have to go in. There is an awful lot of work for the Rural Development Service to do in actually getting everybody together to say how they will manage the land. There are over a hundred different land owners just on the West Sedgemoor Drainage Board area. It's big. It's one and a half thousand hectares with over a hundred landowners, I think. Everybody will need to agree. The underpinning factor is the water management. All the land out here varies so much, the level of water in and around each field. So with a unified hydrological system you are going to have some fields which will become a lot wetter and they will require a different approach to farming them. So that all has to be worked out. The hydrology in a way will be given, if you go to a unified system. You'll know that those fields will be some of the higher, drier fields and those fields will be the wetter ones. So with the individual farmers you have to work out farming systems which suit the rest of their farm, but enable them to manage that land for nature conservation and get their incomes from the scheme.

West Sedgemoor has an important function for flood management. If it was all just left alone it would look a lot different to what it does now, it would all be a lot wetter. Because of the raised river banks and raised river systems that run through the Levels and Moors, virtually every bit of land needs to have a pump on it to pump water up into the rivers, the rivers actually run higher than the surrounding land. So if you didn't have the pumps, if you weren't doing that, water would sit to quite a depth over large parts of the moors. When there is a lot of water it still does, but because of the pumps once the rainfall stops for a while they can get back on top of it and pump it out quite quickly. The last little flood we had here on West Sedgemoor lasted about three or four days, a bit longer on

Wet Moor and Curry Moor. They can really get on top of the flood water. Without the pumps that water would have stayed all over winter. If you go back to pre-War and listen to some of the old boys talking about what it was like, that's exactly what happened. Once you got the first flood of the winter that was it, it was going to be covered in water all winter long and it wasn't till you started to get the really dry periods that the gravity drainage would kick in, when the water in the rivers was low enough to take more out.

If it was like that you'd get a different picture. If the water was allowed just to sit all winter and well into spring those species which thrived in the hay meadows would change. They'd change into a much wetter, swamp, mire, fen community and the species mix in them would change significantly. It would also have huge implications for everyone who lives here. So it's always going to be a question of managing the hydrology, the water-levels, on West Sedgemoor. Man has changed it so much that the implications of just leaving it alone would be enormous.

One of the things we want to look at more is that we have focused a lot of our efforts over the last two decades on the land that we own and manage, and we think that there is a great opportunity to look much wider over the whole of the Somerset Levels and Moors. To help develop systems which benefit and enhance the environment but which at the same time provide sustainable incomes for the rural community here, whether that be through land management or through sensitive tourism, things like that.

We can see the effects of what we are doing with the way bird populations have improved. Snipe for example, as a breeding species. When you are talking about a lot of the birds on the Levels and Moors you have to draw a distinction between those that breed here and those that only winter here. They're two very separate groups, almost two different species. So the snipe that breed here will winter somewhere else and all the birds that we get in the winter are birds that have bred in northern Europe. But our summer breeding population of snipe in lowland Britain is still declining very, very rapidly and has, in fact, disappeared from many wetland habitats that it had bred in in the past, partly because of loss of habitat through drainage. There are only about 500 pairs of snipe left in lowland England now which is pretty scary really. Terrible. But here at West Sedgemoor we hit a low back in the late eighties, early nineties of about ten to fifteen pairs but that is now fifty pairs, which is fantastic, brilliant, and that represents something like 10 per cent of the total lowland population for the whole of the UK. That's actually going against the trend of the rest of the UK which is still in decline. Here on West Sedgemoor, and on the Somerset Levels and Moors as a whole, we are actually increasing the population. And that's because of the whole approach we have taken. You can't just do water management, keep the water-table up for these species, without worrying about land management, too: the ways of farming, late hay cutting, cutting in July and grazing with lower densities of stock throughout the year as well as keeping the peat soils soft from the higher water-tables.

Our land management varies depending on the particular interest in each field or block of fields. So we do have cattle grazing in the spring because it is important for a number of bird species but it is also detrimental for other interests. So things like lapwing and yellow wagtail and a good number of invertebrate species will benefit significantly from having cattle around in April and May, but snipe won't because their nests tend to get trampled and also the botanical communities won't do so well if all the fields have been grazed off in April and May. So you have a mix and the way we manage the land here is we do target, as a farmer would do but for different reasons, fields for different purposes. We have the early grazing fields, fields which are the late hay cut fields and these tend to stay roughly the same from year to year. So you have fields that are traditionally good for snipe, good for the botanical community and they'll be cut for hay in July and August and then after-grazed with cattle, and then you have the other fields, more grassy fields, some of the wetter ones which are really

Opposite: Lapwing and teal flying in to feed, West Sedgemoor December 2005.

good for yellow wagtails, lapwing and they'll be grazed from as early as the ground is dry enough to get cattle on it. But still at a relatively low density, we don't chuck masses of cattle out there, it's small herds, ten to twenty animals in a field, sometimes less than that. And at those densities they are providing the benefits to the birds in creating short areas of grass where the birds can forage and look for their invertebrate prey on the surface and also promote the invertebrate biomass through their dunging. Yellow wagtails follow cattle around, feeding around the dung and where the cattle disturb the ground, pushing insects up out of the ground.

If we are cutting a field for hay in July or August, the cattle come on around September, you need some time for regrowth to come up. They'll move from field to field. A herd of twenty cattle will get through a two-hectare field in two or three weeks, so they rotate around. Then they have to come off in winter, the soil gets too soft and there's a risk to them because of flood. So they'll be out there September, October and November, perhaps on those fields we cut for hay for only about three months of the year. But on other fields they could be out there all through the season from May till November.

It's important to us, a very important part of what the RSPB does, to try to promote and show people wildlife and birds, it's important to our future and to the local community, we need people to support and appreciate what we do. So that's an important element for us here on West Sedgemoor and also on Greylake and at Ham Wall, our reserve in the northern part of the moors. It's been quite difficult, here on West Sedgemoor, to get the compromise right between large numbers of people coming to visit in what is essentially a very quiet, rural landscape and the necessary tranquillity. I mean part of the very reason it's so good for wildlife is that it hasn't got hundreds of people traipsing about all over the place all day long. So we have all struggled to get that balance right, especially on the moor. The woodland areas around the edge are much more robust and that's been where we have focused a lot of our visitor effort and people are able to go and have a look at the heronry and so on. But at Greylake we have a slightly better opportunity to try and show people these wet grassland habitats, and at Ham Wall, our reed-bed reserve, there's a lot of visitor infrastructure that's gone in. Walkways and hides and so on. So it's a question of getting the balance right. We recognise that the Somerset Levels and Moors and our reserves in it are never going to be like our big visitor reserves that we've got in other parts of the country, Minsmere and so on, and we don't want them to be, it's essentially a quiet landscape and we need to keep it that way with sensitive tourism and also with encouraging local people to actually get out and really enjoy what is around them. We've got a viewing platform out on West Sedgemoor now, we got it about five years ago, but we have to use it carefully with not too many people. We do run guided walks throughout the winter and we take people there. And we have a number of local bird-watchers who use it and help us in monitoring the flocks, doing counts, collecting data for us which is one of its major purposes.

That, of course, is a really important element of what we do here. A good percentage of our time, probably 25 per cent, is actually spent on surveying and monitoring and research work. Because a lot of what we do is based on science and knowledge that we have to build up. We haven't lived here for a hundred years and we are very dependent on careful monitoring of what is happening out there, so we monitor the impacts of our management to make sure that what the theories say is actually happening. We have standard survey techniques. You tend to be doing walking routes, a standard transect route, so you don't actually have to stand still for hours on end and try and count each bird! And these routes have to be designed not to take up too much time, so they are fairly efficient transects with a standardised recording system. But we also do a lot more in-depth research so we have, for example, a couple of projects running at the moment, one where we are looking at the land management impacts on a plant called marsh ragwort, which is poisonous to livestock. This has real implications on the ability to farm the land. So we have a four-year research project looking at how some standard farming practices actually influence the density of marsh ragwort, so we can control the marsh ragwort through that without having to resort to herbicide, which obviously would damage other plant communities, or pulling it out which would take forever and a day! So we are doing various things: applying lime, farmyard manure, trying different cutting dates, different drainage — they all have their effects. So that's quite an interesting piece of research we are doing at the moment.

We have another project that's been running for a while now, we're coming to the end of it, and that's looking closely at snipe habitat requirements, trying to refine management for them in particular. And as I said before, we seem to be having some success here. That's particularly where some of the peat soil structure has been degraded in the past and the ability for it to hold water isn't so good — we are putting in sub-surface irrigation channels. In fact, ironically, it's the same as what the farmers would have done to drain their fields but here it's acting to the opposite effect. It's actually bringing water into the fields rather than taking it out. So these drains are about two feet under the surface, milled through the peat, just a hole cut through the peat, no pipes, and these are supposed to last for five to ten years. Then through the management of the water-level in the ditches, management of the hydrology of ditch water-levels, you can feed water into the fields, so maintaining a water-table in the centre of the field which is suitable for snipe. Because the peat soil structure, after it has been damaged, can no longer do that, water can't flow through the peat.

West Sedgemoor is important on different levels: local, national and international, as a wintering and migratory area for wetland birds. There are wetland habitats scattered throughout Europe, and these are extremely important for lapwing, teal, snipe and so on. They need these stopovers on their routes. So West Sedgemoor cannot be thought of on its own — it's part of a global or European picture and, locally, part of the whole Somerset Levels and Moors complex. Many of the ducks, for example, roost in the day on West Sedgemoor and fly out in the safety of the dark to feed on the grassland throughout the moors. If there was only West Sedgemoor the population would be tiny. The Levels as a whole are one of the largest inland wetlands in Europe and they support the flocks on West Sedgemoor. Having said that, it is also important to understand that the roosting areas are critical. Here we have the largest population of teal in North West Europe, 25,000 here, 400,000 in North West Europe. We have 10 or 12 per cent of the total UK population of a number of species and we are also nationally important for the variety of species. Just in this tiny area. What we have here is also a significant extent of the unimproved meadows in the UK and so a nationally important population of insects and invertebrates living here and in all the ditches and rhynes. We have rare snails and beetles including one beetle that only exists here and on one other site. Also, as I said before, the whole area is great for otters and water voles with populations growing for various reasons. The water quality has improved, the run-off is less and the waterways are better managed. And nobody is allowed to hunt otters anymore!

Part of the reason why we are looking at different management patterns, why we are looking at managing wetter habitats, is because of global warming. It seems likely that the lower-lying areas of the country will change, will get wetter. One of the problems is that the jury is still out on quite how much wetter we will get, on what the exact effect of global warming will be. Will it get warmer or colder, for instance? We don't know. But what we are doing is looking at potential habitat changes, working with them gradually over time, trying to keep half a step ahead. We need to look at, to study the whole system from a hydrological point of view, to look at all its parts and connect them.

At the moment we are working really closely with the local farmers to try and help them manage the land — it's a difficult time for them with all the agricultural change that is happening. We also work with the local Drainage Board, with the Environment Agency, with English Nature, to bring the water management towards a modern system which helps the wildlife and the environment at the same time as producing an agricultural system which helps local farmers to get at least part of their income from a viable agriculture.

Trevor Wall, The Levels and Moors Partnership, Moorlynch, 2005

'These are huge issues and the plans are complicated. And the questions of flood management are always alive here, always have been and always will be. What do we do with all the water?'

Trevor Wall is the son of Matthew and Minnie Wall who talked about their lives on the moors in the chapter on peat. Though he was for many years a schoolmaster, he is now the acting Levels and Moors Officer for LAMP, the Levels and Moors Partnership. The function of LAMP is to bring together all the various groups with interests in the area: representatives from the local councils, from the Environment Agency and English Nature, from the Ministry of Agriculture, from the wildlife trusts and agencies and the National Farmers Union, from the Drainage Boards, from the farmers, the withy growers, the peat producers and so on. LAMP helps to support and promote the Levels and Moors as a distinct 'cultural landscape', and acts as a formal channel between the people of the area and the various government agencies involved here. LAMP is now working towards getting the whole of the Levels and Moors extra funding and protection, perhaps under the heading of a World Heritage Site or some such internationally recognised designation. Trevor Wall, born and bred on the moors, is particularly well placed to understand the issues and interests focused here and he started this interview by discussing a matter which hangs in the background of all future planning: what happens to these lowlands if global warming is, indeed, a reality and sea levels start to rise significantly?

What is seen as the critical issue for the Somerset Levels and Moors is the impact of global warming and what we can't do is wait fifty years for that global warming and rise in sea level to actually happen. We have to be looking at strategies for what's going to happen on the Levels and Moors. And the way forward is obviously twofold: you either protect or you allow the sea to come in naturally. Those are major decisions that have to be made and that, obviously, will impact on the people that live in the area: how much land is going to be lost? What's going to happen to farming? What are those people going to do for the future? So I think that that is where LAMP is likely to be in the future.

There's currently a River Parrett catchment project that's running, that also affects the River Tone and related areas, where we are looking at the upper part of the River Parrett catchment that may impact on building the Dunball Barrage at Bridgwater. There's a feasibility study going through now. I think they're investing £2 million in it, there's a huge feasibility study over the next six months going into the idea of a barrage across the Parrett at Dunball, the whole idea which was sort of dropped twenty years ago has really come back. The critical point is how the environmental lobby will react, the ecologists and so on. Years ago the environmentalists were against it. The Environment Agency, I believe, want it and see it as the answer. English Nature are not so sure, so there is conflict between the bodies. I think people who live here are pretty much in favour, people in Bridgwater, on the upper Tone, they all are, and that feasibility study should be finished probably by March 2007 and then decisions will be made, applications for planning and so on. It's a big scheme to stop the tidal waters coming up and to allow the outflow from the Tone and the Parrett out. I mean it's a huge project and there are lots of issues tied in with it. For example, there's a lottery bid in now for Green Waterways in South Somerset, boating and so on linking up from Langport, so you'd maintain high water-levels in the waterways but this could be dropped to allow the flood waters to go out. So there are lots of strategies that are potentially being developed in that area.

The particular issues for nature conservation are the impact a barrage will have on things like the SSSIs on the Levels and Moors and the coastal areas. By 2010, I think, the Environment Agency and English Nature have to get the SSSIs into 95 per cent favourable condition, that's a government target just like schools have targets and things, and the Environment Agency are now — and it's something that hopefully LAMP will get involved with — looking at targeting specific areas and working with specific farmers and putting, I believe, £20 million into getting these 'favourable conditions'

Low tide. The confluence of the Rivers Parrett and Tone at Burrowbridge.

on the SSSIs. This means meeting certain criteria: all the SSSIs — and I think there are twenty-three or twenty-five on the Levels — will form the core or basis of a new Special Recognition area with ESAs around it, forming the next zone and then the rest of the Levels as a sort of buffer area. Each SSSI has got a management plan attached to it, and depending how far the landowner is on towards fulfilling that management plan, that is the percentage that has been achieved. So places like West Sedgemoor are only 20 per cent towards achieving those management criteria, even after all this time. It's difficult. It's things like fertiliser use on fields, water management. Some areas, of course, are already at 95 per cent, but some of the bigger areas like Curry Moor, West Sedgemoor, Catcott Moor, the big farming areas are not meeting the criteria, even though they are within SSSIs. Even though they are fairly rigidly patrolled there has not been enough input to maintain or achieve the required outputs. So that is where this money is coming in. You can see an example of this at Greylake here, they have put a new sluice in but there's a huge amount of infrastructure that's still needed, and the Environment Agency and us at LAMP will be working together to get the message across to the community. That's how LAMP will be working. And it could be difficult in some cases. For instance, for farmers to meet these 'favourable conditions' it could well mean in some instances that they will simply not be able to farm the land. That could be an impact because of raised water-levels. It could mean that land will have to be left or lost, totally lost to agriculture — it will simply revert to scrub — and that then would also create problems, might also not meet these 'favourable conditions' so will have to be mowed or managed somehow.

These are huge issues and the plans are complicated. And the questions of flood management are always alive here, always have been and always will be. What do we do with all the water? Do we flood Curry Moor, do we channel the water over across to King's Sedgemoor, do we bring in new pumping schemes, do we hire the pumps like we did from Holland three years ago, do we buy our own so we can discharge the water more quickly, how will the Dunball Barrage link up? These are predominantly issues for the Environment Agency, all this, they are the people who will have to implement all this, who will be responsible for delivering all this. Hopefully LAMP will work with the Environment Agency to get the message through to the communities, through the parishes and the steering groups. We are now in discussions about this, to get everyone working co-operatively rather than fighting each other. Global warming is the thing. We have to take it absolutely seriously and this was not the case twenty years ago. We may all be sceptical in some way — it's quite easy for scientists to come up with theories and hypotheses — but there is enough evidence now to say that there is a change in our climate patterns and that this will inevitably result in an increased risk of inundation from the sea due to storms, because there is a much higher risk of severe storm events, storm surges coming in, and that's probably initially the greatest threat, what would cause the most damage. The question is how much and what do you protect? Do you protect the towns? Do you protect the roads like the M5? Is the M5 a natural barrier anyway, as it was in the 1980s? And so on. Farm land will inevitably be lost in that area. This is what the Environment Agency is working on. As for LAMP there are issues here at the moment. We might combine with something called the Parrett Catchment Project which in turn might turn into the Somerset Rivers Partnership, whereby we will be involved in the overall water management strategy, with LAMP particularly being responsible for communication. We need an overall objective of where things are going — there are too many organisations with overlapping areas of interest at the moment. I think that's been recognised. That new strategy should be in place within the next six months.

Currently LAMP has been concerned really with getting Special Recognition for the Levels and Moors so that they get extra protection. Protection is the key. To get the recognition for the entire area with the SSSIs as the core. Meanwhile we here spend a lot of time talking to all the people here, the parishes. So if there is a local problem about how the water is being managed, how the floods are being managed, we can pinpoint this. And we have been highlighting the special nature of the area with our Peat

The moors in flood around Burrow Mump.

Projects and Willow Projects and the Apple Projects and so on. We have organised a Willow Fair for the last three years. We've been involved with getting a lot of European funding into the area which has benefited the Willow industry here, for example, so with organising the Willow Fair we get national and international recognition of the importance of that industry, its special nature and this helps to keep it alive. And locally we get schools involved and the children put their projects on our website, like with the Apple Project. We have a lot to do and a long way to go, there's so much that needs sorting out still, but it's all been going on for hundreds of years and I don't suppose we'll ever arrive at a perfect solution. Not yet anyway.

Withies

Len Meade, Basket Maker, Burrowbridge, 1981

'One way of living, one way of making a living round here was on withies. That was a given thing round here. Most of the women was on withies, stripping with a hand-brake. They used to strip and dry them and, of course, the children, so ever they was big enough, they had to lend a hand, after school and at weekends.'

The first record of a basket maker on the Levels and Moors dates from the early thirteenth century, but in ancient times the willow, or withy, used in basket making was taken from the wild — young shoots or wands of willow lopped from the trees. The idea of planting out fields of withies for basket making did not take hold till the early nineteenth century and the first large-scale plantings occurred on West Sedgemoor in 1825. A century later there were nearly 3,000 acres of withies on the Moors. The fact that willow did not mind standing for months in flood water obviously made it an attractive crop for these parts and though the industry has had many ups and downs, it now covers about 500 acres of Sedgemoor.

Len Meade made excellent baskets. Some he made for me have had more than twenty years of hard use. A quiet, polite, dignified man, he worked at his home by the side of the River Parrett and would explain what he was doing, and why, with great exactitude and patience. In his long life — he died in 2004 just a few months short of his 100th birthday — he had watched over many changes and had an intimate knowledge of all aspects of life on the Levels.

One way of living, one way of making a living round here was on withies. That was a given thing round here. Most of the women was on withies, stripping with a hand-brake. They used to strip and dry them and, of course, the children, so ever they were big enough, they had to lend a hand after school and at weekends. The brakes were blacksmith made, 'twas a local thing and they days, you see, we had blacksmiths. They used to bolt the hand-brakes to this railway sleeper and then you just strip 'em one at a time. I did that, ten, twelve years old.

Left: Len Meade at work in his workshop. Giddies, Saltmoor, Burrowbridge.
Above: Basket maker's tools. Top: rapping tool for knocking down and tightening the weave; bottom: cleave for splitting rods along length. Left to right: shop knife for cutting willow rods and splicing them; picking knife for trimming off rods neatly; shears for cutting off excess length; straightening iron for straightening rods; bodkin for piercing rods.

I was working with a chap, Tom Beck, and we used to do drainage, cleaning out the rhynes on the moor, you rake off the weeds and so much silt as you can. And where we were working in some moors, along a drove, you've got a small culvert with a gate that's usually covered with flat stones for the wagons to go over, and you lift one of them and see which way the water's running, and if there's any movement in the water the eels'll always go into the stream, they'll always head into a stream, and we used

Above: Withies drying by the River Tone.
Opposite: Len Meade slewing up.

to put eel traps in under there, cover them up, put them in at night. We used to catch quite a few eels like that, mainly for our own use. A lot of people did that. Then you skin them and gut them and then its just a matter of taste: boil them or fry them or put them in the oven.

I'd been away from the village for a time, I came back in 'forty-eight and I started doing casual withy work, withy cutting, and Tom Beck he was doing casual withy work and we got together and teamed up. I started making these traps under his supervision and I did them all right and he said, 'You took to that quick.' And then I used to be friendly with the late Sidney Grenfield and his nephew Sidney Dare they were both basket makers. Sidney Grenfield was a chair maker in his time whereas his nephew used to make baskets and they asked me two or three times to have a go at basket work, and then he wanted an eel trap and I did that with him a

couple of nights. Then I took some withies up a few evenings and started doing basket work. They were both very helpful. I started off on a type of basket, like log baskets and then the picker baskets.

They used to strip the withies, dry them, put them in the sheds and they would stay there until — 'twas usually a casual worker used to do nothing else but tie them up — they was ready for the basket maker. They was all three foot one inch, down at the big end, at the butts we call 'em, and this chappie would do practically nothing else but go from place to place, tie them up and then the owner of the withies would collect them and then the strippers would be paid so much per bundle for doing them.

Another way they used to do them, especially the white withies in the spring, was straight out the withy bed, and then they would have been tied in three foot four inches round the big end. 'Twould be so much for stripping on the bank. Before any diesel pumps most of the withy-growing moors was flooded in the winter and that meant you couldn't get in to do the cutting until sometimes till April and then the sap was up, you see, they was ready to strip, straight away. They used to use boats. Matter of fact, I suppose 60 per cent of they withies was brought out by boat because the moors was a bit splashed. The droves were so bad that you couldn't get in, they'd cut down so much, big ruts, and the horse and cart wouldn't be able to get in, so therefore you'd bring a boat alongside the withy bed and put 'em in the boat, and drag the boat out to the hard road and then, you know, they would come along with the horse and cart.

You could punt if you had a good ditch, but if your ditch wasn't very good, you know, shallow, silted up, then you had to put a rope on him and drag him. You could haul somewhere about forty-five or fifty bundles of withies, depend on the size of the boat. You could go out and put your anchor and unload and pack out, carry on like that; anytime between end of November and March, it just depended on the conditions.

I think it was good for the withy beds to get flooded, especially if your soil was on the light side. The withies like a nice firm ground to root in and the ideal, really, is when you start off a withy bed, the second year, is to cut 'em right down to ground level and let 'em come up out of the ground. If you don't, if you let 'em come up too high, they get springy, as you try to cut them the root springs around. If you've them ground level then it's nice and firm and they gradually spread, the withies spread out from the ground. That's why so much of it has to be done by hand. They have a machine, but there again you really want somebody to go round behind to tidy it up, a lot of people aren't satisfied with it. They days, going back, they looked after their beds better than they do today. Labour was cheap, a lot cheaper than what it is today. The stumps used to be tidied up after cutting, then the weeding — we used to go and break off the bindweed, withywind we call it, that had to be broken off. If you've got a bad withywind patch then you've got a bare patch in a few years. It'll kill the stump even, in time, smother it, just smother it.

It has always been a very expensive crop to harvest 'cause there's so much hand labour, so many tasks. First you have to cut them, then you have to boat them to the hard road or today you haul them out with a tractor, and

Above: Charlie Keirle cutting withies by hand.

Opposite: Lunch in a withy field. Charlie Langford and Emrys Coate on West Sedgemoor.

then you bring them home. You've got to grade them into sizes, tie them into bundles and then you've got to boil them. Then, nowadays, you put them through the stripper, then you've got to dry them, then you end up with tying them again. You see there's so many times you've got to handle 'em, and the weather plays a big part, especially in the drying. They must be dry, you can't put them away till they're really dry — after they've been boiled and stripped — or they'd go mouldy. They'll cover with a white mould even in a few days, it's the same with baskets.

Usually about April you put stock in the withy beds and they bite the grass down really short and then the withies, when they start, probably about mid-May, the withies'll come away fast and keep above the grass. It's a good idea to get cattle in there, especially if it's a bit wet, their feet tread down the turf, make it late starting, therefore the withies get quite a few inches above the weeds. They used to be against sheep one time, they used to think the wool collected round the stumps, I don't think they are so particular these days. The withies start growing around the middle of

April, if the bullocks was in that'd keep them back till the middle of May, and then 'tis unusual to have a frost hard enough to do any damage.

It's not nearly so much as it was sixty years ago, many of the bigger growers have disappeared. I know there's a few big ones now, but that time there was about three or four recognised merchants in the district that used to buy off the smaller growers. And some of those bigger merchants would buy land and cultivate it, which meant time, and then plant the withy bed and then rent it in alternatives: seven, fourteen, twenty-one years, for someone that wanted to start on their own. Then the rent was paid, you see, when the withies was sold, the merchant had the privilege of buying the crop back. The man had to keep it as a viable withy bed in that time, such as doing the ditches and keeping the weeds down and all that type

of thing. It had to be looked after. Of course, then again you got spraying to do. You get a leech that starts from a brown beetle who lays his eggs and what we call a leech hatches out, not really a leech, the larvae of the beetle about a half, a quarter of an inch in length. It could go up right around the young and tender leaves, eat them off, and therefore if your centre bud is gone then you get four or five shoots come out below, its practically useless. You've always had to do a certain amount of grading, grade out stuff that isn't usable.

It's very hard work and not very rewarding, especially back sixty years ago. When the first War was on the sale increased, then again soon after there was a slump and the prices dropped again very fast. Some people do try to combine a bit of withy growing and a few cows but I think, today especially, you want to give your undivided attention to one or the other, things have changed a lot. You would want to grow somewhere about six to eight acres and then it would have to be a thriving withy bed.

On this border soil round Saltmoor, Stanmoor, a withy bed, if well looked after, could go on for forty, fifty years, but if they're not taken care of, if you let the bindweed take over, then they don't last very long. Disease has always been a problem. You get this blight, you get aphids. The aphids come in the withy beds practically before anywhere else for some unknown reason, and then there's another insect we used to call the elephant, and that one was an absolute replica of an elephant and had a sucker like a trunk, and he just sucked the sap out of the withies and a few months after when they were being harvested, you see these great burs on them, you know, and you used to have to throw them back for seconds. These days now I suppose a lot of that goes back for hurdles, but once 'twas a dead loss, they were useless.

Practically all of the withy work has been piecework — so much a score, so much for twenty bundles. 'Twas the same with tying, always piecework, contract work. You'd go and weed a withy bed, p'raps it would be, just

Left: Basket making, Burrowbridge. Ready to slew.

Opposite: Upsetting and waling a log basket, Burrowbridge.

depends what the acreage is, so much per acre to do the weeding. That was all hand work with a small sickle and that would be so much per acre.

In basket making you usually had Black Maul for doing the siding up and that type of thing, you know if you was doing a bigger basket you'd want a bigger withy stick and Black Maul doesn't get very big. After a couple of years they fine down a lot; that's when you like them for siding because they're sleek and very pliable and durable. And then you had to go to Champion Rod or one of the New Kinds for staking. The Old New Kind was a good one. They were straight and they would border down nice. There was two New Kinds here we used to use and Black Spaniard, not a very good working withy, and then you had the osier, but you always dried them off without stripping. It is a withy as such, but not as hard. Whereas a Black Maul is just as hard when it's been stripped as he is brown, the osier is always brown, with the bark on, it's no use stripped. There again there is variation in osiers, there was the Briney Osier, that was hard, but on the whole they used the softer kind. A lot of them would be used in willy baskets. Going back in time the coal merchants, they usually had a few willy baskets about, because they used to do the rounds every week in winter, some places they put in perhaps a couple of tons, loose, and to save bagging it up they would take it down to the weighbridge, take it straight to the customer and have willy baskets and shoot it out. The same thing used to happen when the barges used to bring the coal or the brick rubble up the River Parrett on the tide. You always had quite a few willy baskets and then they'd have a lot of people carrying in. I remember seeing the barge load of coal when we were going to school, nine in the morning, and when we came out at twelve o'clock, they'd still be carrying in. I suppose they days there were more willy baskets used and picker baskets because all the apples was picked up by hand, potatoes picked up by hand, so much of it was.

A tree withy is different from the ones we grow in the withy beds, they were used one time for chair legs because going back, I suppose possibly over eighty years, they had no end of these people here making wicker chairs, that really started off here. Chair makers, so many of them was chair makers they days, and then you had to have a three-year-old tree withy for the legs. Of course, they was always growing the tree withies to make thatching spars to thatch the houses and ricks. They'd pollard the tree and the sticks'd grow out from the trunk. You do see it now, though the sticks aren't used so much, not like they was. Of course, there wasn't the house thatching in this district like there is in neighbouring ones but there was always the rick thatching and therefore the tree withies was very handy for that. They days it was very unusual to leave the withies in the withy beds till they was three years old, 'twas uneconomical as there were so many of the withy trees grown along the ditches and rhynes. And 'twould help to keep the bank up, the bank of the ditch, the roots would help that because cattle tread the ditch in pretty bad where they go to drink.

There was a lot, one time, laundry hampers, and when apples used to go away from this district we made half bushel, bushel baskets, for dessert apples. 'Twas unusual for the cider apples to go away, they were never sold other than loose, there again you had your baskets to pick them up or to measure them. You have your willy butt on your weighing engine and if you could get a half-hundred weight in, then you adjust your weights and allow for your basket, weigh them out and count your baskets. You had a half bag or a quarter bag and then you had a larger one, a four score, that would hold eighty pounds of apples or potatoes.

I dip the withies in water two or three times in the evening when its cool and throw them down on the grass and then perhaps come out first thing in the morning and dip them again. Then, when I'm ready to start basketing they're pliable then. Of course, you have to dry them, the people who grow them and process them have to dry them, so to make them pliable you have to soak them again, and by dipping them like that they keep a good colour. If you leave them in the water too long they very often turn a bad colour. By dipping them you retain the bright buff colour. A buff withy is one that's been boiled then peeled, a brown withy is a natural withy, with the skin on. Your white withy we cut when the sap is up and they'll

Stripping withies.

strip easy — but you can't cope with so many and the rest you put in a pit or ditch. So long as they got access to water they'll keep growing for a long time. When the sap is up — that's usually about the beginning of May for a pit withy — why, then the skin'll come off easy. White withies aren't used so much now as they used to be, one time there was quite a demand for whites. So many clothes baskets, laundry hampers, butcher baskets, display baskets, so much of it they days was in whites.

The drainage has altered so much, especially in places like West Sedgemoor. Back in my young days there was no pump there, the flood water used to wait till the river went down and then it used to run out,

Les Musgrove stripping withies.

which was a good thing from one point of view: it used to run out in the spring when the spring tides was going and the elvers used to go in there because there was an old oak door and when the water went down in the river and it was high in the moor, the water would push the door open and the elvers would go in the moor. That's their natural feeding ground and there they'll grow into eels, then they'll come out in the flood water, in the winter, and go back to their spawning grounds. Curry Moor was another moor, although they had a steam pump up there, it had a door where the water used to run out in the spring and when the door was open the elvers'd follow the water back. Because that's what they're looking for, the moor water.

The bad thing about it was for withy cutting. Sometimes, if it was a very wet winter and a late spring, late in drying off, it was so late before you could get out to get the withies off, you couldn't do no withy cutting till the water went away. Curry Moor and Sedgemoor, round that part, and Northmoor, there used to be water in the fields most of the winter, until we got the diesel pump. Land must have improved in value because you run keep-stock out there on that border ground for most of the year now. One time in West Sedgemoor there must have been 1,000 acres of withies; West Sedgemoor, Wickmoor, even in Saltmoor there was six, eight withy beds one time. All gone. So much labour, there used to be so much hard labour in them.

Michael Musgrove, Withy Grower, Lakewall, Westonzoyland, 2006

'Dad always said that when he started, a bundle of withies would pay a man's wages for a day. Now we're getting about twenty pounds a bundle. You can't work for that. It's three times that now. That's how it's gone. You've got to turn out more to make the same.'

Stripping and tying withies.

The sweet, distinctive smell of boiling withies hangs over Lakewall, and drying withies line the road. Michael Musgrove prepares his withies here, and stacks them in bundles ready for the basket makers and buyers from across the country and abroad. He and his wife Ellen run the business now, but he started working with his father, Les Musgrove, whilst still at school and has seen the trade evolve and change. Though more mechanised now, growing, cutting and preparing withies is still hard, physical work. Harvesting starts in November and runs through to March, the cuttings for new beds must be planted in spring, the stacking, carting, boiling, stripping, drying and tying lasts through the year. Though a withy bed can last for forty years it has to be kept in good heart and constant war is waged against the 'elephant' mite and withywind.

Michael: My dad died two years ago in March. In 2004, I started to work on the withies with him while I was still at school. I was always up here weekends and after school. I used to drive the tractor round and things like that. And then every night — 'cause Dad used to do stripping most days, he had other people working for him doing the sorting and things like that — every night after school I'd come up, get the little tractor, back it down, pick up the withies he'd stripped and go on spreading them. So every night I used to spread these few withies, see. I was an expert at spreading before I left school! Spreading them to dry. I was always helping, always knew I would carry on with the withies.

My grandfather, as far as I can find out, did bits of all sorts and my dad started off on farm work but they always had a few withies. But then they went on doing more withies and used to buy in withies and prepare them, then they bought a few more withy fields. They started off mainly doing

tree-sticks, cutting the young branches off the withy trees. They had an old boiler where the other one's to now, an old galvanised boiler, and they'd boil them off and strip them. No one does that any more, there's no money in it, though we do get asked for tree-sticks sometimes. They work all right, they bend all right. But we grow other varieties now instead and just leave the rods to grow on in the field for two years. They grow much straighter and cleaner.

When I left school you could make a living at it. It was harder work then — the physical side of it is a lot easier now than when I started — but you didn't have to do so many withies to make a living. The price wasn't too bad then. But now — with all the foreign stuff and whatever — you can't really charge an awful amount for the withies, you just couldn't sell them. Because of competition. There aren't so many people doing it as there was either, so what we've had to do is turn out more withies to make the money. Dad always said that when he started a bundle of withies would pay a man's wages for a day. Now we're getting about twenty pounds a bundle. You can't work for that. It's three times that now. That's how it's gone. You've got to turn out more to make the same.

We've bought a cutting machine rather than cutting by hand as we used to, that's made it a lot easier and quicker, and we grow more withies now than we used to when I left school. It's doubled, the acreage. We had about twenty-five, getting on to thirty acres, and now we're growing nearly sixty. We've got withies around here, Westonzoyland; we've got withies down at Lyng, three fields there, one by the road, one down by the lay-by, another one down Hector's Lane, out through there; we've got a field, six acres, out there on South Moor; we've just planted eight acres here beside the house; we've got thirteen acres at Langport; and then we've got one field in Curry Moor and one in Hay Moor — one right beside the river bridge which we don't own but we buy the crop each year, and then another over the bridge and down the drove and we've got three acres there as well, we own that one.

We didn't own that much before. We used to buy Mrs Talbot's withies, up Lyng, every year and others, we didn't really have that much when I left school. Since then we've tried to buy our own land. We've saved up, bought a field when it's come up, withy beds when they came up, and we've made more money by doing that. If you can buy the field reasonable, that is. It seems a lot of money, say six acres at nearly £20,000, but you haven't got that outlay every year and it's finished with. So we've saved up and done that and it's made it easier.

The field out on South Moor, about six acres, was arable land. We bought that and planted it. We planted the young one at Lyng the year before and then we managed to buy the one next door and we just planted that last year. We're not the biggest withy grower around, Coates are the biggest, Hector's quite big but he hasn't got so many now, has sold off some of his fields and that, and where he was doing just hurdles, he's doing more river bank work now — live willows for river banking — and

Opposite: Stripping withies at Stathe.

they've laid off a lot of the chaps and are just concentrating on doing that. They never did many baskets, Hector's, mainly the hurdles, and Coates do charcoal and baskets.

We send our withies all over this country and all over the world. We send them to Ireland, lots to Northern and Southern Ireland and, last year, we've done Denmark, Germany, America, South Africa and I'm just doing an order now for New Zealand. It costs more to send it there than what the withies cost. But they still want them. They can't really grow them. They can buy Chinese stuff, which is probably nearer and certainly cheaper, but they snap like a carrot so they don't want to use them. We've sent withies to New Zealand for years. And Ireland.

There are fewer growers now, only four or five left, but the market is out there, you've just got to find it. We sell more now direct. Before, we just had a few firms that we supplied, see. We had Brighton Baskets, they made all dog baskets, cat carrier baskets; then we had Burdekin's in Yorkshire that does cane furniture — he was like a wholesaler, so he'd buy a load of withies and then sell 'em off to people in his area, sell 'em on again. Then there's Hill's in town, Bridgwater, where they make the balloon baskets. So we just had like four or five people that bought withies off of us and that was it. A hundred, two hundred bundles at a time. But now we send nearly every day direct to people that want, say, two bundles, five bundles, twenty bundles, small orders like that. And not just for basket making. We sell to schools, just for artistry sort of thing. They make lanterns and things like that with the children, that's quite big, specially up country. You know, they make the frames out of withies, they're so lightweight, cover it in tissue paper, put little torches inside and they make lanterns. Just before Christmas that's quite a thing. So the market has changed, it's changing all the time, going away from basket making, to schools doing that sort of thing, art projects and that. And projects in the playground: they make domes and tunnels and things using live willow, get the kids all involved making it and then, of course, in the spring it grows. And it stays there. We send a lot for that. Mind, the baskets is still mainly what we do, supplying withies for them, 80 per cent is still that, but it is changing.

My only worry now is that we've got all these withies and we've got to sell 'em. You can't go pushing the price up and then be stuck with all these withies if they don't sell. We've got a couple of chaps working here now and we've got to find their wages each week. All they do is mainly sorting, I do everything else. The withies come straight in from the field and have to be sorted into sizes, foot sizes. Say a basket maker wants to make a log basket — he'll want eight foot staking, all depending if he's slewing or randing. Slewing is using three or four at a time, randing is going round in single weave. It's the patterns.

Mostly what we grow is Black Maul, you still can't beat it though we do grow other different sorts, too. The only thing with Black Maul is that they get diseases: rust, aphid problems. But it's the best withy there is for workability. Coates have ripped out a lot of their Black Maul and are growing other varieties that are faster growing and more disease resistant. That's alright for charcoal, they just want straight pieces they can cut up and burn. They don't need it to work, though. We've got other varieties of triandra — Black Maul's a triandra — like they grow in France and they're not too bad, Noir de Villaine, we got a patch of that, and they look quite nice but they just don't work so well.

Ellen: They're a darker skinned rod than Black Maul is.

Michael: You can't really boil 'em. If you boil 'em and strip 'em they'll snap like a carrot. Originally we had them to do white withies — cut them, put them in the ditch and strip 'em when they start to sprout — and they do strip quite well but they don't work so well. So what we do now is cut them, and we pull all the big stuff out for the people who want them for river banking — the sevens, eights and nines go for that — and the smaller stuff goes for baskets and withy sculpture and that. They're green when cut and they are dried as usual but they work quite well after they've been steamed. So they go in the boiler and aren't boiled but steamed and they turn a really nice black. Then they're dried out on the wires like the others, though they take a bit longer, about two weeks. So the black withy you see in baskets and that is Noir de Villaine.

We used to put stock in the withy beds, but not anymore. We can't get them. Only in the one field that we still cut by hand, the field's that old that the stumps aren't in rows anymore, they've come up everywhere, big stumps as well. We've got someone who puts cows in there and they'll pick it out bare in the spring. Lovely. Then the withies all shoot out again. We'd have them in our beds but the farmers can't be bothered now. Years ago there was more cattle around, I suppose. We had a farmer up at Wick who was always on Dad's back, couldn't wait to get them in there. Now there's too much grass around, they just don't need it.

The methods are much the same as they used to be but we did buy a new machine, a Polish stripping machine because withies are a big thing in Poland, or they were. It's quite good, actually. It's got two drums going round and you don't have to hold on to the withies to strip them any more. Not like when you had to hold a handful and feed them in, you can do a whole bundle now, spread out the whole wad, clamp the tops, strip the butts and then take them out and do the other end, clamp the butts and strip the tops. We got that about four years ago and we should have had it ten years ago! But Dad was never keen on it, never keen on anything like that, didn't want the cutting machine, didn't want the stripping machine. But times have to change and I couldn't do it now like it was. It was alright when me and Dad used to do the stripping together all the time but I couldn't do that on my own. Even with the new machine I'm stripping for twelve hours a day sometimes. I stay and try to finish the whole boiler-full — I try to do two boiler-fulls in a week. It all depends on what sizes the withies are in the bundle but there's roughly 200, 250 bundles go into the boiler at a time.

Dad didn't even like the tying machine and we've had that for years. He wanted to tie the bundles all by hand. But you can't do it. If I'm on my own

Opposite: Les and Michael Musgrove boiling withies, Lakewall.

I can tie sixty or seventy bundles in a day with the machine. It would take at least two days to do that by hand. With the cutting machine, Dad just didn't think that it was as good as the old way, the machines don't leave it so tidy as cutting by hand. You can't cut them tidy enough with the machines, they've all got to be trimmed off afterwards. You have to keep up a few inches above the stumps with the machine and you can't leave them like that because they need to grow out straight from the stumps, from the stool. Most of the growers would go over the stumps with a really heavy-duty topper, a bush hog, and bash 'em down, but they don't like it. We have a machine with saw blades on now, so we go in and trim off the stumps really nice and tidy. It's like a saw-bench turned on its side with two blades, so you can do two rows at a time with the tractor. Fantastic job it makes and it's quick — if you've got a good bloke driving the tractor. Even my dad had to admit it was better.

These things take getting used to. Like with the new stripping machine, it didn't work too well to start with. And we had to get three-phase electricity and that cost £6,000 just to swap it over but we had to do that. Ellen managed to get a grant to help us with it, nearly the only grant we ever had. All the farmers round here get ESA payments but we can't get anything. Because we use sprays on our crop, they say. They're changing that to the Single Farm Payment now and we thought we'd get something but no. Yet arable farmers spray their crops and they're going to get their grants.

Ellen: Because we have a permanent crop, because we don't physically rip out our willow beds every season.

Michael: We managed to get a grant from the woodland grant scheme for planting our withies out here. Well, for half of it. We planted the first half and the second year they told us that we couldn't have it, that we shouldn't have had it in the first place because it was only for biomass willow, for energy. But not for basket-making materials. And there's so much wildlife in a withy bed, you wouldn't believe it. We planted that field next door, it was only a grass field before, not very interesting, and now there are all sorts. There's a barn owl we got in the bottom shed who flies over this field every night. And the snipe that we got in there! They go up and the sky is black with them, there must be fifty or more in this field. And the skylarks in the spring in every withy field! When we're picking up withies, all you can hear while you're there is skylarks!

But I do have to spray against the withywind, the bindweed. It doesn't like it but it will grow again, it'll just hold it back a bit. But it's a real problem, especially with some of the older beds, that's why I'm trying to plant up some new fields. All these old ones have got bindweed in and it makes it hard work. They'll pull down the withies, just pull them flat and we've got great bare patches in some fields because of it. You have to try and do something to fight it. I spray two or three times, perhaps, against that and the aphids. You see farmers out here who run about and spray non-stop. I don't go and spray the whole lot, only bits and I've only got my little sprayer. I check the withies carefully.

Black Maul gets this 'button-top' from their own special aphids that come and sting the withies two or three times a year. I know the dates, more or less, when they're going to do it, so I only spray then. Others spray a lot. That's also why they're ripping out fields with Black Maul and planting up with other withies that don't get the disease. All withies aren't the same you see, different sorts of triandra, different sorts of viminalis, faster-growing ones, fragilis albas and so on. Lots of them. Well, Black Maul and Noir de Villaine are triandras, *Salix triandra* Black Maul or *Salix triandra* Noir de Villaine. Only triandras get button-top, this particular insect only stings triandras, but we have to have them because they are the ones the basket makers want, the best ones for working. If I was doing charcoal I could grow others.

Ellen: We can't afford to, really. A lot of these schools and places want something that's fairly flexible immediately, with Black Maul you don't even have to soak it. Depending on the project. Some of the other varieties hardly bend at all. But we've been asked for other sorts, too, a number of different varieties that are better for other kinds of work, like living willow hurdles for river banks which they're using now to stop erosion.

Michael: The best for that is Flanders Red, fragilis alba, it's more of a withy tree, very hard. So we have to know which varieties to plant. But they're usually easy to get growing. After we cut the withies, we'll sort out some eight foots, keep them alive in water and then in the spring we'll cut them up into sets, ten-inch pieces from the butt end. So we'll cut five pieces, say, from an eight foot, the rest is too thin. You want them about pencil size. Then you just push 'em in the ground. Rows two foot two inches apart and about eight to ten inches apart in the rows. We planted that eight-acre field out, all by hand, of course! We planted mainly Black Maul, about two acres of Flanders Red, some different viminalis varieties, capreas. They like those for making domes and arches of live willow. Trouble is with all of them it takes three years to get a proper crop. For the first year or two they'll just send up a few shoots. Though they grow tall fast, eight or nine foot in a year. Well, only a few months really, 'cause I'm not trimming them off till June, so that's June, July, August and then they're finished. They're doing nine foot in three months. They don't grow much in September, perhaps the first week a bit.

Ellen: I think the only thing that grows faster is bamboo.

Michael: But it's a long-term thing. You have to think three years in front. So, yes, we're planting for these domes and tunnels and that but will they want them in three or four years' time? Will the fashion have changed? It's a chance you've got to take. We've been planting up withy varieties with different colour barks, trying to save me having to boil them. The only reason for boiling and stripping is to get the colour, the buff colour and, anyway, some of other varieties don't work well if they've been boiled and stripped, so you've got to sell them with the bark on.

Ellen: You've got no idea what you're going to get out of a field. I mean, Michael can judge what the tallest withies are, he might say that there's a lot of eight foots in the field, but as far as the rest of the other sizes you haven't got a clue till they're all sorted by hand: fifty bundles of three foot? Five bundles of five foot? So it takes a lot of work: the two chaps here do sorting, mostly, all the time.

Michael: We're selling more direct, ourselves. The phone's going every day. Most of the people we don't even see, they just ring up and order this, this and this. Years ago we had our four or five main customers, they had 100 bundles at a time, say. But now we're selling all these bits. We've got to send them all off, we get a lorry coming nearly every day to pick them up. They have to be labelled and wrapped in cling film. All the computerised stuff and that, I couldn't do it. Ellen does it all.

Ellen: It's time-saving but far more expensive than it used to be. We have to be competitive. There's a lot of baskets coming in from China, absolute rubbish but they're cheap. So we haven't put our prices up for ages!

Michael: You're half afraid to. We undercut all the others anyway, but we don't want to put off our customers. So it's twenty pounds a bundle, usually. And in a seven foot bundle, say, there's 500 or 600 withy rods. In a three foot bundle you're looking at 2,000 or more rods, in a bundle of stripped buffs.

Ellen: It's really the customer base that has changed most. Whereas willow used to be a necessity it's more of a craft thing now. It's become more of a leisure industry than a trade, if you like. We do still supply a lot of basket makers but even they don't make for agriculture and so on as they used to. But still they do make really good, strong baskets that'll last for years.

Michael: You've got to find that new thing, like I was saying, the river banking, lanterns, kitchen drawers. Well, they're not all new but taking off again, some of them. The basket makers have to find whatever it is people now want and we have to be here to supply them. The other thing they're doing is coffins now. Hill's — that's the Somerset Willow Company — are making coffins. We supply them and they do look fantastic. They're far better than wooden coffins. People round here have had them and they did in the old days, too, but not nearly so much. It's all environmentally friendly more now, so willow is perfect. The one we had done for Dad was fantastic. He'd always admired the coffins Hill's made and the one he had, he'd handled the withies in it just days before.

Industry

Maud Gould, Clarke Shoes, Street, 2005

'I never thought of what I'd do. It never really occurred to me because automatically a lot of them did go in the factory. I mean my sister worked in the factory, my cousins worked in the factory, I got cousins and practically all the family who worked in the factory.'

The town of Street grew around the sheepskin and shoe industries. From the early nineteenth century, as the need for an agricultural labour force declined, many of the people of the Moors and Levels sought work in the factories, especially in Clarks and Morlands. Morlands went into receivership in 1982 but Clarks still has its headquarters in Street, though it has not made any shoes there for some years now. Maud Gould, like many hundreds of others, spent her working life, forty years or so, with Clarks and, now in her eighties, remembers it all vividly.

I was Maud Walters and was born at West End Street, my father was Alec and my mother Elizabeth. Then, when I were about eight months old we moved to Brutasche Terrace, because Dad was a labourer in Clarks and worked in Clarks nearly all his life and he put in for a house. I suppose when they were married it was awkward to get houses like it is now. And he was lucky to get a Clarks house down at Brutasche Terrace, number 8, and that was where I was brought up. I was brought up mostly around the factory, if you can understand my meaning, because I was brought up on the doorstep, me and my sister. We were there right from when I was a baby till I was nineteen or so. I had a marvellous childhood down there, everybody helped everybody else. Money was not plentiful in those days, I suppose my father brought home about two pound a week, we thought 'twas a lot of money. That was his wage from Clarks and the house rent was, as I remember it as I got older, fifteen shillings a week. And we had a great big allotment where the car park is now. Clarks provided the house, they provided a lot of the houses round Street, there was Grange Road, Brutasche Terrace and so on and my father helped to build these all up here, they were all Clarks houses, they've all been sold now. There was the swimming-pool my father helped to build, the outdoor one, he helped to build that, he helped to build Hindhayes school. It was all Clarks, you know.

Above: The Closing Room at Clarks. (Archive photograph courtesy of Clarks Shoes).
Opposite: Mrs Maud Gould.

Of course, Clarks being Quakers they had the foresight, I suppose, for the workers, that they had to do something for them, to keep the industry going and by building all these houses it helped them to keep the people working there. So my father was on the maintenance, not in the factory, and my uncle, he was a bricklayer working there on Clarks' private work-force, you know. There was Mr Packer, he was another bricklayer, Ronald Barber as foreman and Mr Wormald, he was head foreman. But before him was Henry Clark. They worked in the factory to do the maintenance and all, like if the drains were blocked they had a plumber, their own plumber. They had everything at hand. I can remember the swimming-pool. I used to watch it being built every day because in those days Father never had a flask, not a Thermos flask like they have now. So every day I used to walk up the High Street on my way to school and I used to take a bottle of tea up for Father so he'd have a warm drink.

I never thought of what I'd do. It never really occurred to me because automatically a lot of them did go in the factory. I mean my sister worked in the factory, my cousins worked in the factory, I got cousins and practically all the family who worked in the factory. But when I actually left school I worked first for the CWS tannery, the Co-operative Wholesale Society, where they made the leather.

I went to the County mixed school, well it was the Board School then, where the butcher's shop is, there's a plaque up there. It was the first school in Street, then they moved from there when they had the big one built, where Living Homes is now, that's where we were all educated. Of course, there wasn't the number of children then like there is now. There was only about four classes upstairs and four downstairs. Almost the whole of Street was to do with Clarks then, or the CWS tannery. And there was Bartlett wagon works. Then they had Morlands as well, they were all relations, all Quakers. So not many pubs. There was only the Elms and the Street Inn and the Legion and the Unity Club and the Bear. But the Bear was dry, that was temperance. You could go and have a cup of tea or orange juice. There was like a constitutional club, the Goss House, that my aunty used to be caretaker of. You could play billiards or read the papers, but they never allowed no drink in there, all you was allowed were packets of crisps!

My father was a Streetonian and my grandfather was too, but he was an outdoor man, didn't work for Clarks. He never wore a coat or nothing all winter and summer. He was one of these men that did roam, he did roam the moors and that. I know he worked on the railway. But my grandma came from Walton. My father was born at Beckery really, Glastonbury, but he lived in Street all his life.

When I started work at the tannery I was measuring the skins. I was fourteen. I was learning how to grade the skins and that. We had great big machines with little prongs coming out of them to measure the skins and, I suppose, it was so much a square inch. That's how they did sell it, see. You push the skins through the machine and you've got a treadle to help it go through and then you pull it out and write out how many feet it is and so many inches. It had a clock dial up over the top. A great big long machine. I did that all day long, feeding skins into the machine to measure them. Then I went on clipping the suede skins and that went to Yeovil to be made into gloves, at the Yeovil factory. They did a lot of glassy kid, too, at the time, for shoes for the outside part and they used to do linings, as well, lining leather. We were starting at eight o'clock and I was finishing at five, every day. But the children that went to the Continuation School, the Strode School, they did do two half-days a week in the Strode School for sixpence and Clarks paid for them. But I didn't have that because I never went there.

Then I was grading the skins. That meant I had a pair of scissors — and my poor fingers used to be all blisters — you had to cut the rotted part out and if there was a mark in the skin you had to cut it out. To grade the skin higher. I was in the warehouse part and my first pay packet were fourteen shillings a week for a forty hour week and I used to give mum ten shillings and keep four for myself. I never smoked and never drank and you couldn't buy so many clothes because they were all on coupons, on ration. I stayed there for two years and then my father said, 'I think you could do better by going in to Whitehead's'. That's Vickers Armstrong's, that's the munitions in 1939, 1940. They took over the whole of the Big Room at Clarks and a couple of sheds out across the yard where I worked to. I worked in the copper department. We had to make copper pipes for torpedoes and we used to put stoppers, like, on the end and the screw to screw it all up and then we used to shine them up. They used to be ever so shiny, they never had to be dirty or nothing and they looked real lovely after they were done. Then we had to bend them all in shape, because you can't just put them all in and screw them up, you had to bend them to the shape they had to go because they had to go all in round the gyro and round different things in the tail sections of the torpedoes. And they never had to be a thou' out. Really accurate. I was the only woman over there and there were five men. Two were tinsmiths, two were coppersmiths and the other was a carpenter and were all in the same shed. I stayed there the whole of the War, well just until things got a bit quiet and we knew that the War was going to be over and then we were all of us — a lot had been sent over from Clarks into the torpedo works — sent back into Clarks.

My first job in Clarks was to fold over the leather on the shoes, various handwork and then I went on rubbing the back seams of the linings down at the heels. I had an old-fashioned thing with a handle and two pieces of wood and you'd put the thing on and put a drop of water on it and rub the seam out. So it wouldn't rub the back of your heel. And then the stitchers come along and stitch the uppers to the linings to go round the top line of the shoe. I stayed on that till we all got split up. I was fortunate because I stayed in the old Silflex block. They were building the Grove by then, that was the welting part of the factory. That's where my husband worked to.

But anyway after that when we went into the Silflex I was under Flo Parsons. Now Flo was a nice woman, she was strict but if she could help you she did. I'd got married you see, but my War marriage broke up and I had a baby, and after I had the baby she sent and asked me to go back and I went back. I was only on part-time to start with and, well, after that my mother and father looked after the baby because my father got ill and couldn't work. So I was like the breadwinner for the whole family at home. I was twenty-two when I broke up with my first husband. So, any rate, I worked at the factory and gradually, as my son Michael got older and went to school, I went on full-time. I'd got married when I was nineteen, at the end of the War, to someone from Wolverhampton and I went up there for a bit but I hated it. Every minute of it. I loved the country! He was in the Army here in Street, all the soldiers were stationed here, that's how we met. All the lorries were all over the place, Somerton Road was Nissen huts, there were soldiers everywhere! Goodness knows how many lots of soldiers we had. We had the artillery here, we had the engineers (that's where my husband come from), we had the Gloucesters, we had the Americans, black and white Americans. Street was full of soldiers! We had New Zealanders here and my mum and dad wrote to two New Zealand boys for years and they came and stayed with us.

I didn't go up to Wolverhampton till he was demobbed but I only lasted three months. Then Flo let me go on short hours, which was good of her and I was always very grateful to her. And I had my mum and dad to help, thank God! I didn't want to send my boy out to nowhere. So I brought him up and I worked in the factory. I was about twenty-one when we moved to Southleaze, just before Michael was born. And we moved there because my father used to go up right inside the big chimney you can still see in the town, to sweep it. And one day he'd just come down when he bumped into Mr Clark, that was Bancroft Clark's father. And he said to my father, 'Oh Alec, you're dirty,' he said, 'have you had a shower?' And he said, 'Yes, sir, I've had a shower but I want to ask you something.' And he said, 'What's that Alec?' And he said, 'Do you think you could put me in a bathroom down at Brutasche Terrace? We haven't got one down there and now I've got to get back home and get in the tin tub!' You know, with the copper, like they did in those days. So anyway it wasn't but a fortnight later when Mr Fitton — that was the man in charge of Clarks Estate — sent for my dad. And he went up there and Mr Fitton said, 'Alec, Mr Clark has offered you a house in Southleaze. It's got a bathroom.' But my dad said, 'I don't know, I don't know if I can afford the rent. I'll go home and talk to my wife about it.' Because the rent was one pound a week! Anyway, we did go out there and we never looked back. And he had his bathroom.

The next job I did in Clarks after the linings was they put me on hand-lacing and cleaning and then after that I went on skiving. That's taking bits of leather off the shoes to make it soft. I mean you had a knife to take off little bits of leather, trimming it off to make it softer and also easier to stitch. This was when the shoe was all in pieces still. And then people did fitting bits of different things like putting on duponts and all that, that's like little bits of paper in different places in the shoe to make it stronger. Like a paper, called duponts. And then they used to number them, every twelve pair had a certain number. After that they'd stick the fells on, that's like a lining that you stick to the shoe and they used to do that and sometimes just put the half-lining in.

After I did the skiving — I was on that for a good time — I went on ironing pieces onto the shoe, you know, like this velcro stuff that you can iron on. I used to iron bits on there to make it stronger. Then they stitch all the linings on, like the top line, and then they'd go down for assembly then, to have the last put on them after they'd come from the closing room. Then the men'd last them and put the soles and heels on. But that was all done in different departments. I was in the closing room, that was all the uppers, to stitch all the uppers. I did a little bit of stitching but not much.

After we moved to Silflex an entirely new system came in: you had to measure the stitches, so many stitches to the inch. And afterwards you had to do so much of that in a time, like piecework. There was 100 performance and 133 performance, and if you were on 133 you were earning good money, if you were doing 100 that was just day work. Every piece was measured and they did work out how much time twelve pairs of shoes should take. You might have to do it in seven minutes. That was the 100 performance. If you did more than that you could make more money. You had men come round with stop watches and they'd time you. They had clipboards. And there was three different men'd time us to get the picture right, because one might be a slight difference. So they'd put them all together and work it out from there. If you had a slow person and a medium person and a quick person, they'd put all that together and work it out from there. That was what I was told. That started to come in and I reckon that was the worst day of our lives there. They brought in this new system called the PA system. It was all right money-wise but 'twas slavery really, you know what I mean, it wasn't a bit like the old days. Though some girls were terrific, they'd earn good money then. Everything was done on conveyors then. So we had a girl stood down the end of the conveyor and she used to put the work on the conveyor and send it up.

When the new lines did come in, summer, winter and autumn, like with the sandals and so on, they'd check us again. Though they had the sandal room then. And they opened up other factories and it all got distributed to different places. We had summer and winter shoes, though the boots were made up in Minehead to start with but they went to Bridgwater and then all over the place.

Well, one of our girls left and said would I like to take on her job with the union so I took it on from there. I wasn't anti-union but I wasn't so much politically minded. I only went on it because I felt I could help people. The Boot and Shoe Union. Wilf Simmonds was on there. I was the representative in that room. I must have been nearly thirty then. I used to sort out if some of them couldn't earn their money on this timing, used to have to get them all re-timed and that. Or if there was something they didn't like we had to sort it out and go in the office and argue about it. It wasn't like the olden times when Mr Stanton used to be in charge of them doing the shoes. It wasn't such a big turn-out then. We used to go into Mr Stanton and we used to quibble and he used to let us have, perhaps, a ha'penny on twelve shoes. But it wasn't like that afterwards when they set the clock on you, you could ask for a re-timing, see, and all sort of things like that. Like when girls would do their work wrong or were worried about something. You see I had been a Street girl and I knew a lot of their mothers and I knew their families, see, so it wasn't only the union work I did do, 'twas like agony aunt work! One time I had eight girls pregnant all in the same room! That was before the pill came in. But believe me, it wasn't all the girls' fault, some of it was the homes they come from. And some of those tales I wouldn't like to tell you because I wouldn't want to have it put down. But whatever happened between me and them, I've had girls come on my doorstep crying.

I used to take them up to personnel — we had a very good personnel woman called Miss Featherstone — I used to take them up there or go to the factory nurse, and I used to tell them and they used to see to them. And they'd sort them out and then they'd have their jobs back afterwards because that was most important, most important, and then they'd come back in and we'd never mention it after that. Now I had one poor girl, I'd just been up the office to see about another one, and I came back and I said, 'I hope you aren't going to be the next!' And she said, 'I am! And I don't know what to do about it.' I knew she never had no mother and father. She said, 'I told my brother this morning and all he could do was swear at me.'

She said, 'I've got nowhere.' So I took her on up to personnel, to see Miss Featherstone and they helped her a great deal. But that poor girl! I don't know how she stayed the work because she wasn't well. And then she had her baby in the hospital and that girl left that baby in that hospital and walked out. Now I'll tell you why she done that: because she knew she couldn't keep the child, she couldn't cope. Some of these girls were heartbreaking. Some of them did get married to their men, some put their babies up for adoption, some of them put them in homes. It was very sad. I had one mother stop me up Street one day and she said, 'Maud, I've been waiting to see you.' I thought to myself, 'Oh dear, I wonder what's going to happen now.' But I said, 'Oh, have you?' And she said, 'Yes. I want to thank you for what you done for my daughter. I couldn't have done what you've done.' So, you see, it is the approach, and I think having my baby and coming home like I did — and I had good parents — made me able to cope and to understand. So being a union representative was far more than just about work. I was hardly in my seat sometimes. I was supposed to be on the line and doing my work as well. Though in later years I was able to get signed on, on day work. If you got a flat rate they'd pay you that flat rate and you wouldn't lose out even if you were not actually working on the job. But that took a bit of time to come in, happened a bit later on with the union and that. We really all sort of worked together. For instance, there was one girl doing her work wrong one night and they sent for me just before we were going home and I spoke to her and that. And I said, 'Now, you go home and take a tablet and go to bed and I'll see you in the morning.' And I went to see the foreman and explained that she was doing her work wrong because she was worried. And we did sort her out. She's married now and got three children.

I continued doing my union work all through right till I left the factory. I worked for Clarks for forty years. I took early retirement and came out at fifty-five and I'm eighty next birthday. And I've still got strong links with the factory by the pensioners and that. We still get together every other week. I've only just come off the committee now. Last week, funny, I was coming out the Post Office last Friday and I saw one of the girls and I said, 'I'm sorry I never spoke to you at the Clarks party, because I can't get around very well now.' And she said, 'Well, I've been in and had an operation but have a happy new year and thank you for all the years you did for us in the factory.' Now, that was lovely!

I stayed on various jobs. After we were in Silflex for a bit, they decided that we were all going to amalgamate into one big room, so we all went into the Big Room, they used to call it. We all went in there. But that was a bit hard because there was a union rep one side and I was the union rep the other side and I think it caused a problem, though it did work out in the end. I were a bit put out. But I went to see Malcolm Cotton who was a very nice man and listened to what you said. And he said, 'What can I do for you, Maud?' And I said, 'I've come in to give in my notice. There's been a bit of an upset at the union meeting and I got hauled over the coals for something I didn't do. They got the wrong person.' So he said to me to think it over but I said no. I said I'd rather get out of it. And that night the woman who caused the trouble came up to my house and apologised to me. And then they asked me to carry on and I said, 'Well, because that woman came and apologised, and to think that she was good enough to do that, I don't mind staying on.' And then I took it all over and I had about 200 girls. I was their representative.

We had trouble in the Big Room when we went down there first. The conveyors used to make an awful row! I think that's why we're a bit deaf now, why we talk so loud! Mr Lance Clark were down there just after we moved and said he was pleased with how it all went because within quarter of an hour all the girls were at their seats working. I mean you have a move like that and it was quite good. But I said, 'I don't think we're going to get so much out of it! The only ones who are going to get something out of it are they up the chemist's with the headache tablets!' And he said, 'Why?' and I said, 'Oh, those conveyors make a terrible row!' Anyway, I don't know what they did but they were alright afterwards, they put them right. But they were terrible! The row were terrible. I mean, you sit there for a while!

After we were in the Big Room we were sent up to Lock Hill because they put us in sections again. I was up there for six, seven years. Then, before I retired, we went back to the Big Room for a bit. At Lock Hill we did the men's shoes all the way through: the cutting, the closing, the making. That's the whole shoe. There were about 200 of us there, all in the one place. We were doing the overflow from what they were doing in Weston-Super-Mare. The cutting is when the leather comes in, all in great sort of shelves, and then they take the leather down, whatever they want, say lining leather, all in a big roll and then it's all measured out for the cutters. Then they cut the linings or the outsides or whatever, it can vary, and then they go through a process and then they come into the closing room. Now the closing room is all the stitching for the uppers, not the soles. All the different parts of the shoes are in pieces when they come in, they're flat and the linings is separate to the outsides. I was on the linings. They were going to do slippers at first at Lock Hill, Grecian slippers, that's the men's leather slippers, you know, but we didn't do that. They decided to do proper shoes. So with the linings one of the jobs I did was I went on the latex. Sticking the linings down, because at the finish they didn't sew the linings, they stuck them and we latexed them. You see, it went like that. Automation! Then we put them all together, the different parts. If you look at a shoe, like the one Frank's got on now, you can see all the parts and how they're put together. All the outsides have to be stitched and the ends of the seams are thronged, what's called thronging, they used to do that by hand. Then here's the top-line stitching and that's hammered over and here's the fancy stitching and you can see how they did it. After the linings and the outsides are all together you can see the shape of the shoe by then. Then they go to the lasting, put on the lasts, and then they all get vulcanised, I call it vulcanised — they might have a different name to it — the soles get put on and the shoes are sealed all the way round. So there's probably six different pieces of leather all stitched together. Not in all shoes, mind, some might be four, it varies. And every lot of stitching would have a different girl doing it. On each shoe, right from the beginning to the end, you might have more than twenty people working on it. And here, on Frank's shoes, this is bag-top, the linings is turned over, they aren't just stitched round there, you see. That's not to make them stretch so much. And then they're all stitched down further. As I said, we was doing all this for the factory at Weston and then Weston got short of work so they closed Lock Hill. But we had a happy time there. I was there for seven year, from when it started till when it finished.

Then I went back to the Big Room again and we were doing work for Bridgwater, ladies shoes, but there wasn't much of that, they closed Bridgwater and then they started closing it all, right the way through.

Automation come in. After the War automation come in, that was the trouble. It was never the same again after the War. They have these new machines now to do the work. What I feel sad about is all the old skills have gone. I mean, going back years, you had someone like old Mr Whitcombe. He was a lovely hand-sewer and he used to do hand-sewn shoes and they were lovely. And to look at it today and to think that machines do it! Some of those shoes he used to stitch were lovely. That's a part of history gone. I don't expect there's a person in Street now that can do hand-sewn shoes. And I can remember years ago when our next door neighbour used to do the ballet shoes for Clarks. And he used to do them at home and put them on a long pole and all those houses up Orchard Road have got places out the back where they used to have their workshops. They all used to do their work at home and you used to see the women and the men taking them in on long poles in the factory. That was when I was a little girl! But competition came in serious and that was the trouble. I can remember when they started to send out the work to the other factories and that. Of course, now it's all gone abroad. It's the money! They don't do the making here in Street any more. Do you know, I've literally seen men cry because they've lost their jobs! A few of us went up the office because we were concerned about it. For the young ones coming on as well. Now they're working on the computers!

Mind, Clarks have done a lot for Street, they've helped us with education and that. We had a happy time, a happy childhood. I had my ups and downs same as everybody else but I enjoyed my work and I thanked God I had the work and earned money to bring home. And my husband earned, too. I've been married now to my husband Frank for forty-odd years. I was married to him when I was thirty-two. We've done eighty-one years at Clarks between us. He was doing the welting, that was stitching the upper into the sole. He was a welter. He came from Henley, near High Ham, over the moors. I met him through the factory and through football. My father used to be groundsman at Street football club, this was before the War, and my mother used to do all the washing! We never had no television in those days. All we had was the cricket and the football and the hockey in Street in those days. We only had a wireless when I was about nine years old and my mother thought it were wonderful because we had a wireless. We used to take the batteries round to Mr McMillan, sixpence to have them filled! I think if my mother come alive now and knew I had a deep-freeze and a video and a telephone — well!

When Clarks split up again and they were going to send us to other places and that, I asked for retirement. They took all our work away and took it to Weston and they were going to put us with Bridgwater but Bridgwater never had much work and they closed down next. They gradually closed them all down, Plymouth and all, they all went in their time. There were six of us left at the same time, we were the oldest. I could have stayed on but I didn't want to, I'd had enough. So I retired when I was fifty-five. I went down school, then. I loved it there with the children. I worked in the kitchen and cleaning, down at St Crispin's. I worked there for five years till I was sixty and I loved it. But none of those schools would be there today if it wasn't for Clarks. My great-granddaughter is up at Hindhayes now and my dad helped build it when I was a little girl! I haven't moved far! All my life from the time I was born has been round by the factory.

Setting skins to dry.

Chris Tinnion, Sheepskin, Fenland Sheepskin, Bridgwater, 2005

'There's another real problem: we're all getting old! That's a real problem. There are no young people coming into the business, not into management or the workforce. And the buildings are old, and the machinery!'

The Fenland Sheepskin factory is housed in a huge warehouse in the maze of the Colley Lane Industrial Estate in Bridgwater. Inside, vast vats bubble, great drums like cement mixers turn and steam, piles and hillocks of sheepskin lie ready for tanning and sorting, ancient and peculiar bits of machinery dye, dry, measure and prepare sheepskins gathered from across the world. I talked to Chris Tinnion, the managing director, in his interestingly frayed office, under a curling map with pins stuck in surprising places — Novi Sibirsk, Tomsk, Pyatigorsk — a reminder of past booms in the sheepskin trade. It is a trade that has deep historical roots on the Levels and Moors for good reason. As Chris Tinnion says, tanning sheepskins needs two things: sheep and water, and both were in plentiful supply on the Levels when enterprises like Clarks and Morlands got underway in the early nineteenth century.

The whole thing goes back to Morland's. My brother and I were both directors at Morland's and there was a guy called Brian Jones, a tanning specialist, he was getting skins tanned there and was a consultant on the tanning process. When Morland's went bust in 1982, I think it was, this

place here was their footwear warehouse. They were looking for new tenants, we were all looking for jobs, Brian was looking for someone to tan his skins and we got together. He had the company already, he was based in Spalding in Lincolnshire, that's why it's Fenland.

So it all stems from Morland's and that had been going for years, from 1820 or so. They were connected to Clarks, the families were connected. You see, they were based here on the Somerset Moors and Levels because there were sheep and there was water, the two things you need for tanning sheepskins. Clarks actually started off making slippers from sheepskins and then developed into footwear generally. And it was a big industry here, all that. Before they went bust Morland's were employing about 1,500 people. They had a site in Glastonbury, one in Highbridge manufacturing slippers, and a site in Redruth, in Cornwall. After the War they had a place in Bermondsey doing specialist sheepskins for the fur industry and they relocated that to Cornwall, sometime in the sixties. The GLC, Greater London Council, gave them a grant to move out.

My father came down from Manchester just before the War and was chief engineer at Morland's. He became a director of the company and both my brother and I followed in his footsteps. We were the only people on the board who weren't members of the Morland family. I started in 1966, worked there for fourteen years and then came here. I started off in charge of footwear production, then was in charge of all production, footwear and coats and Andrew, my brother, ran the tannery. So, when we started off here, because I had a degree in maths they told me I could be the accountant. So I am! But I manage everything these days. We've got smaller and smaller so everybody does everything now. Our turnover's shrunk from £4,000,000 to £1,000,000. At our peak we were employing fifty-five people, now it's thirty-five.

Now we are making some sheepskin products, though very few coats — people don't wear coats anymore — so we make rugs, cushions, bed-throws, beanbags and so on. But the bigger part of our turnover is skins for other manufacturers. So we do skins for footwear to go in boots and also for a company called Morland's, funnily enough. A different company on the site next to Morland's, bought them off the receiver. The whole thing gradually ran down except for a contract to make sheep-skin floor-rugs for Rolls Royce and Bentley. When they sold off the site — which is still empty and has had enough money spent on it in feasibility studies to rebuild the whole place twice over — they moved to a small factory in Walton where they make these particular car mats. So we supply the skins.

Opposite: Dyeing drums at Fenland's.

We get some local skins, from Exeter and Tiverton, but the rest of them come from Australia and America. We use the American ones for the car mats, they are bigger and have very fine wool. We import the skins raw and tan them.

Tanning is a chemical process where the protein in the skins combines with a chemical — we use chromium — and that stabilises it. Otherwise it would just rot. So it's a chemical change to the proteins which stops the rotting. The ancient, traditional way was done with things like urine. So the skins are shipped all the way to us from Australia or America in containers and we process them for various products. It might seem a long way to bring them but it was always, till now, economical. But it's interesting the way the world's going. It's becoming less economical now. Now that China has emerged onto the world stage, has become big, they are taking an increasing proportion of the Australian sheepskins. Obviously, it's closer. So, over the last few years, we have tended to become more localised. More localised in terms of our supply because we are using more and more local skins, and more localised in terms of our customers. It's interesting how this goes.

Some years ago there was a Russian boom. Their needs were being supplied by Turkey and the Turks were buying lots and lots of UK skins and that forced the price up. Now that the Russians are developing their own business — and with the Chinese who are on their doorstep — that demand for English skins has dropped off. At one time we exported skins and coats to Russia. We took over a company in Taunton called Tans that

had a small tannery. They closed down and we took over the production side. One of their major markets — this was in the days of the Soviet Union — was Russian embassies around the world. All Russian ambassadors and their staff got paid in US dollars and they were quite wealthy. They liked to buy sheepskin coats and take them home with them. So Tans had a market of all these embassies, quite a big market. When Gorbachev broke all that down and changed the world, most of those people — and they had something like 2,000 in Cuba alone, embassy staff, technicians and so on — all these people went home. The chap in Tans used to go out to Cuba and do a lot of business, he'd pick up an order for a few hundred coats. Anyway, there were a lot of dollars floating around in Russia at this time and some of these Russian customers who had been employed at embassies around the world, became our agents in Russia and developed businesses there. Mostly in coats but also in skins. So we had agents all over the place, in Tomsk and Novosibirsk in Siberia and in Pyatigorsk in the Caucasus and so on. The other thing that happened at the time was that a couple of trading companies in Amsterdam and Berlin — who were buying fluffy wool skins to make collars for coats which they were exporting to Russia — also bought lots of skins from us.

Well, we had four or five years of that, the boom years, and then came the crash in the rouble engineered by George Soros. And that was the end of that. The business stopped almost overnight and we went from working a six day week to working a two-day week — such are the effects of geo politics! Our turnover dropped from about £250,000 a month to £80,000. Just like that. So we went on short time and the people who could stand the reduction in their wages stayed and those that couldn't went. And that was it, really. But what just saved us was that at that time the rug business picked up in the UK and so with that and the footwear and now the sheepskins for Rolls Royce and Bentley we have got back on to full-time working.

Opposite: In the factory at Fenland's.

Above: Sorting skins.

So now we are doing, processing, about 100,000 sheepskins a year. About 40 per cent from Australia, 25 per cent from America and 35 per cent from the UK. And that local element is growing while the Australian side is dropping, mostly a matter of price. But it's not going to have much effect on sheep farming in the UK: we might buy, say, 30,000 or 40,000 skins out of a total kill of 10,000,000. Not many skins stay in this country now, they are mostly exported for the leather trade. Around here there used to be so many companies, large and small, associated with the sheepskin business, quite a lot of small coat manufacturers and so on. I mean, it had long since stopped being a purely local industry — by the 1930s Morland's were already importing skins from all over the world, from South America, from Australia, South Africa. But there were a lot of people working here, what with Clarks and so on. We have just about clung on. We have lost a lot of the big contracts, the big store groups have gone to China. This is mostly for rugs. Basically, the Chinese have just come along and told them that they'd undercut any price they were being asked. We cut our price to John Lewis by 15 per cent and still lost the business. That's 15 per cent this year on top of 5 per cent last year. They've just undercut us so much. We'd had that business for ten, twelve years.

But it's funny how business is effected not just by geopolitics but by fashion. The rugs were declining anyway, the business for floor rugs, because the fashion for floor rugs was going out. They became popular when wooden floors started to be the thing, carpets went out of fashion and rugs came in. That's past it's peak now. So John Lewis have just taken the view that the market's going down and they'll squeeze as much money out of it while they still can. So it's fashion, too. Not so many rugs, not so many coats anymore. Kids don't wear coats. They go round in heated cars and work in heated offices. I don't wear a coat! Just for football matches and the races!

There's another real problem: we're all getting old! That's a real problem. There are no young people coming into the business, not into management or the workforce. And the buildings are old, and the machinery! Looking forward, that will be as much of a problem as the markets. Actually, at the moment we've got a reasonably strong demand, a reasonably good outlook in terms of demand for the product. But can we keep the machinery going? And the place intact? We have had a tricky time finding people with specialist skills, you can't just pick them up off the street. Things like engineering. We've some really old machines like the one for measuring the size of the skins, the pinwheel, that's over a hundred years old. We bought most of our stuff from Morland's: the drying racks, the tanning drums. They didn't mean to sell it to us, we bought it through an intermediary, put it all on trucks and drove off through Glastonbury. Then turned round and brought it back here! That was in 1982 — at that time the company that sold the stuff to us was also in business in tanning. Then they closed about ten years later.

Our spin-driers came from a couple of commercial laundries and the things that look like cement-mixers are dyeing drums, also from Morland's. That's the main machinery we got from them. Then the wooden vats are for soaking and tanning. You put the raw skins in there, that's the start, the first thing. That's about the only new equipment we've got, we actually had them made on site. So you soak the skins in water, then tan them with chemicals, chrome and stuff — we also do an aluminium tanning for the white rugs — that makes it stable and heat resistant. That's important because then you take the skins and dye them at nearly boiling point. If the protein in the skins wasn't stable it would shrink in the heat. So you soak it, tan it, dry it — dry clean it to take the grease out — then you dye it in the big drums, dry it again and then finish it off on the suede side if it's a suede or on the wool side if it's a wool product.

Originally all our people were inherited from Morland's, even now it must be about three-quarters. So they've learnt their skills over a lifetime. We are now the only company in Somerset doing this work, tanning sheepskins, and one of only two in the whole country — the other's in Devon. Years ago there were twenty or more. That's how it's gone. We've had so many ups and downs. I wouldn't want my kids to come in. We've had so much competition round the world. First it was the Spanish and Italians, then the Turks, now it's the Chinese. They all had cheaper labour costs and didn't have to bother so much with things like their effluent, no rules, no one worried about it. The other problem is that if you buy a hundred skins, you'll always have a bit of wastage, that's what can kill it. Unless you can get rid of the last 20 per cent you're struggling. You make a good margin on the first bit, it's what you do with the rest. In China, apparently, they just throw it away! Their costs are so low. The raw material itself has no cost, of course. It doesn't cost anybody anything to produce a sheepskin. They're producing lamb or mutton. Logically, the value of that skin lies in what the tanner can do with it minus his production costs. But our costs have been heavily effected by the cost of disposing of effluent and such, fuel oil, electricity, rates — all of which have rocketed up. Our rates alone went up by 13 per cent last year. If it wasn't for the fact that the cost of the skins themselves have come down, we'd have shut up shop.

What we have managed to do is have customers who want a quick response. If, say, the skins are wanted for Rolls Royce and ordered on

Opposite: Tanning vats.

Monday, they can have them by Thursday. Now you can't do that from China. John Lewis, see, would give us an order now for next October. By then the Chinese would have time to come in and do it cheaper. The other thing is the internet. I mean we don't sell there — we keep away from the general public — but we have quite a lot of customers who do. We just couldn't handle the enquiries but we have a customer, for instance in Cornwall who sells hats, gloves, boots and so on, he is on the internet and he has a mail-order catalogue. He increased his business by 30 per cent last year. He's spending about £15,000 a week with us and is doing well. We couldn't have predicted that and we couldn't have predicted the Rolls Royce business — we've been doing that for three years now. That's about £10,000 a week now. Couldn't have anticipated that.

So there's sufficient growth with our existing customers not to go rushing around for new ones, particularly as we have limits on our capacity with our staff, limits on what we can finance because it's a fairly stock-intensive business. We carry five or six months' supply of skins at any one time, that's say 50,000 skins in stock now as we're doing about 100,000 a year. That's gone down from 200,000 a year. But that's still a huge amount of capital tied up, we just couldn't expand again. We haven't got the finance, the machinery or the people. It's a question of squeezing what we can from what we've got.

I mean, we have tried and failed to find engineers to work on the machines. The old specialists are long gone. What do we do? Well, it's interesting. It's quite possible that we'll start to look for people in Eastern Europe, countries like Poland. I mean Poland has a tanning industry and it has quite a high labour presence in Bridgwater. It wouldn't be totally nonsensical to try and find specialist skills there in engineering and in production. It would take a bit of a leap in the local mindset but, actually, it's one of the more possible things to do. Even if we wanted to find a youngster here to train from scratch, they just aren't interested any more. In fact, there's a huge foreign contingent of workers in Bridgwater now. If you drive round you see a lot of cars with Polish or Lithuanian number plates. Even our local laundry is Portuguese. It really has changed in the last few years. That's the future.

There's people here on this industrial estate who make containers, plastic pots and things, and have just built a new place on the next road up from here. The whole factory was built by South African engineers, the steel was shipped in from Russia and it's now staffed mostly by Eastern Europeans! That's it in a nutshell. People who say we shouldn't have immigration just have no idea. Half the industries in this country would close down without them.

Opposite: A 100-year old pinwheel machine used for measuring the size of skins.
Right: Making up skins, Fenland's.

Strapping, Cider & Eels

Dickie Macey, Strapper, Drayton, 1981

'My first job was rook starving... Then I was ploughboy... then went delivering coal. Then I went delivering papers. Fifteen bob a week. Then I went strapping, I suppose I was sixteen. I was a strapper. I'd pick out a job anywhere: laying hedges, digging ditches. You were your own boss, you did piecework.'

Dickie Macey died some ten years ago and there are no more strappers working now on the Somerset Levels. Not so long ago many found work clearing and digging the rhynes, drains and ditches which criss-cross the moors. They woxrked by hand with their staff-hooks and spades for the Internal Drainage Boards and local farmers. Almost all of this work is now done by machinery: hymacs and tractors and, on the main rivers, draglines, dredgers and high-pressure hoses which shift the silt off the banks. The work was hard, often wet and cold and most used plenty of cider to help them through the day — Dickie was so fond of it that he had it delivered to him by the postman. Like many strappers, he'd find any kind of labour that he could, hedging, harvesting — anything for a daily wage — and he would supplement his income and his diet by catching rabbits, birds, eels and elvers, all of which were in plentiful supply across the moors. His way of life had made him down-to-earth, quick, humorous and fiercely independent.

I've been here in Drayton for thirty-five years, my parents came from Curry Rivel. My father was a quarryman, he quarried blue lias stone. I was only six years of age when he died and I be coming up to seventy-four. I worked in the quarries myself for some years. I had to take out twenty square feet at ninepence a foot, and you had to wheel it sometimes twenty to thirty feet high across the planks and the planks were nine inches wide. You had to push the wheelbarrows across. Piecework. Then I didn't care for that job much and went across to the Channel Islands on the potato job. I saved eleven pound in six weeks.

When my father died my mother got parish pay, they called it, half a crown a week. When I was fourteen years of age I started work on a farm. My first job was rook starving. The boss showed me where to go and

then I went sound asleep, first day. The rooks was getting in on the corn what was down and we had to keep 'em off by shoutin' and that. All day long on your own till they cut the corn, six weeks or two months. Out there shouting at crows for two months. 'Twere that or starve in them days. I got ten bob a week, that was the pay then. Then after that when they cut the corn they had the three horses and I rode the front horse, keep them in line. Then I was ploughboy, led the front horse. Nothing else to do here, up and down the ground all day long. Then come in and feed the horses before you had your own food. I only stayed there a twelve month, then went delivering coal. Then I went delivering papers. Fifteen bob a week. Then I went strapping, I suppose I was sixteen. I was a strapper. I'd pick out a job anywhere: laying hedges, digging ditches. You were your own boss, you did piecework.

Above: Wassailing, Drayton. Dickie Macey is holding the lantern.
Opposite: Clearing a rhyne.

Out on Sedgemoor we used to take a rhyne out there, throw a rhyne. You had to stand on boards in the bottom of the ditch because if you

Above: Clotting for eels on the banks of the Parrett. A bundle of worms is attached to a hook in the end of the line and the eels are flipped into a tin bath that floats on the river.

Opposite: A family of elverers on the Parrett.

stood on the peat you'd go right down; so we had to stand on boards all the time to throw the muck out, clear out the rhyne. There were a lot of strappers in they days, worked in the willow beds, anything that came along. Cut the withies, trim the stump, weed 'em. Once the water came in on the moors it would stay in six months, you couldn't cut withies or nothing, all under water.

If you was clearing a ditch, hooking and shearing, you'd have a hay knife with a long handle so's you could stand up on the bank to trim your bank down, then you'd have your crook to clear it out. What you call your ditch crook. Throwing and clearing was different. Throwing a rhyne, you only had a shovel and got down in the bottom. You used to have to bay it off first to keep most of the water out, you'd have to bail it out first and then go in right after, but you can't stop water like that, so as soon as ever it got up so high then you had to go and put another bay further on. You'd stand on your board and throw the mud out over the top with your long-stemmed shovel. We got paid so much a rope or chain, whatever the case may be. A rope is seven feet and a chain is twenty-two yards. No standard rate. Sometimes when you went after a job you'd say to your mate, 'Now, look here, we got to go down Sunday afternoon when no one's out there.' Because if somebody had seen you out there they'd say, 'Dick Macey's after thic job, we got to come down a bit lower.' There were plenty of strappers around they days. The farmers'd try and get the lowest price. We got a lot of trouble when we was doing it for the Langport Internal Drainage Board with the expenditures. If you was daft enough to give 'ee a tip then you had another job, but if you didn't you wouldn't get a job. He could give you a job all right, so after I been paid I'd give him a couple of bob. Well, 'twere a lot of money in them days.

Working for the River Board you had to tender for it. They'd send you a tender form. I've cleared main drains many a time, Midney Pumping Station right up to middle drove and goin' up to Kingsbury. And rhynes.

Opposite: Eel clotting or reballing.

Not on the river and I wouldn't now, I couldn't work with them lazy objects on the River Authority, I'd sooner be out the way. That would get me down quicker than anything, to be there and waiting for time. You had to know how to take a job — and the heart in doing these jobs is taking it — if you couldn't get your money in be Wednesday the job was no good to 'ee. 'Cause there's no holidays wi' pay and you had to put your own stamps on and all for those days you'd lose 'cause of the wet weather. Earn your money by Wednesday because you could bet you was going to have a couple of wet days. I've done that on Curry Moor, Wick Moor, Aller Moor, West Moor, South Moor, every bloody Moor. Shearing and crooking or throwing. Throwing was better paid because 'twere a messy job, getting in the bottom of those rhynes. No rubber boots in they days. We wore what they called the three-quarter boots, If you let the water go over the top of those you was wet for the day. You had to stand on your board, especially out West Moor, West Sedgemoor because it was nothing but peat there. I came off me board many-a-time, especially after dinner! You had to have somebody to help 'ee, to get 'ee out. The more you splutter about the worse you'd go down. The more suction you get. You'd always take a jar of cider down with you, that was nothing, a gallon. Everybody had cider in them days. They wouldn't go without in them days. I wouldn't. I don't.

If you could do a good job you always had plenty of work. I was never out of work, never. Even today I could get plenty of work. It be different industrial places. They got it too easy today. There was no dole, no social security. You had sick pay. Matter of fact sometimes when you couldn't get no work when it was flooded out on the moors then you had to have a bad back sometimes.

If you was out in the moors withy-cutting and had to come on home eleven, twelve o'clock, I suppose a gang of us used to go in the pub and dry off there in front of the fires. When there was good fires in the pubs. Didn't take no notice of the wet really, though I may be suffering a bit for it now in me leg but never mind about that.

I've done a bit of well-sinking in me time. Pick and shovel and put a windlass up to carry out the spoil. A water diviner'd come and find where to dig. I tried but was never no good at it, but me half brother 'ee could find it all right. A willow stick or a thorn stick or a blackthorn held in the hands and as soon as he come on a spring, the stick'd go over and over. There was only two or three could do it; you've got to have enough 'lectric in 'ee, haven't 'ee? So they say. You'd always find the spring on the highest spot; you'd never believe it would you? They had some idea of how far down to go but they wasn't always right; a real expert could tell how many gallon was going through there a minute.

I'd do anything. I've dug graves. As long as the money was there I didn't mind what I done. I did a bit of thatching. Not house thatching but ricks. The last one I done was down at Midney here. You'd get 'em come up with the horse and cart and put the straw up on the rick or mel for you. A rick is a hay rick and a mel is a corn mel.

I did a bit of rabbit trapping up on the Mendips. I practically done everything on me own. Poaching. Out with a ferret all night long. I've sold many up the King William at Curry Rivel for thruppence a time. That'd buy you a pint of cider, then. I could get thirty or forty of 'n a night.

I got tons of elvers, in the spring tide. Go down on the river bank and catch them in nets, not to sell really, though sometimes you'd get sixpence a basin. I've caught many an eel though, in me time. Deuce of a lot of eels. Clotting. I've caught as many as six eels at one time on one clot. You could get twenty or thirty pounds. They make a lot of money now out of eels but I just made a bob or two, sell 'em to locals. You had an eel, say a pound and a half, you could make a bootlace out of 'n, for your hobnail boots. They were tough. And the handles for the timmern bottles what we used to carry the cider in, most of they was eel skins. Firkin or timmern bottle, it kept cooler in them than what it did in the stone jars. I do like eels! I prefer them stewed, meself, drop o' cider along wi' it, flavour it up. I always use wood ash to skin 'em. One or two do catch 'em round here and they can't get on wi' the job so I do do it for 'em. Your best time to catch eels is in May month, you can catch them day and night then. And the first lot of rain you get in a thunder storm, then they're all over. But after that for a night or two they won't hang on to the clot because they've had a feed with all the extra stuff come down the river off the hills. You can catch 'em with a night line. Just chuck out your line in the river and peg 'n down the side of the bank. A hook on the end with a piece of eel and then you'd get a big eel, mind. A lot of people used young birds, sparrows or anything. I'd never do that. It's the best way really but then I couldn't just go and kill a little sparrow and put 'n on a hook, not meself I couldn't. Then you know you got a big eel, a small eel wouldn't touch it. I done a lot of eel spearing. You could do it down any rhyne where you fancy an eel's to. About the second week in September you finish with clotting because the eels start going back to the sea. You get a few staying in the moors but they get down in the mud. The best time for eel pecking or spearing is in the summer when the water's low, and you can see the holes where the eels go in the bank, and if you peck in there you can get out eels galore. But after that, after you've made the water mucky, well then you can't see nothing and you're just pecking all the time blind. I've caught two, three eels in the spear at a time, cause you've got five sprongs you see and they get in between. 'Tis illegal now.

I did a lot of shooting one time. My best bird as a wildfowl was the teal. Not much on 'n I know, but still. I've killed starlings before now, ate them. But when you shoot a starling to get that bitterness out you pull 'ees head off straight away and then the bitterness do come out. Now you've got a dog, I don't care what sort of dog, a retriever or anything, and you've got a devil of a job to get it to retrieve a starling. He won't touch it. But I never fancied rooks, never eaten those. If I 'ad one I should want a pheasant to stuff 'ee with!

The hares used to like it in the moor, too. Though I was never so fond of a hare as a rabbit, too strong for me, unless 'ee was no bigger than a rabbit. The only times I got caught was twice in one week, and that were for riding a bicycle without lights! I enjoyed everything but I used to like the old ferreting be the moonlight night, the old owls up over shouting away. I always took me cider along with me but no smoking. They could smell it. I always had two to three ferrets with me. I'd put one in one end of the burry, one the other. I'd have to sit a few hours sometimes, mind, but keep quiet. I'd never dig for a rabbit in my life, nor a ferret. A ferret could kill a rabbit and get up behind it and he's penned back be another rabbit. He's got to eat he's way out. It could be a week before they come out! It's happened to me.

I was after some rabbits one day on this farm and the daughter come up to me and asks if I've got permission. She says, 'What do you do with the rabbits?' and I says, 'We give 'em to the old pensioners.' An' she says, 'Isn't that nice.' I could hear the bugger I was with behind the hedge laughing. I can tell a lie; there's others, if you do look 'em in the eye, they're apt to smile, but I don't smile. But I'm very open. What I got to say I'll tell 'ee straight out, no messin'.

Donald Coate, Dairyman and Cider Maker, Helland, North Curry, 1981

'I 'spec' they'd get rid of a couple of sixties in a week, years ago, the old-fashioned cider drinkers. I used to go night times. I never used to drink much cider then, too powerful. Anybody not used to drinking cider 'ee 'ad two pints or two pints and a half, I doubt 'ee'd get home!'

Donald Coate died in 2005. He had spent his working life on the moors as a dairyman, though he'd turned his hand to most things. What he liked best, though, was cider, perhaps not so much the drinking of it as the making of it. He loved the conviviality, the sociability of the whole process, from the gathering of the apples to the putting up of the 'cheese' and, especially, the well-earned rest after the apple juice had been pressed out and barrelled up.

Father used to work for a farmer, used to do a bit of milking and withy work, cutting, weeding, spraying, and he used to strip the withies by hand, before the withy-strippers came out. There were nine of us — none of them ever used to work here on Sedgemoor, they always went out to work. When they left school they went into service at gen'leman's houses and that, that was the girls; the boys went on the building work. I was the only one that stayed here, the only one ever worked on a farm.

I used to do hand milking when I was thirteen, weekends and that, and did hand milking for twenty years before the milking machines came in after the war. Then I 'ad to help cleaning out and feeding and that. My father always did it the old-fashioned way, hand milked. I left school when I was fourteen to do the dairy work. Last June I was made redundant — they didn't want the milk see. I used to milk 130 cows more or less by then. In the old days, in the thirties, you had a big dairy if you had fourteen cows! We 'ad pigs and sheep and that too. We used to fat a pig every year; the hams we used to hang them up in the chimney corner here. We used to 'av different men coming round killing pigs. I didn't like to see it being killed. I used to go in the pigsty and help catch 'im but when 'ee'd drag the knife out I used to turn me 'ead and walk away.

We used to have to walk to school, Wrantage, two miles. We carried our sandwiches with us. But after we was eleven we went to North Curry. But when there was floods we used to go upstairs, it was like a sea all round here. I've lived here all my life, never been away from it. Only time we went out, we went over grandfather's for Christmas, down their place. When the floods were up he used to come down with a boat, we'd get in the boat and he'd row us out to the road. Most years we used to have it, the water. It'd come in two or three times a year. We just had to go upstairs and hope for the best. We'd stay up two days, a day and a night, and come down again. This year Boxing Day it came in about eleven o'clock. So I stayed up till half past two in the morning and packed the furniture all upstairs.

Hasn't changed so much round here. Though the elm trees is gone. But practically all of the old families is still here. And the cider orchards 'av gone, almost. In the old days every farm 'ad its own cider press and its orchard.

Morgan Sweets used to be the first apple, didn't never make so good cider as ordinary cider fruit. I mean the cider was all right but did not have so high a colour. Used to reckon to drink that before we'd drink the proper cider fruit, after eight weeks we'd drink it. If you put the cork in too early, you'd burst the barrel with gas. We used to pick the apples in the daytime and men used to come after they'd finished work night times, and before we had the 'lectric out there we do it by candlelight.

There'd be two turning the mill, one making the cheese, one putting the apples up in the mill and another man shovelling the pummies to the one making the cheese, the apple pummy or pulp. Years ago we used to buy the straw, what you call the liner bundles. The straw was long then, went through a thrasher. When the combines come in we used bale straw. By using bale straw we made a wooden frame and put the straw inside the wooden frame and put a layer of apples in level with the frame and you rise the frame up, another layer of straw, more pummies again. Used to put up seven layers of pummies. We press it down then we 'av a hay knife and cut 'im round and give it another pressing. Some years you'd make a lot more than another. A good year you'd make five to six hundred gallon. We used to have friends come and drink it. If you had a poor year that'd 'av to last you through till you get another good crop. Years ago they wouldn't go to work if they couldn't have their cider. The younger generation never take to drinking cider. I drink a mug at night time with my supper. Too acid for me. Father, 'ee'd live on cider. 'Ee'd drink a gallon I suppose. If 'ee'd drink anymore he wouldn't do no work.

Some would take a quart bottle to work, there was some'd use a gallon jar and some'd take a firkin, like a cider barrel, hold a gallon. Sunday morning they'd come around. We used to have our own orchard here, and grandfather had another orchard over there and we used to have those apples, then we used to buy apples off of different neighbours: Crimson Kings, Sweet Blenheims, Tom Putts and Kingston Black. That's one of the favourite apples. Must be all sweet apples, you couldn't put a Bramley in there, you'd never drink it. It'd come out like vinegar. But you never get no sweet cider — 'tis all more or less one palate. If you put picking fruit in, the cider'd never work. Let 'em fall off themself, put 'em in bags. You'd 'av to leave 'em in bags about a fortnight and then you'd see 'em start to turn rotty, not too brown, and then it's time to put them up and you'd get most of the juice out, you know they fit to put up then. You put them up too early and then you never get too much juice out of them. You have to see they don't get black rotty, you have to throw them away. Before too many years you won't be able to get them any more. The factries got their own orchards and the people here, when the apple trees fall down now, they don't replant. They don't bother, not now. Nobody now wants 'em, they don't bother to put young trees back.

We do generally put up about half a cheese and then they say, 'Well, I think it's time we had a drink.' And then you go back and sit down and smoke a pipe of baccy or a cigarette, have a few drinks and then they'd say, 'Well, I think its about time we made another start.' We used to start roughly about seven and sometimes we was out there finished by half past nine, ten o'clock, then another hour sitting down drinking, telling jokes and that. I can never remember them.

If you have a cold the best thing for a cold is hot cider and ginger, if you go to bed on that you'd proper sweat. Oh yes, that'd warm you up, bring the colours up. In the cold, in the winter, you'd put a poker in the fire, make it 'ot and put the poker in the pint of cider. Take the coolness off. 'Twas practically all cider once. Where you'd see two cups of beer you'd see thirteen cider cups. There used to be one proper cider house in the village. The landlord used to go round them that made cider take a sample and see if 'ee think 'ees customers'd like; then, of a Sunday morning, 'ee used to go up and bring down so many barrels of cider. Used to buy the barrels at the wine merchants, always reckoned rum barrels were the best. I 'spec' they'd get rid of a couple of sixties in a week, years ago, the old-fashioned

Opposite: Don Coate and Fred Cousins outside Don's cider barn.

cider drinkers. I used to go night times. I never used to drink much cider then, too powerful. Anybody not used to drinking cider 'ee 'ad two pints or two pints and a half, I doubt 'ee'd get home!

If you get the apple trees out in blossom in May and then you get rain to make the blossom wet and have a frost, you haven't got the apple crop, the frost will get the blossom. Sheep is the best to keep the grass down tight, you couldn't keep the cows, the animals, in there or they'd pick the apples off and choke therself, they would do, they get back in the throat. They eat too many you have to get the vet to treat 'em, they get half drunk. Cows break in, animals break in an orchard of apples, they blow up, they can die in less than a week if you didn't have the vet. He injects them. The cow wouldn't last too long if he had too many.

When we was all quite young Father used to keep on at us 'cause we used to 'av bits of straw, suck the cider up off the press. 'Ee used to say, 'Get away you young sods!' Proper pastime sucking apple juice off the cider press — 'twas nice and sweet like honey. We always used to do that, suck the cider up off the press round the channels. 'I'll hunt you all in the house in a minute!' When we was about eleven years old we'd watch where Father was and go in quick and used to turn the tap on, half a glass out of the tap — he was away to work — would make you a bit giddified. They could always tell if you'd bin drinking, they'd smell your breath, me brothers and that. You'd tell a lie, that you 'adn't been out there. We was all the same, for devilment. All Mother would say was, "T'wont do for I to catch you in there again.' But Father never said nothing, 'ee used to like it 'eself. He'd get irritable if he had too much, couldn't live wi' 'im, just keep outside and hope for the best. Everything'd never go right, no matter what you done, 'twern't right. 'E 'ad 'is own way.

Opposite: Don Coate at work in his cider barn.

A Life on the Levels

Cuthbert Hurd, Burrowbridge, 1982

'They all used to do farming, a bit of farming, cider making and all this business. There were a lot of orchards, now 'tis all gone... You could go in barton and see rows and rows and nothing else but apples, tipped out with the horse and putt before the bad weather...'

Cuthbert Hurd was my neighbour and my introduction to local matters. Most of our frequent conversations were carried out across a road and over a hedge, entertaining some of the residents of the middle reaches of the River Parrett. Occasionally, Phil from over-the-other-side would join in and then any passing tractor or cyclist might stop to see what was what. Eventually, after many years, I managed to coax him indoors into my kitchen to record these few extracts from his endless tales, but this was not his natural habitat and he seemed to need the larger theatre outside, where he could lean on his stick by the river bank and gesticulate across the moors. I only once went into his house, to say goodbye to him when he was dying, though he had frequently promised me a musical evening after the chimney-corner was mended (imminent for twenty years), and he'd finally found his banjo.

Cuthbert, Cuffy, was born and bred, lived and died in Burrowbridge and knew the land about and all its people intimately. He also possessed keen opinions about the wider world and was a great natural raconteur who gave, and demanded, entertainment from any conversation. He spoke the local language fluently and, at first, before my ears were properly tuned in, this could lead to some confusion. It took me a while to realise that 'zen' was not a state of oriental contemplation but a building material, sand, 'red zen' being particularly good for making cement; that 'voles' which had to be 'hunted up' at night were not some herd of small fluffy rodents peculiar to the district kept, perhaps, for their valuable pelts, but common-or-garden egg-laying chickens or fowls. I have tried to render his speech here to give some of the flavour of its vigour and distinction, without resorting to abstruse phonetics or horribly eccentric spellings. Of course, this is what is always missing with written oral histories: accent and tone. Cuffy's whole way of talking was inherently and quite intentionally comical, at least when he was in good humour. Indeed 'comical' was a word which he fre-

quently used to describe anything even slightly odd, different or strange (its once normal dialect usage) so that any passing reference acquired an edge of hilarity. My dog was a 'comical article' ('article' was a favourite word for any thing, creature or person), my pigs were 'comical articles' when they escaped and I had to hunt them back in. In fact, almost any event that wasn't entirely predictable or any person he hadn't known since birth was bound to be 'comical' and probably an 'article' too.

Cuthbert's family had lived in the village for generations and his grandparents, parents, uncles, aunts, cousins still all lived within 'three parts of a mile' throughout his childhood. Though he never had children himself, his nephews and their children continue in the village. He grew up working the farm within a tight-knit group of relations, looking after stock, haymaking, picking up apples for cider, cutting withies, catching eels or elvers, ditching, carting the mud from the river or the muck from the beasts to lay on the fields, busy with the never-ending round of work on a typical small farm on the Somerset Moors. Even in his eighties he was still up at half past four in the morning and by the time I had settled down to breakfast he'd be cycling past my window on his way home after getting a drop of milk from his nephew Henry, urn dangling from his handlebars, nearly ready for a bit of lunch. He took some time to get from one edge of my window frame to the other, and how he managed to stay upright on his bicycle going quite so slowly was a great mystery. He drove his car at roughly the same speed. The pace of modern life was a subject which never failed to engage him, the 'hurry, hurry, hurry'

Above: The Waggon House, Ham Lawn Farm, Westonzoyland.
Opposite: Cuthbert Hurd, Sharman's Farm, Burrowbridge.

of some driver who went down our lane a bit too fast would have him out by the hedge, shaking his head in pity and disdain, as he looked out upon a scene which was seldom animated by more than a couple of cows and a passing badger. He very much enjoyed holding up whatever traffic there was as he saw his wife Jean out onto the lane, a complicated manoeuvre which took a considerable time as he went back into his house to fetch whatever essentials she had forgotten for her journey of 500 yards to the chapel, where she played the organ to a congregation of two or three.

Cuffy died in 1988 and Jean some few years later. The chapel is now a private house, the church has the same problems as many churches in small villages throughout the country. There's no post office any more. Houses are too expensive. But the pub is still going strong, the primary school continues to flourish, despite being one of the smallest schools in the county, and though many of the farms around have become much more modern — old fields sown with improved leys, hedges cut down and ditches filled — withies are still grown and baskets made, a few apples are still gathered and the odd drop of cider drunk, the sea still runs up the Parrett from the Bristol Channel, the rhynes are still lined with willow, alive with herons, ducks, moorhens and swans, and every winter the floods pour out over the moors. There is still much of the life here that Cuthbert Hurd would recognise. And his 'chimney-corner' still has not been mended.

I was born here, Father come from Ham Lawn where he were born to, Uncle Fred were born down there and Uncle George were born down there. Also Aunt Lu and Aunt Sue. I can't find the photograph — I've been lookin', I've been lookin', I've been lookin' — which I'd love to come across one day, because all my aunties and uncles down at Ham Lawn, they were out over on the river bank frying pancakes on this old-fashioned coal stove, and there they were just scooting around and eating these pancakes, and they had a photograph and I've got 'un somewhere. That's where my father originated from, Ham Lawn, and Uncle Fred what lived here. Uncle George stayed there. 'Ee took it over from Granny and Granfer Hurd, you see.

Aunt Lu used to live up at Shepherds' Drove corner, then she shifted. All the family were within three parts of a mile, a half mile. And me Aunt Sue used to live at Bridgetown, Totnes. She married a gen'leman and he were a builder down at Totnes. I went down there once, me sister and I, I shall never forget it. And, of course, we took down about three or four dozen eggs and all this. Me sister had a parcel and I had a parcel, eggs and different things and all of the rest of it. But the few days that we was there we never seen an egg of ours, nor nothing else, we 'ad to 'ave bread and butter. We were goin' to stay the week but we didn't. We said to Sue that we'd 'ad a letter from mother to come on home because they'd started haymaking. This was an excuse fer to get away because what we 'ad to eat down there wouldn't keep a mouse!

Me mother's father and mother used to live down at Lake Wall, up be Westonzoyland. Me sisters and I'd walk down there, we never 'ad no bicycles then, 'twas walk, run and walk and run, and we always wanted to go down Granny's down thur because she used to wear the old-fashioned white bonnet wi' a bit of ribbon, and me uncle used to wear the old black hat, something like a catholic vicar's. They used to sit outside all the day. The house is ripped down now.

They all used to do farming. A bit of farming, cider making and all this business. There were a lot of orchards, now 'tis all gone. Hooper's Mead Orchard is still there but there were Long Orchard, he's all ripped out.

Opposite: The Fish House at Meare, built in the fourteenth century, was one of a number of important fisheries on the moor. In one year over 5,000 eels were caught here in Meare Pool, along with many other freshwater fish. They were an important part of the economy on the Somerset Moors.

Loads of orchards. You could go in barton and see rows and rows and nothing else but apples, tipped out with the horse and putt before the bad weather, and then when the bad weather'd come 'tweren't no odds about a bit of snow and this, that and the other, when they were in the heap, 'cause they'd heat a little. Then you could go out with your shovels, one in front o' the waggin, one at the back o' the waggin, put two bags over the waggin where you was both to so's they wouldn't go down through the holes, and there you are.

That's the waggins we used to have for our one-day treat to Burnham. That was back when the Sunday school was back here to the chapel. And me Uncle Fred was a terrible Chapel man, and me Uncle George. Father wasn't Chapel so much, he and Mother was more Church. Anyway, this one-day treat was the only holiday we 'ad o' the year. All we schoolchildren and Sunday-school children and this, that and 'nother would sit up one row here and one row there. Uncle Fred used to hire a horse and go up to the chapel and took us all laughin', singin', laughin' and all the rest of it, only eager fer to get into Bridgwater fer to get in this train. Oh, 'twere lovely! And we did go from Bridgwater just to Burnham and if we could poke our heads out the winder 'twas beautiful! So then we did go down to Burnham and go down on the sands and then we 'ad to catch a certain time back to the Railway Hotel in Bridgwater. I remember George Slocombe was one of the hostlers in there, that was when they 'ad the carriage 'n pairs. And when the travellers did come down by train they had to be outside. When Father and I had the pony and trap for to go to Bampton Fair, the last Thursday in October — I think we went there once, right up till Father passed away, when 'twere fairly fine, and that were only once I can remember, all other times 't 'ad been raining in torrents — we had to be in Bridgwater to catch the five past seven down to Bampton. We done it every year because he used to go down and buy some young sturks, probably they were bull sturks, steers.

You may have one or two South Devons but they were generally North Devons, the deep red ones, the South Devons were the lighter reds. And Mr Isaacs down there, he were a cattle dealer, and also Mr Beadle, he used to buy 'em of us, they lived at Crediton I believe it was. They used to hunt these store cattle in. Maybe they was about eighteen months, two year old. Then when you did have 'em up from Bampton, off they big high hills 'n this, that and 'nother, and bring 'em up on this ground, well, in about a twelve month they had got big steers and fat fer to go. This ground is rich, you see, richer than what that was over there. And then you could go down to the float in Bridgwater, the docks, and John Robinson's had a cake mill up the top, and you could go down there with your horse and putt. You'd take the bit out of the horse's mouth, undo your pole-strap so the horse could put he's head down from the brichin' block, and the foreman'd put down a tub o' cake in front o' the horse so's he could have a good feed. Well, that were 12 per cent linseed and you'd have the 12 per cent linseed, come home and put it through your cake crusher. You did 'ave your bag an' you did 'ave twenty-two tubs all wi' some notches in the bottom to keep them up off the damp, and holes to let the wet down through, so's he wouldn't be wet, not very wet, and you'd turn 'em up in the afternoon so's to go down and see 'em and feed 'em.

Father generally used to have eighteen to twenty to twenty-two, all beef cattle. Come back here and fat 'em and off they'd go. To get them back from Bampton we used to go down, see, and we did get down and catch the train when 'ee did come down from Yeovil. Old Bill Doyle, the cattle driver — he used to have on a big thick jacket wi' all the poachers' pockets and an old silvery bowler hat and carry a vurkèd stick — and 'ee used to be one of the cattle drivers. Father always used to engage 'ee 'cause we used to meet 'n down to Taunton and then he used to come in the train along wi' us to go down. Uncle George sometimes was along wi' father, sometimes father and I did go on our own, and then, when you made a deal, you had to go back into the White Horse with p'raps Mr Isaacs, and have a drop of whisky and make the deal and come out and see Bill Doyle. He'd be round there — 'course the cattle were all through the streets then, not like 'tis now. Well, right, so as ever the deal were made, come out, and old Bill, 'Woah, now then, come on lads, mind yer backs!' And he'd go round with this old vurkèd stick, 'Yiiup! Yiiup! Yiiup!' And up we goes up the station, and Father and I, all three of us, all up through the streets. People had to keep back out the way; we wasn't th' only ones, mind, there were several there. And we had to put them in the train. They were put in the cattle truck, then you 'ad to go back in th' office and sign and that and pay for the delivery at Athelney Station. Well, then we 'ad to get them back up home. Sometimes do come me sister in 'er bike, Father used to have the pony and cart and I were on my bike, and all's what we had to mind to do was to try and keep them out the ditches or out the river. The river was most dangerous, you zee, because if they get on the river we'm liable to lose them. So all three o' we used to be up on the bank, one here, one here and one there, and keep 'em back. Arter we passed the corner we was OK. Sometimes you'd 'av a floater mind, though we never lost one through it. Well, then after we turned away from the river, we was in our glory. We always used to put them in the field down Whitlake's Drove there called Square Ground because 'twere clay bottom, yer see, and when they got in on the clay bottom that was something similar to where they'd come from down on the stones down Bampton, because 'twas all stony, you see, and brooks, where they'd walk through. And 'course this was what they'd try to do out on river out here, they'd go down o'er the bank and they were goin' through a brook. But when they got down they'd sink down through the mud. That's what you 'ad to keep 'em out fer.

And then p'raps you'd halve them: ten in one ground, ten in another, whatever the case might be, after they'd got used to it. Well then, soon's ever you'd shift 'em and put 'em in another ground where there were turfy bottom, you could go down in th' arternoon and p'raps find two or three and you 'ad to pull 'em out. Because they were in this turf. We used to have little gangways, what they call wardens, where the beasts can go down and drink. Well, then we used to dig out this 'ere things with spades and shovels and old ditch crook, and then pull up this dirt, and then if the bullocks were goin' along here sometimes 'ee'd see this open bit — what we did call wardens — and then probably if he could get 'is feet up he may 'ave a chance to get out. But the banks used to be high. Well then, if thik warter was lower down and on the slope 'twould give 'em a chance to get out, till they got used to it. We'd cut them in one or two places along the banks. That's what we used to do. Course, you go up here where you go into Somerton, where is the river the Yeo, there where 'ee come down through to meet the Parrett, right through Somerton there, if you had 'em up there you didn't want ter take no notice, 'cause they get down in there and all's they were on were stones, but here you had to be careful. You get 'em on the turf you very often'd 'ave to pull 'em out. Well, sometimes now, too. Now last year Henry lost two. They can't move, see, 'tis so soft.

There used to be twenty-two people worked in this river at one time and they all had little shovels. The foreman were Mr Thrasher. And they used to throw up loads and loads of zlime, up on the river bank, and then you'd come up wi' your horse and putt and you did get eight or nine of 'em at a time shovelling and throwing this zlime up on this putt for 'ee to haul away, to put on the fields. 'Tis lovely stuff. Especially if you get it throwed up when 'tis new, that's that soppy stuff, then you want let it bide two or three year for it to dry out. We hauled down a layer of zlime then a layer of stall manure, layer of zlime, layer of stall manure, and so on, then mix it up all together in a big heap fer to go up over with the horse and putt so high with it. And tip yer putt and off you did go and get up o'er it again. As you tip the putt you didn' tip 'n right up, tip 'n half way and then it'd run along so as you could go up o'er again. And then, in the spring of the year, haul that out on the fields, in heaps here and there, and then you had to come along with your four-sprong vork and spur it, with a shovel sticked down in ground beside you in case you got too much little bits in one place — and you had to have the shovel for the little bits — throw it all about.

I can remember down there when Tommy Keefe used to cut the grass with the two horses — well he's man did cut for him — 'ee did do the sharpening of the knives. He used to have two clips wi' screws on and the knife used to have to go on the top of the five-bar gate with a clamp here and a clamp down here so's to hold 'n , so's he could vile. And we'd done this particler ground just down Whitlake, down there, down Whitlake's Drove. Dampitt's Drove is the first, then Mare's Drove, then Middle Drove then Little Drove. And Tom Keefe come down there — and you want to see the beautiful White Dutch that come up there, white clover not the blue, you did get some blue in amongst it but 'twer nearly all white — and he said, 'There you are Harry' — me father's name were Henry, he did call'n Harry — 'There you are Harry,' he said, 'we can cut in this 'ere field. If you live till you're two hundred and I live till I'm three, you'll never have a better shear than this.' Beautiful grass! And that was that manure and that salty zlime, makes that difference. Oh, 'twill grow for a pastime. Now that's a funny thing, you go down my orchard there, where the stall 'n barton's to now, you go across the ditch and into the next field, and he's like coming out of cream and goin' in margarine. The difference with just the ditch between in the quality of the ground to thic 'ere one over here. The zlime you see. The zlime's been hauled over there, hauled over there, hauled over there. Father used to have I over there wi' the horse and putt and he did tip so much round each tree and now when you had a gale come on this weight did keep 'em from rockin' about too much.

You had the white and the blue clover, then you had some good corn. When we did the haymaking we used a two-sprong vurk and the old mead-rake. And me father's first swaff-turner. The first one he bought was when the Bath and West was up Weston-Super-Mare. He were put on the train at Weston and delivered up Athelney Station. And I had to go up with the horse. You'd throw your back chain over and do up your hameses and your brichin and on home. When you did have the swaffs from the mowing machine, well, instead of you using the mead-rake fer to turn it over fer it to dry, this thing'd do it. Well, when they started haymaking I was home from school more 'n I was up school. I had to tell Father if the attendance officer had been there and I'd come home and say he has, well, then he'd keep me home a week, nearly a fortnight and then the attendance officer'd come down here and ask where I were to. And then Father'd say, 'He been very bad and we thought he had the measles.' Or whooping cough or something or 'nother but I'd been out haymaking! I were eight, nine. I had a little rake, the wheelwright made I a little rake. There were me brother out in front, then me vather, then me sister, then me mother and I was the nipper. I did come on behind. One swaff for me brother, one swaff for me vather, one swaff for me sister, one swaff for me mother and a swaff for I. Sometimes I could hardly pull 'n over and me father'd come back and help 'n go along, and we five'd go right round the outside of the ground till we turned 'em. That's till we had the swaff-turner.

We never had a mowin' machine, not in they days. They used to go round, 'Do you want a piece of grass cut?' 'Yes, please.' What was it? Ten bob? A pound? 'Twasn't very much. I remember once they was out Hooper's Drove, Mr Tom Keefe and his man. Of course I, with the little bicycle, I had to take up their breakfasts in a long basket. Mother had a long basket, something like Old Ninety used to carry, the cake man that used to walk from Betty's into Bridgwater down Bath Road, all up through Moorland, up round Burrow, down round here, down round Andersea and back to Bridgwater again wi' a basket o' cakes; and he'd call in the houses goin' along p'raps you'd have two, p'raps somebody else'd have two and if he sold up he'd go along and he did walk like a jerkin' horse and singin' and hummin' all the way. He looked old, and yet he wasn't very old, always singin' and laughin'.

But when they was up Hooper's Drove, Mr Tom Keefe and his man, I had to go up wi' a basket similar to what this cake basket was, with their two breakfasts and a jug of tea, two cups and this two fried breakfasts. Out to the fields on the handlebars of me bicycle. Off I goes, out Hooper's Drove. Mr Keefe was there whetting out the blade for his man what was goin' round. So he said, ''Allo, me son.' I said, 'Mornin' Mr Keefe.' He said, 'What you got there then?' I said, 'I got your breakfast.' He said, 'Let me have a look a minute.' He pulled back this nice tea cloth, looked at it. He said, 'Where's your vather?' 'Oh,' I said, 'he's up in barton, up there milking.' 'Well now,' he said, 'you go back on thic 'ere bicycle, my son and tell yer vather he been and fergot something.' Back I go. Father said, 'Oh hallo, you been out with the breakfast yet?' I said, 'Mr Keefe told I to tell you, you been and vergot something.' 'All right, come on in here along wi' I.' So I had to go in the cellar and fill up a gallon jar. And this was seven o'clock in the mornin', mind. I had to put him in a little bag and up to the back and out to Mr Keefe. Aha! Up she comes out of this 'ere jar, out comes the cork, up she goes, goggle, goggle, goggle, goggle and 'ee had a good swig off of 'n, wiped his old lips and had another go. 'Tweren't about quarter past seven in the mornin' then. 'Twere hot mind and 'twere goin' to be hot thic day, I shall never forget it. When the man come up with the mowin' machine, 'Whoahup!' So he stopped 'n. Undone their pole-straps, kicked up a bit o' grass. He caught hold of this jar and he had a couple of good swigs.

'Right ho then Mr Keefe I'm goin'...' 'Whoah! Whoah! Whoah!' He says. 'You come here, don't go on, my son, not yet.' Well they emptied that gallon between 'em. 'You go back and tell yer vather for you to bring 'ee on out again, so's we shall be all right till we zee him.' So I had to go back again and say, 'Vather, they want another jar of cider.' 'They an't drink 'ee?' Well they 'ad! Off I had to go again wi' another gallon! Then they'd sit down and tuck in to this 'ere couple or three eggs apiece o' 'em, gurt piece o' ham, p'raps two pieces, from the ham that were hanged up in the chimney's corner; they'd get back all this with fried petatee and pepper and salt and then the tea would be out in the ditch, that warn't no good, they wanted the zider! So as I growed up my father very often used to say, 'Cuth, where's that jar to?' 'Oh!' I'd say, 'Mr Keefe got 'ee!' Dear oh dear, you fancy, seven o'clock in the mornin'! All they little jokes you did have a good laugh for ages and ages. Strong as horses they were. He'd cut his hand p'raps, down 'cross the blade and he'd go down along the hedge and if he could see a cobweb, he'd put a cobweb on it. Still carried on, no stiches. A deep cut.

There was another thing in all this haymaking. P'raps there'd be about five of 'n come in to help Vather only purposely to have their zider. I did do the odds and errants and all this business being only a youngster. So we had the one horse and waggin, you did have up a load of hay, undo yer waggin line, then three or four of 'em'd go o'er one side — you had to pull up in the hayrick — and about two, three'd push that load over and you had to go on wi' the horse and waggin to the three more down in the ground and load up another. And this lot had pitched this up on the rick. All in this gurt heap. Tug! You had to tug like blazes, fer to get it out! 'Cause we never had the eleevator. 'Lot of people had this old-fashioned eleevator. It all had to be pitched. But they'd go to a load and push 'n over. Purposely so's you could go on another fer to get it in quick before the weather did alter. Any spare time they did always come in purposely fer to have their zider.

In the village the chapel people, bar one or two, would hardly ever go to the church, because they thought that they were more religious than what the church people was. Now up at Stoke 'tis all the other way about. They do want to co-operate wi' one an another. What 'tis like other places I don't know. Church people probably used to go in the pub and have a glass of beer and of course chapel people didn't. Uncle George and Uncle Fred'd go up to chapel and pray and sing hymns and this, that and 'nother, and 'twere wonderful! They'd come straight home and go out in cellar and have some zider. Oh yes. They did drink it but when they were out they didn't show it. Oh no. If you were goin' in pub, 'There, now, look at that. Do you mean to tell I they'm religious?' And then they sat at home and drink p'raps a darn sight more than you or I what do go out open and have it. This amused I! They did never drink nothing! Oh no! I used to call 'em Chapel Ishmaelites! Out, they were angels. In, 'twere different. 'Tis better now but back along 'twere different altogether. There were the narrow-minded business of it. You wouldn't see Burrow Chapel Sunday school down the church, nor the church down the chapel.

I suppose the main things we did were fatting beasts, a little milking and zider making. The zider making were very good then. The orchards were filled right out with trees. Father used to go up Kingsbury to buy his young apple trees and he always used to like to buy Morgan Sweets. If you buy a Morgan Sweet he do grow faster than either another one, and you let him bide about three or four year and then have them grafted. Cut off the heads and then they do go on the tips of the apple trees and cut off so much of the zider apple, what they call grafts. They used to do a tremendous lot of grafting. They'd graft these zider apples, well different sorts, but mostly zider apples because there was a sale for zider, 1s 6d a gallon. That was one of the ways you did earn a shilling or two to keep you going. Your milk was only five pence or six pence a gallon, till the years went along and they started to put it up a little, but zider was a wonderful thing for around here. We used to make a deal wi' the Cross Rifles, in Frank Smith's day. He was a wonderful fellow for zider. You rack out with your buckets and then have your funnel in the barrel, and then you'd have four barrels up on your waggin and off you did go wi' it. And in the summer you had to be down there about five in the morning and get your horse all ready, see that your waggin were all right and your barrels covered up, keep the zun off of 'n. Then you unload and load up your empties and go in and have some beer and a piece of bread and cheese and very often he used to give me a packet of fags.

When we had thic barton built I used to have to go down Dunwear and fetch bricks. I don't know how many thousand times I been out there! You had to carry a gallon jar of cider for the foreman. But I had to look out for the steam photon what were coming along because they'd draw up and the driver's mate would run arter the waggin, just push open the bag and slit the rope and have this gallon of zider and away do go; and when you got out there you never had none! The driver of this steam photon used to stop out under the beech tree up Burrow and fry the breakfast. I got up there and had breakfast before we went in school. If we know'd they were goin' to stop we used to go on purposely for to have a bit of breakfast. Anyway, I hauled thousands of bricks from the brickyard. First of all I had to haul the brick rubbish for to mix along wi' the mortar for the foundation. Charlie Stacey's father down on Lake Wall 'ee built the barton. They had the fir poles for the scaffolding.

The barton was filled up full of zider and straw up over up in the loft. Well, then you had to go up there and you had a piece of board wi' a vurk in it, a vurkèd stick, and you go up there with a reed comb and you used to have to comb out the straw for thatching yer ricks. Father always used to go over Mr Tom Keys's or otherwise Charlie Miller's over to Thorngrove over there, because the straw were growed out of a place what they called Cutley and 'twas all beautiful, nice straw over there, sweet for zider making. The sweeter the straw the better the zider. If you had a bit of stone ground up a bit, it did keep nice and gold and if that was harvest in nice weather and put in the mel, 'twere lovely! It did come out nice and sweet, you could smell it. But if you had a lot of rain on it 'twouldn't be so good, not for zider making. A lot of people used to use it then and then they could never make out why 'twas their zider warn't much good. You wanted lovely, nice, gold-colour lookin' straw and sweet. Father used to pull 'n back and smell 'n and if he 'ad one he thought was a bit mildewed or anything like that he put 'n back one side, then he'd come for thatching, use it for thatching. But then today it isn't like the old McCoy. There's this mixed up and that mixed up, chemicals and all this business.

We didn't get flooded here, but all South Moor were flooded, yer see. And just the same up here when the bank broke up to Curload up here in two places, in 1929. The flood mark is still up the Pigeons, how high it went in the houses. It were all in the houses, all up through there running all over, here, there, everywhere. With the River Tone, a little way beyond the station, of course the bank were only bricks, you see, and it had this tremendous weight of all the water in Curry Moor and all the rivers. Edward Storey and I had a boat and we got in the boat and we pushed this boat all the way up through to the station, put 'n outside the station gates, went across, got up on the bank — it were flopping up over he beside the Athelney Inn, the road were flooded, the whole moor were flooded and it were right up there in the bar and everything — and there was a ladder out on the river bank and you could go up on this ladder into the Inn and go in the room up there and we had a glass of beer.

Up here to Stathe 'twere flopping outside the ceilings of the bedrooms.

That was the worst one that ever I've known because the bank burst, you see. Well, of course, they've improved upon it now but that was a flood that was. Any amount of people from London and all round cities and all that there, were sending clothes and different stuff. Well, then when the flood water went out — they cut the bank up there to Stathe you see so's to let it out a bit faster — when it all cleared out and this, that and another, there were flood relief. And people would come round and value your stuff and all this, that and another, and any amount, throwing old bicycles out there that wasn't worth two pences, they claimed for them bicycles! 'Twere a bit if an artful turnout but 'twere bad at the time, mind.

The houses were all damp for ages and ages. People had to go about in boats and if they had cattle and that, they'd evacuate them over this side. And when South Moor flooded they had to live upstairs and have boats fer to go anywhere. That was when the engine was up beside the river. The pumping engine. He had to draw the water from all up here round Chedzoy, this side of the road like, and all up Westonzoyland and right up to the river. Now, the other pump here he couldn't pump very well in high water. Very often there was a bit of a lark about this 'ere games, 'cause when Cliffy Thyer used to keep it out there, they were busy thrashin', he and his brother Benny, and old Mr James Baker were living over to Othery — he used to be a wonderful chapel person. So, in the winter all this used to be flooded 'cause they were only little rhynes and they wan't very wide; and if there were weed in 'em to stop 'n, the water'd come all in over the ground, so it was all flooded down over. Anyway, Cliffy were so busy with his thrashing machine, you see, so he get up about four, five in the morning, throw in a lot of coal, away goes the old black smoke out of the chimney, you see, well then, 'bout nine o'clock, half past nine, he'd shut down the engine. He used to leave he's wife to throw on more coal. He were out thrashing, a lot of the times, pretending he was pumping, but the engine warn't running, he warn't drawing no water but owing to pumping in the morning he was still drawing a little. And they thought he were pumping when they seed the black smoke come out. Mr Baker did come out of he's house and drive up so far as Grove Hill and he could look straight out across to the chimney and he see'd the black smoke coming out and thought he were pumping. Well, then they got the twig of it and there were a bit of a bust up about it and Cliffy had to bide home.

Once, when we put in the eel net up here in the rhyne when they did start pumping, we had a huge catch up there. Now, me brother did skin 'em and I remember a lady asked I for some and I was pretty nigh all the day skinning them eels. I used to hate it! They did come up and curl round your hand. Anyway, I managed a few for her. My brother — Mother'd cook 'em — he'd sit down and he'd eat sixteen. Ordinary sizeable eels. I didn't like 'em, nor elvers. Now I wouldn't touch 'em with all this pollution in this river. But I didn't mind catching 'em.

I remember catching elvers for Dick Tucker's father and I never seed a man eat elvers like 'ee, never in me life. I did go out and catch these elvers with the old dip-net, March, April when they do come along, and after they were scalded and washed, mind, we had a four gallon bucket — you could measure your milk in him — well, I had 'ee brim right up and they were all solid elvers washed clean. He'd come down, he used to have a big moustache and an old black hat like a trilby but more like a duck pond, more round, and nice, thick clothes and a long coat. 'Oooooh!' he did go, 'Mmmmm! Well done, Cuffy! Now, do you think there be any chance for any more?' He'd go home, he'd have a gurt frying pan, he'd cook a gurt frying pan full, he'd put 'em out on a gurt dinner plate, pepper, salt, mustard, two, three eggs mixed up, he'd get down this lot and have another lot next morning and then he were down after some more next day. Eat elvers! He'd eat 'em for a pastime! I never seed a man eat 'em like that.

I've worked on the rhynes for to earn a shilling or two. Along wi' Jim Hucker over here to Thorngrove. Tony Bowen were the expenditure then. He were the expenditure for the moor, go round and see that the rhynes were dug and collect the rates, a nice feller he was. You did have your staff hook and your rake and you did trim it down. You also had a shearing knife. You did start out here to Cutley, where the rhynes do start from, and

Above: Building a bay across the Parrett. (Archive photograph courtesy of Mr R. Heard)
Opposite: Reed bed, Westhay.

work your way down through right out to the pumping engine. The Board payed us to keep so many rhynes as what you could clear of weed. All the hedges was here then, big thorn hedges for shelter and that, and happen we had to go down between these and throw out a bit, wasn't very much in there sometimes so we had got on a bit. And old Jim'd have a mood in his head and we had to go peck-'n-tossin' across the rhyne, wi' coins. I did have a stick stuck in over here and he did have a stick there, he'd throw so many coins across to I and if he had more coins tighter to my stick than what I did to he's stick, he had to toss over his side and I had to let these bide. And if he's coins came down nearly all heads or tails I had to throw my heads or tails across to he. And opposite. We done this over the rhyne, Sometimes a penny'd go in there and I'd say, 'Oh dear, we'd better-ways stop this.' 'Cause we only had 32s 6d and ninepence had to come out for a stamp. 'Twere a lark. Wonderful feller to work with, Jim.

With the drainage 'tis certainly better than what it used to be. But there's too much cut down and not enough planted. They'm cutting down all these lovely hedges which they'll be sorry for one day. I don't mean to say that if you' ad an old withy tree lyin' o'er the ditch or rotting, that's a different thing. If it did snow and you had a high hedge you had a bit of a shelter for to go up beside of. Now 'tis all down about six inches, 'tis getting more like ranches every day. Now 'tis all goin' and goin' and goin' purposely for to have an inch more ground. There's nothing there to break the wind. Whereby you'd see a nice hedge where the cattle could get in under for a bit of shelter, now 'tis much as ever a sheep could have shelter, there's the difference. It could be leaved, the hedge, just trim up the sides of it and then they'd have a nice shelter for some beasts up there in the spring of the year. You'd hardly tell the wind were blowing. Now, 'tis all gone to ranches.

In the summer, fer to keep back the water in certain places, they used to bay it down here and up Shepherds' Drove. Some way down towards Bridgwater they used to have a contrac' out on the River Parrett, and they used to contrac' who'd put a bay across there when the tide didn't come up for above three or four days, or only just make a little bit of tide. Well, you had to have fourteen, fifteen, twenty fellers down there with wheelbarrers, diggin' out the side of the bank and putting in a gurt bay right across, like a dam. They put 'n right across each side till you come in the middle, and then they'd have a gurt heap of zlime there each side ready fer to put in middle, and then they had to go like blazes, wheelbarrer arter wheelbarrer arter wheelbarrer to stop the water. To pen the water back up here towards Burrowbridge. They used to let it in up Shepherds' Drove — there's a clapper out over there — and also out to Moorland Farm from thic clyse up there, and this did have to go in the ditches and all over the moor when the hot zummers was, so's the cattle could drink. They had to put a bay right across the river. You used to have long zummers then, hot as blazes! If they could hold 'n for a day extra that was a day's extra water goin' on the moor. The moor could get quite dried out. Then the tide did get higher and higher and higher, then all of a sudden you'd see the bay break and up comes the water and down goes the clappers so's not to have the thick water in.

Sometimes the banks did slip out in the river. Well, then they had to go down and dig off all the outside and throw that up and bank it back up again. But what the draglines do do now, or thic blower, well they used to have to dig all that, throw so much up over, so much out in the river, all with little shovels. All the year round all the way up right through, right down to Bridgwater and right up so far as the locks here on the Tone and up so far as the locks up to Wick. And then they'd go on the points and take off all the points the river do bend round, wherever they thought was a bad place, then they'd go on to another. That was constant work. They got 32s 6d, but then a large Player was eleven pence ha'penny, a loaf of bread, I suppose, tuppence. What is Player now, thirty bob? This is where 'tis to.

When we were going to school, when Mr Brazier come here, we didn't know what a football was. We had an old iron hoop and we used to scoot her all up the road till we got up school and then we used to have to hide 'n in Ernie Kiddle's hedge. Then we used to have tops and you'd try and get round your father for when he did go in Bridgwater, Wednesday, to the market, to get 'ee a bit of whipcord. A bit of whipcord for to hack this top along. We used to call them 'winder breakers'. Very often if you hit 'n too hard, he'd go through somebody's winder. But, nobody was there then! Not playing tops! They were all walking. 'Oh! Whose top is this, come through the winder?' Nobody knowed! So when Mr Brazier comed there first he said, 'Well, boys, what's your sport.' We said, 'Marbles.' We knowed that and we knowed this hoop lark and the tops, that's about all what we knowed. 'Don't you never play football?' 'No, Sir.' I'd never seen a football. So, first day he was there he away did go on this old Matchless motorbike and went in arter this football and come back.

We were well away! Joe Muggins had to be in charge of blowin' this ball and he had the laces and you had to have thic needle for to thread him down. Not like they be now, all wind in 'em. Somehow or other I were so anxious fer to kick about this ball I sticked the bloomin' needle in the tube and down 'ee went. I didn't do it a second time, mind you. Out we goes, all with hobnail boots on. Kick anybody in the leg you'd pretty nigh break their leg! So out we goes. This one were on 'n, t'other were on 'n, three or four were all on top one another purposely fer to get this ball and see how far we could kick 'n. Then Mr Brazier went up to Stoke and bought these goal-posts out of his own pocket and we were goin' to get up concerts for to help pay for 'n. Then fourteen or fifteen of us had to go out with spades and shovels, and fer a little bit of wood he made us dig a hole all out round, so and so. We got wild. We said, 'What the devil do us want a gurt hole like this for? We'm never goin' to have a kick today.' Then one'd work hard and t'other one'd work hard, purposely fer to see whether we could kick this ball through the goalposts. Then, eventually at last, we finished near enough. Then out comes Mr Brazier with his whistle. And all of a sudden he said, 'Now, I want the forwards, the half backs, the backs and the goalie.' So he had to pick us out. Oh, we couldn't see a bit o' sense in that! Not a ha'-porth. 'Cause one had to bide over this side and other had to bide over thic' side and you had to pass'n! Next mornin', 'Can you see any sense in that?' 'No.' I couldn't see no sense either 'cause we all couldn't go after it. Weren't no odds if there were fourteen of us all on top of each other so long as we could get the ball and just kick it. But when we come along day after day you could see what the game was more about. So, eventually at last, he begun to see that we were gettin' a bit better and could pass 'n a little, and he said, 'I think I'll fix up a match.' So he went up Stoke St Gregory to see Mr Musgrove. 'Course, they'd been playing up Taunton against the schools there several years, knowed all about it. Anyway, we had a game. They was scorin' goals be the pastime and 'course we lost, something nil. After they got through four or five, old Sid Boubier were in goal, Sid started crying 'cause he let so many go through. And then we played Aller, Langport, and so on. I think we'd played about twelve or fourteen matches and we lost 'em all and then we drew once. That were a little bit better!

Opposite: Burrow Mump.

Bibliography

Ashworth, Nancy, *Voices From the Peat* (Somerset County Council, 2004)

Body, Richard, *Agriculture: The Triumph & the Shame* (Temple Smith, 1982)

Burrows, Ray, *Beckery Burrows* (Research Publishing Co., 1978)

Elworthy, Frederic Thomas, *The Dialect of West Somerset and East Devon* (English Dialect Society, 1875—88).

Fort, Tom, *The Book of Eels* (Harper Collins, 2002).

Havinden, Michael, *The Somerset Landscape* (Hodder & Stoughton, 1981)

Hawkins, Desmond, *Avalon & Sedgemoor* (Allan Sutton, 1982).

Hoskins, W.G., *The Making of the English Landscape* (Penguin Books, 1977)

Mellanby, Kenneth, *Farming & Wildlife* (Collins, 1981)

Rose, Cuthbert Arthur, *Wedmore's Moors & The Enclosure Acts of the 18th Century* (Cocklake Farm, 1982)

Shoard, Marion, *The Theft of the Countryside* (Temple Smith, 1980)

Somerset Ornithological Society, *Somerset Birds* (SOS, 2005)

Southerland, P. & Nicholson, A., Wetland, *Life in the Somerset Levels* (Michael Joseph, 1986)

Williams, Michael, *The Draining of the Somerset Levels* (Cambridge, 1970)

Glossary

ADAS	Agricultural Development Advisory Service
barton	enclosed farmyard, sometimes of barn and house too
brake	a V-shaped metal fork for stripping willow rods of their bark
buff	boiled and stripped willow, brown with tannins released by boiling
butt	trap made of withy for salmon, also known as putcher
butt	thick end of withy wand or rod
blower	high-pressure hose used for washing silt from river banks
brichin	harness worn by horse in shafts of wagon
cheese	layer of apple pulp and straw for pressing for cider
clatting/clotting	method of fishing for eels with bundle of worms, same as rayballing/reballing
clapper	sluice-gate
clyse	sluice
dumpsy-dark	twilight
elver	baby eel
ESA	Environmentally Sensitive Area
expenditure	expenditor. Official of Drainage Boards overseeing work on moors
flatner	flat-bottomed rowing-boat
glassy kid	glacé kid, a kind of leather
gripe	shallow, open drain dug at intervals across fields
hameses	strong curved wood or metal pieces strapped to horse's collar
home-screetch	mistle thrush
hyle	little stack of fourteen drying peat turves
IACS	Integrated Administration and Control System
maul/mauler	very heavy long hammer for knocking in stakes
mump	a spade-sized block of peat cut from ground
osier	willow, usually Salix Viminalis, producing coarse rods used especially in hurdle-making
pecker basket	basket used often in agriculture for picking up apples, potatoes etc.
picker basket	see: pecker basket
putcher	see: butt
pummy	apple pulp
rayballing/reballing	see: clatting
reap	special withy basket or deep, round tray for boiling shrimps

rhyne	ditch on Somerset Moors and Levels, forming field boundary and usually ten foot wide or more, smaller is a ditch
ruckle	a drying stack of peat turves, usually a thousand or so
spit	half a mump
Steba	peat-cutting machine
SSSI	Site of Special Scientific Interest
steam photon	phaeton, light open carriage drawn by horse. Here, steam-driven lorry
sturk	bullock
swaff	swathe
thick water	flood water, enriched by silt from rivers and rhynes
timmern bottle	wooden bottle for cider
turve	a block of peat, one third of a mump
unridding	top layer of soil and grass which must be removed before peat begins
vurk	fork
winrow	a row of turves stacked for drying
warden	cut in bank of rhyne or ditch to allow cattle to walk down to drink
willy basket	deep basket made of withy with two handles opposite on rim, not side
withy	willow
zider	cider

NARROWBOAT

Life

NARROWBOAT
Life
DISCOVER LIFE AFLOAT ON
THE INLAND WATERWAYS
JIM BATTY
ADLARD COLES NAUTICAL
BLOOMSBURY
LONDON • NEW DELHI • NEW YORK • SYDNEY

WEST SUSSEX
LIBRARY SERVICE
201619652
Askews & Holts 29-Jun-2016
386.48
WITHDRAWN FOR SALE

Adlard Coles Nautical
An imprint of Bloomsbury Publishing Plc

50 Bedford Square
London
WC1B 3DP
UK

1385 Broadway
New York
NY 10018
USA

www.bloomsbury.com

ADLARD COLES, ADLARD COLES NAUTICAL and the Buoy logo are trademarks of Bloomsbury Publishing Plc

First published 2016

© Jim Batty, 2016
Photographs © Jim Batty, 2016

Jim Batty has asserted his right under the Copyright, Designs and Patents Act, 1988, to be identified as Author of this work.

All rights reserved. No part of this publication may be reproduced or transmitted in any form or by any means, electronic or mechanical, including photocopying, recording, or any information storage or retrieval system, without prior permission in writing from the publishers.

No responsibility for loss caused to any individual or organization acting on or refraining from action as a result of the material in this publication can be accepted by Bloomsbury or the author.

British Library Cataloguing-in-Publication Data
A catalogue record for this book is available from the British Library.

Library of Congress Cataloguing-in-Publication data has been applied for.

ISBN: PB: 978-1-4729-2708-8
ePDF: 978-1-4729-2710-1
ePub: 978-1-4729-2709-5

2 4 6 8 10 9 7 5 3 1

Typeset in 9.5pt Life Roman by Carrdesignstudio.com
Printed and Bound in China by RRD Asia Printing Solutions Limited

Bloomsbury Publishing Plc makes every effort to ensure that the papers used in the manufacture of our books are natural, recyclable products made from wood grown in well-managed forests. Our manufacturing processes conform to the environmental regulations of the country of origin.

To find out more about our authors and books visit www.bloomsbury.com. Here you will find extracts, author interviews, details of forthcoming events and the option to sign up for our newsletters.

For Karen

Love of my life, who throughout the writing and photographing of this book has acted as a sounding board, critical ear to sporadically read passages, honest eye to a myriad of pictures, and enthusiastic supporter at every bend. What a happy adventure this life together has been! Long may it continue.

Acknowledgements

I would like to thank my mom, Brenda, whose own independent spirit encouraged me as a child to become a free-ranging explorer of neighbourhoods and forests, and set me up for life. And I am grateful to my dad, Chuck – whose ash remains passed to a river many years ago – for his reflective and playful nature, which has always inspired and helped me to enjoy my own restless spirit.

I am indebted to Paul and Eileen Garner, Dave Godwin, and Dave and Gillie Rhodes, who so warmly invited me aboard their narrowboats to talk about their lives afloat, plied me with tea, and then graciously stepped aside while I photographed the intimate interiors of their floating homes. This book is so much richer for their contributions.

Narrowboat Life was inspired by questions. I would like to thank all those gongoozlers that took the time to stop beside our boat and ask about life afloat, offer an interesting external view of the boating world, or simply say 'hello'. It has been a joy.

A special thanks goes to Tim Coghlan and Paul Bennett at Braunston Marina, who unwittingly rekindled our hope of finding a narrowboat of our own, with their welcoming and helpful encouragement well beyond the call of duty.

A tip of the cap goes to Louise Stockwin at The Canal Museum Stoke Bruerne, who graciously granted permission to publish my photograph of their marvellous Bolinder engine.

I would like to thank everyone at Adlard Coles Nautical who have helped polish the brass work on this project and navigate it through the publishing process. I am especially grateful to commissioning editor Jenny Clark and senior editor Clara Jump for their ever-cheerful guidance and advice, and thorough responses to my many dozens of questions.

Life would not be the same without our fellow boaters, who through lively and illuminating conversations over the years have shared their knowledge and, in this way, contributed to many of the ideas that have found substance and flourished between these covers.

Introduction 8

1 What's it like... living on a narrowboat? 18

Step aboard... A boat of two halves 36

2 How safe is it? 42

3 Is it cold in the winter? 60

Step aboard... A recycled, repurposed narrowboat 76

4 How much did you pay for your narrowboat? 84

5 Why do women do all the work? 104

Step aboard... A roving canal trader 116

6 Did you paint it yourself? 122

7 How green is living on a boat really? 132

Step aboard... A well-read ark 152

8 Does he (the cat, dog, parrot) live on the boat? 158

9 Four canny questions... about continuously cruising 168

How do you receive post? 171

How do you see a doctor? 174

How do you use the internet? 177

How do you hold down a job? 178

Glossary 186

Index 191

HAZEL
LORD VERNONS WHARF
No 58

INTRODUCTION

ABOVE: *Entering a lock standing on the cabin roof requires expertise and clear communication with the helmsman, near Wilton Brail, Kennet & Avon Canal.*

'Inland waterways boating is a curious mixture of heritage and 1950s community spirit fused with modern eco-awareness and cutting-edge technology.'

Living and cruising aboard a narrowboat within Britain's intimate inland waterways is a special way of life. If you are up for it, each season can become a great adventure. Living afloat often feels like cheating at 'ordinary life' and it is a common sentiment among liveaboards that moving back on to land is difficult to imagine.

When you live aboard a boat you can choose your view and change it as you like. Of course, it helps if you enjoy waterside scenery! If you like variety in your company, the waterways offer a genuine, helpful and enormously interesting and diverse community. If you value independence, you will find scope for expressing it in spades. If you enjoy the outdoors, or pine for the countryside, you will discover it right there outside your portholes and one step from your deck. And chances are that making a boat your home will lessen your impact on that beautiful environment, almost by default.

The boating life usually requires you to expend a bit more physical energy than you would living on land, something most boaters consider a good thing. Driving the boat and taking it through locks requires stamina, and at times a little extra oomph. As does relaying your groceries from a shop across town to the canal or river ... along the towpath ... and into your galley.

Continuously or intermittently cruising (as opposed to being permanently tied up on a fully-serviced residential mooring) is a form of living off-grid and requires a certain level of self-sufficiency to be viable and comfortable. Water and diesel tanks need to be routinely topped up, propane canisters replaced, waste emptied, electricity generated and the engine serviced. None of these things are beyond the wit and skill of anyone, it just takes a little planning.

There has recently been an increased interest in living on boats for economic reasons, especially as house prices continue to climb beyond the reach of many hard-working people. The fact that a second-hand boat can be bought for one-tenth of the price of a second-hand house makes you sit up and think. If you already own a property, the maths seem loaded in your favour if you dream of a quieter, downsized life. Of course boats are not houses, their value rarely increases, and living in a corridor-sized space seriously inhibits natural urges to consume your way to happiness.

I think my best advice would be: live on a boat only if you really want to live *on a boat*. That said, it's difficult to know beforehand what this is like, so one of my aims in writing and photographing this book is to help you decide whether living afloat might be right for you.

PREVIOUS PAGE *Narrowboat at the end of the rainbow, Great Bedwyn, Kennet & Avon Canal.*

BELOW *A well equipped stern.*

The big BOATY questions

This book has been inspired by, and attempts to answer, a host of questions I have fielded from a huge variety of curious, excited, bemused and uncomprehending strangers, friends and colleagues about what it's like to live on a narrowboat. After six years of cruising and living aboard a 53-foot narrowboat it has been fascinating to discover that the same core questions surface time and again. I have also found it thoroughly satisfying that many of these inquiries are not of the sensible 'how-to-do-it' variety, but playful, whimsical, even sceptical queries about the waterways lifestyle that reveal genuine insight.

There is the near-inevitable, 'Is it cold in the winter?' It seems that half the population worries about being chilly, damp and miserable aboard something akin to a floating tent. This is counterbalanced by the cheeky, if observant, 'Why do women do all the work?' Then there is the wary, 'Is it safe to live on a boat?' and the down-to-brass-tacks question, 'How much did you pay for your boat?' (or, more tactfully, 'What's a narrowboat worth?'). But there is also the spontaneously gleeful, 'Does *he* live on the boat?!' (pointing to your cat, dog or parrot). A surprising number of aesthetically-knowing towpath wanderers ask, 'Did you paint the boat yourself?', while those concerned about the environment often enquire, 'How green is it, actually, living on a boat – you run big diesel engines don't you?' Finally, there are the canny continuously cruising-related questions, such as, 'How do you receive your post?' and 'How do you hold down a job if you are always moving?' Read on, for all will be revealed.

More generally, towpath passers-by have also expressed curiosity about what narrowboats are physically like on the inside. How are the rooms laid out? Do you have proper appliances? How does everything you own fit into such a small space? To address these sorts of questions I approached a variety of liveaboard narrowboaters with beautiful and interesting boats, to see if they would be willing to talk about their boat's interiors and clever features, and how their layouts supported their different lifestyles ... and allow me to photograph their floating homes to show off to the world!

Well, I think it is a tribute to the friendliness, goodwill and flexibility of liveaboard boaters that everyone I asked was thrilled to 'invite us aboard' to give us a peek behind the portholes. For this I will always be grateful, and I am really excited to include them in the special *Step Aboard...* sections. I have also included an inside view of our own modest 53-foot narrowboat, to demonstrate how liveaboard space can be truly maximised. I hope you enjoy your visits.

The inland waterways are home to a variety of fascinating liveable craft. My experience is of narrowboats, but most of what you find here can be equally applied to living on and evaluating widebeams ('wide narrowboats'), motor cruisers and small Dutch barges.

RIGHT *Widebeam reflected in the cabin side of a narrowboat at West Mills, Newbury, Kennet & Avon Canal.*

BOBBIES GIRL

'The more we looked, asked questions and pried into boats' inner workings, the more discerning we became.'

LEFT *Approaching Blake's Lock at Reading, where you leave the River Thames for the River Kennet, and the Kennet & Avon Canal.*

The QUEST for a LIVEABLE boat

My partner Karen and I enjoy our narrowboat as much now as we did during those fresh autumn days when we first moved on board. We spent four years looking at second-hand boats before finding *the one* – a boat we could fit into, enjoy and afford.

To begin with, we corresponded with brokers and private individuals, sifted through canal magazine adverts, scrutinised boating websites, and simply walked the towpaths and chatted with whoever looked 'boaty' and knowledgeable. I even visited a couple of boats with 'For Sale' signs in their windows on the Thames – travelling by inflatable kayak. Astonishingly (it now seems) we visited well over a hundred boats: in marinas, down lost cuts, tied up on fast-flowing rivers and abandoned in backwaters. Of course, the more we looked, asked questions and pried into boats' inner workings, the more discerning we became. We also felt more confident about organising a survey and making an offer.

If you think that the boating life might be for you then there is some real, hands-on guidance in this book to help you to understand what you're looking at when faced with a boat, and evaluate what it's actually worth. This should save you time when deciding which boat is exactly right for you and how you want to live on it.

BELOW *Winter sun setting on Harefield Marina, beyond the suburbs of west London. Only shallows separate the marina from the Grand Union Canal, giving the appearance of cruising across a lake.*

The PHOTOGRAPHY

By intuition and profession I am a photographer and graphic designer. I have been making and capturing images of Britain's inland waterways for over a decade, originally by following the towpaths on a mountain bike loaded with a camera and some camping gear, then with an inflatable (and portable) kayak, and now from the comfort of our narrowboat home nestled deep within the waterways world.

Most of the photographs here reflect our recent cruising patterns throughout the southeast and south of England, taking in the Grand Union Canal and London, the River Thames from tidal London to Lechlade, River Wey Navigation, the Oxford Canal and the Kennet & Avon Canal.

The colour, nature, heritage, craft and people of the inland waterways are a photographer's dream. Even if you decide that living on a boat may be too confining a lifestyle for your taste, I hope you experience some of the joys these beautiful and fascinating waterways offer through this collection of photographs.

Jim Batty
West Mills, Newbury, 2016

ABOVE *Mirror like reflections in the River Thames near Beale Park at sunset.*

RIGHT Flat Bottomed Girl *setting off into the Oxfordshire countryside at dusk, Oxford Canal. Punny humour has a curious habit of mixing with the sublime on the inland waterways.*

GRAND UNION CANAL
FLAT BOTTOMED GIRL

What's it like... LIVING on a NARROWBOAT?

1

Living on a narrowboat is a **WONDERFULLY ROMANTIC** way of slowing your pace of life down, being intimate with the British countryside, having the freedom to shift your view as and when you desire, while being part of a **GENUINE AND COLOURFUL COMMUNITY**. As a nice counterbalance to all this, it can also involve a bit of work.

ABOVE *Butty and motor: a remarkable narrowboat pair breasted up at Braunston, Grand Union Canal.*

'... the sight of a floating toy-box dressed up in crayon colours can only inspire romantic wonder at what it must be like to call such a thing "home".'

PREVIOUS PAGE *A line of liveaboard narrowboats tied up along the Kennet & Avon Canal at Great Bedwyn.*

BELOW *Bowler hat on a tug. Some boaters do like to dress up!*

BOTTOM *Two tipcat and button rope fenders on the stern of a traditional working narrowboat.*

ROMANTIC and simple, sophisticated and cutting-edge

Beauty can be found in the inland waterways vessels themselves – still influenced by traditional boat-building design and decoration going back to the 18th century – brightly alive with painted roses and castles, diamond patterns, contrasting primary colours and stripes, flashes of brass, seductively curved bows and graceful cabin rooflines. In a world dominated by the immensity and impersonality of its public buildings, transportation systems and maze-like bureaucracies, you cannot help but envy the contained, human scale of a narrowboat, decorated with playful panache and personal style. Whether viewed from grey urban ramparts or the green verges of open countryside, the sight of a floating toy-box dressed up in crayon colours can only inspire romantic wonder at what it must be like to call such a thing 'home'.

Charm can also be found in the language of the canals and rivers. Common terms include: 'winding' (pronounced like the blowing wind, meaning to turn a narrowboat around); 'tumblehome' (the slope of a cabin side); 'butty' (an unpowered boat usually towed behind a motor); and 'crabbing' (driving a boat forwards at an angle, usually into a stiff wind.) This is a world where 'galleys' and 'gangplanks' and 'gauges' and 'gunwales' still regularly feature, as do 'stern glands' and 'stop-gates', 'rubbing-strakes' and 'weed hatches'.

And if you look with a sympathetic eye, a certain allure can be found in the industrial heritage that surrounds these inland waterways. Its history can be read from the regional variety of its architecture: bridges, locks, warehouses, quays, tunnels, aqueducts and canalside cottages. It can be enjoyed through the clever mechanical apparatus at locks that still continue to keep the system running and boats moving.

Despite these idyllic aspects, it would be a big mistake to equate living on a narrowboat with living in the past. Inland waterways boating is a curious mixture of heritage and 1950s community spirit fused with modern eco-awareness and cutting-edge technology. If you decide to live by candlelight on your narrowboat it will be little remarked upon in the boating community; most of your neighbours will understand the romantic attraction. But they themselves are far more likely to be investing in convenient, low-voltage LEDs to minimise power consumption.

RIGHT *Couple aboard their narrowboat at Little Venice, Paddington Arm of the Grand Union Canal, London.*

ABOVE *View of the Victorian Gothic Old Vicarage at Kintbury framed by a side hatch, Kennet & Avon Canal.*

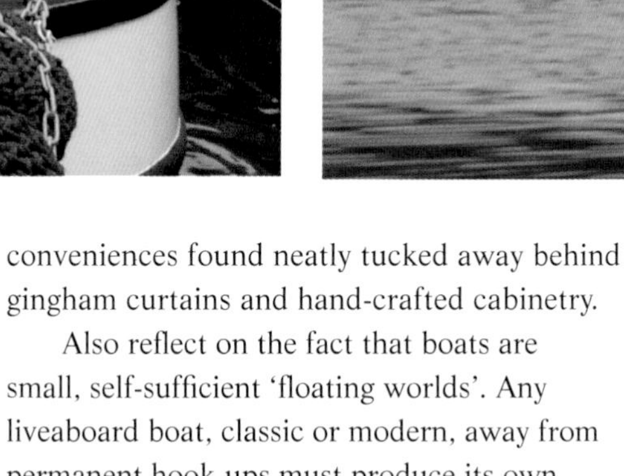

Consider some of those great, traditional-looking narrowboats you see chugging along the cut, with a cosy boatman's cabin at the stern and decorated with lace curtains and brass fixtures, colourful hand-painted signage across their cabin sides, and a classic Gardner, Lister or Russell Newbery engine slowly thudding away in their engine rooms. Look a little closer though – perhaps at the back of a cupboard or beneath a bench seat – and you will probably find an electronic 230-volt inverter tapping a large hidden bank of batteries to power a microwave oven, washing machine, stereo and flat-screen TV – conveniences found neatly tucked away behind gingham curtains and hand-crafted cabinetry.

Also reflect on the fact that boats are small, self-sufficient 'floating worlds'. Any liveaboard boat, classic or modern, away from permanent hook-ups must produce its own electricity, sustain its own water and waste systems, and create its own heat. This is pretty elemental stuff that most land-dwellers take for granted. When you live off-grid, securing these simple necessities is the key to comfort ... and, occasionally, survival.

This is where the traditional, romantic aspects of living on a boat meet the needs

ABOVE *Truly mobile – a canoe, bicycles and wheelbarrow loaded on to a cruising narrowboat near Shillingford, River Thames.*

of the 21st century. While most liveaboards welcome a simpler, independent, hands-on lifestyle that brings them closer to nature, modern technology contributes to this on-board self-sufficiency and comfort in a big way. Each boater decides for him- or herself how simple or sophisticated they wish to make their journey.

Technology ensures that those who want, and can afford, to be 'plugged in' while on the move can do so. Most people will attempt to ease their lives aboard with the help of *some* devices from an ever-evolving list of inventions that includes: inverters (that 'invert' 12-volt battery power to 230-volt mains power), 'hand-luggage' generators, intelligent battery-charging systems, solar panels and wind generators, laptops, satellite-seeking TV dishes, digital entertainment centres, 12-volt marine fridges and freezers, spray-foam insulation, diesel or gas central-heating systems, electronic toilets, e-book readers and tablets, solar-powered radios ... you name it! While making your life afloat easier and more comfortable, some of these devices will also save you money over the long haul and some will lessen your impact on the canal and river environment.

SHANTI
514408
SHANTI

It depends on HOW you LIVE on it

What it's like to live on a boat also depends on how you live on it. You may be a continuous cruiser – moving about the system and stopping in one place for no longer than 14 days (as required by your boating licence). Or, you may prefer living aboard tied to one place, such as in a marina or on a permanent canalside mooring. You may combine the two, cruising in the warm spring and summer months and heading back to base when it gets colder. Alternatively, you may continually cruise most of the year but take up a temporary 'winter mooring' between November and March. Or you may find a pied-à-terre mooring, where you can live aboard your boat in a marina and enjoy its services for a certain number of days per week, month or year, and spend the balance of your time cruising.

LEFT *Urban living, Paddington Basin, London.*

BELOW *Living in stripy style on the bow deck of a widebeam.*

'One of the biggest reasons boaters love their residential moorings are the people who live afloat around them.'

Permanent moorings:
MARINA OR ONLINE?

If you do find yourself with a permanent residential mooring (and they are not particularly easy to find), it may be a fully serviced one – with electricity and water supplied straight to your pontoon or jetty; shower block, toilets and launderette available on-site; a pump-out station close to hand; and a parking spot beside your boat. It may even have a post box with your boat's name on it. Alternatively, your permanent mooring may be very basic – simply a strip of bank to tie up to – where you must factor into your plans regular excursions to fill up with water, empty toilet waste and recharge batteries. There is, of course, every permutation of these and other boating services to be found in between.

The level of services available will play a large role in how you live on your boat. Plugging the boat into the mains allows you to use electricity in a similar way to how you would on land: plug things in and turn them on. It means you don't need to worry about keeping your leisure batteries fully charged. You can unthinkingly use high-draw appliances such as washing machines, microwave ovens, hair dryers and electric space heaters, or spend eight hours a day on your computer. But, note, not all *at the same time*. Of course, don't forget that you will need to budget for the associated cost-per-unit electricity bills. Having a secure parking space means you can operate a vehicle and rely less on public transportation. For many, permanent moorings are simply handy for work, schools or visiting family. Full-service residential moorings can make life very easy indeed, but will deflate your average wage packet by 10–20 per cent for the privilege – even more in south-east England and on the Thames.

Apart from convenience, one of the biggest reasons boaters love their residential moorings are the people who live afloat around them. They are part of a community in which most people help each other and often socialise together.

RIGHT *Every sort of narrowboat and variety of mooring can be found at Braunston Marina, Grand Union Canal.*

ABOVE *Typical view from a narrowboat (typical weather!), where you stand below the waterline.*

TIME
CARTER-WILSON
BRAUNSTON
DAVIES' FAMILY
11

LEFT *A variety of working and liveaboard boats on the Tring Summit Pound at Bulbourne. It is here that the Wendover Arm joins the Grand Union Main Line.*

BELOW *The enchantment of private moorings – in this case the scope to develop a variety of timber-framed outbuildings and a garden, and to tie up another boat.*

Marinas and secure residential moorings themselves will all have a different character. Some are friendly and relaxed, others seem more 'professional' or officious; one might be a bit neglected but calm, another very much a working boatyard, still another remote and sleepy, and so on.

Most marinas that host liveaboards, whether formally or on a nod-and-a-wink basis, restrict their numbers and distribute them among the pontoons between leisure boats that are visited only occasionally throughout the year. Oftentimes, one of your liveaboard neighbours will work part-time for the marina, keeping an eye on things when the office is shut and helping out with general grounds or boat maintenance, or working in the chandlery.

BELOW *Narrow- and wide-beam boats on quiet, almost secretive, residential moorings of Salters Cut, an arm of the River Chess above Batchworth Lock at Rickmansworth, Grand Union Canal.*

Some liveaboard boaters feel a little claustrophobic in marinas and prefer to find residential moorings online: tied up end-to-end along the canal. Usually these moorings are 'offside' – the side opposite the towpath – and have their own private and secure entrances. Normally they have fewer services than marinas; they may not have electricity, water points or secure parking. They can, however, provide the same community spirit as that found at a marina and may offer a small strip of property alongside your boat where you can set up a few deckchairs, park a couple of bicycles, pile a winter's supply of coal, store a canoe, or maybe even house a garden shed and support a few rows of vegetables. Online residential moorings certainly support their fair share of garden ornaments and quirky sculpture!

In some formal residential moorings – whether marina or online – you will need to pay low-band council tax, depending entirely on local council policies. And note that security of tenure on marina moorings is almost unheard of, so you must be the type of person who can 'get on' with a variety of people and be happy to abide by a marina's regulations.

LEFT *A colourful liveaboard pair of narrowboats, named* Tarred *and* Feathered, *near Dockett Point, River Thames.*

ABOVE *A pretty boat tied up to a flowery bank, near Horton, Kennet & Avon Canal.*

'Open-ended cruising allows you to live in some of the most beautiful and inspiring landscapes in the world…'

Continuous CRUISING

Some boaters prefer to continuously cruise rather than orient to a single 'home mooring', moving every couple of weeks from place to place. Some continuous cruisers, especially those who are retired or have a mobile form of self-employment, set out to cover the entire inland waterways system over a number of years. Others continuously cruise a network or 'ring' of canals over long periods or cycles, perhaps returning to favourite stretches every year or two or on a seasonal basis. Some continuous cruisers barely cruise at all, shuttling up and down a short stretch of canal from bridge to bridge, just moving enough to keep waterway wardens from shooing them on.

Continuously cruising can be hard work at times: driving the boat and locking in all weathers, walking a couple of miles for groceries, finding pump-outs and making repairs on the move. But it offers some of the most exciting, spontaneous, wondrous experiences that turn life into an adventure.

The freedom to change your view at will and the ease with which you can merge with the countryside is open to anyone with a boat, but it is most poignantly associated with continuously cruising. Open-ended cruising allows you to live in some of the most beautiful and inspiring landscapes in the world, where cattle or sheep peer into your lounge from fields of buttercups, breakfast blackberries can be plucked from the hedgerows, herons fish opposite your boat in the morning mist, trout hover sleepily within crumb-throwing range of your side hatch, and night-time skies are utterly black and pricked with ancient constellations. These are the places most boaters would like to escape to, and they are the places where continuous cruisers linger.

ABOVE *Public moorings (on the left) at Abingdon, renowned for welcoming boaters on the River Thames.*

RIGHT *The Thames towpath in Oxford comes alive in the early morning mist during term time.*

TOP LEFT *Cruising with tender in tow, Kennet Mouth on the River Thames, Reading.*

FAR LEFT *Couple cruising aboard their traditional working narrowboat on the Grand Union Canal, Northamptonshire.*

The LIVEABOARD community

Liveaboard boaters form a genuine, coherent community, which is rather remarkable given how strikingly diverse a group of people it contains. Every conceivable type of background and range of interests is represented and it has become almost cliché for boaters to list people with exotic professions they've met living on boats. We know writers, engineers, mechanics, architects, web designers, alternative-health therapists, artists and musicians who live afloat. Most recently we have become friends with Nick, a particle physicist.

Naturally, as in any extended community, the boating world also has its pirates and those living on the fringes. We also know people who enjoy a very simple lifestyle of hedonism sustained by ad-hoc work, foraged fuel and the occasional rabbit or bird poached for the pot.

Despite the differing lifestyles, most boat people 'pull together' when it counts. All liveaboards have boats in common. More importantly, though, we have all made that heady decision to make that boat our *home*. This step almost automatically signals a certain independence of spirit, flexibility and healthy disregard for mass consumption – although this might sometimes be difficult to perceive through the mounds of detritus on some cabin rooftops!

Those who persist with a liveaboard way of life will usually possess a good level of tolerance, an appreciation of the outdoors, and a growing set of skills and knowledge about keeping a boat afloat, running and comfortable that they are willing to share with others.

BOTTOM LEFT *Breakfast amongst friends at the annual Braunston Historic Narrowboat Rally, Grand Union Canal.*

BELOW *Galley and glassware displayed in an old sash window mounted on this converted working narrowboat.*

STEP ABOARD...

A BOAT OF TWO HALVES

The interior of this beautiful 70-foot narrowboat is unusual in that its forward cabins are thoroughly modern and bright, while the stern is very traditional decorated with castles, roses and antique lace, and houses a showpiece vintage diesel engine. Paul and Eileen Garner live aboard and cruise their boat throughout the inland waterways during the six warmest months of the year, and migrate to their flat in southern Spain for the winter. Linking the two lifestyles is a campervan that further expands their nomadic horizons!

The couple have lived on a number of boats in the past and eight years ago downsized from a Dutch barge, preferring the cottage-like cosiness and flexibility of a narrowboat. Given all that boating experience, combined with the fact that Paul has fit out the interior almost entirely himself, the living space is exactly suited to their needs and way of living.

Both work seasonally, Paul fitting-out boats for the marina where they winter their own boat, and Eileen helping English-speaking customers negotiate and buy property in Spain.

The boat has a large raised tug deck at the bow covered with cloths – an enclosed canvas canopy that offers a protected outdoor space with room for extra storage and a place to get out of wet gear and muddy boots when it's raining. When the weather turns bright the canvas can be rolled back either side to offer four adults and Freebie, their border collie x whippet dog, room to relax in the sun and enjoy the passing pageant that is narrowboat life. Paul has previously parked a fully-dressed Harley Davidson out here while cruising, taking land transport along with them.

BISTO
READY FOR THE COURSE

Through a pair of doors and down a few steps is the open-plan lounge and dining/work area. What strikes you first is the brightness, due to white panelled walls above the gunwales complemented by light oak floors and ceilings. Vertical tongue and groove panelling below gunwale level, painted a dusty rose colour, adds visual height to the cabin. A matching leather sofa further sets the modern tone. Oak display shelving and cabinets, on either side of the entrance and along a wall, prominently show off models and sculpture of some of their passions: motorcycles, 1970s American muscle cars and British birds. The steps contain more storage as does the under-deck compartment behind them, including a library.

Between lounge and galley is a solid oak dining and work table and chairs and Eileen's rocker – a favourite piece of furniture that has followed her through three liveaboard boats.

The Heritage range that separates the lounge and galley is a real setpiece. Its not only a beautiful cooker, but also the narrowboat's main source of heat. The central position means that it keeps half the boat toasty warm directly, while the remote cabins benefit from a series of radiators fed from the stove. It also provides hot water.

The galley is particularly bright when its two large side hatches are open. They illuminate the wide worktops on either side and invite you to linger and gaze at the surrounding landscape. There is lots of clever storage in the form of cabinets at base- and eye-level, drawers and open shelving. A neat illusion is the half-width drawers with full-width fronts that slide out from beside the sink. The galley is equipped with under-counter 12-volt fridge and freezer and the boat has a powerful inverter to ensure the microwave and a good stock of small kitchen appliances make cooking easy and enjoyable.

The walk-through bathroom is something of a masterpiece. The entire wall over the vanity cabinet and loo is a mirror – with a porthole cut out at its centre! This fragile installation was the only part of the fit-out that Paul left to other experts. The embroidered porthole bungs were made by Eileen.

The toilet is an ultra-modern portable unit. Opposite is a space-saving P-shaped bathtub with a shower at one end and the wall above is covered with a luxurious granite laminate, again with a porthole at its centre. In the ceiling is a glazed Houdini hatch that channels in daylight and hinges open to let fresh air in and steam out.

The sleeping quarters have a cross-cabin double bed. The foot of the bed is folded up during the day and covered with one of Eileen's hand-embroidered quilts. At night it is dropped down across the passage and the duvet tugged into place, a process that has become habit and takes about 30 seconds to complete.

This cross-cabin configuration offers lots of space on both sides of the bed and room for a small bedside table and lamp each. It also gives good access to two full-height closets with accordion doors – a substantial unit

'The walk-through bathroom is something of a masterpiece and the embroidered porthole bungs were made by Eileen.'

F
260
240
220
200
180
160
140
120
100
80
60
40
20
120
100
80
60
40
20
0

that separates and insulates the cabin from the engine room next door. The right closet holds clothing, while the left incorporates a large calorifier (hot water tank) and acts as an airing closet with deep slatted shelves above. Brilliant idea! At roof level over the bed are small built-in hanging cabinets of oak, and another Houdini hatch in the ceiling gathers more daylight and fresh air.

The boat is also well designed for visitors. Visiting friends or family can be put up on the double sofa bed in the lounge, where they have access to the loo through the galley. While another person or children can comfortably sleep in the boatman's cabin at the stern, and use a compact portable toilet in the engine room that is neatly concealed beneath an embroidered jacket.

Through a door in the sleeping cabin lies the engine room, completely dominated by a magnificent 1931 Gardner 4L2, 38hp traditional engine. It is a marvel of mechanical engineering and to the interested eye the full process of internal combustion can be traced. Spotlessly clean and shiny, we could have eaten our lunch off of it, though Paul insists it actually requires little upkeep.

The engine room itself has two large side hatches and is attractively decorated in a sort of 'marine industrial chic'. The walls are covered with narrowboat festival plaques that Paul helped design, vintage metal signage and coiled ropes. The cabinets and trim are scumbled in traditional faux wood fashion and overhead swings a heavy-duty lantern and a couple of playful mobiles. Discretely attached to the wall are a pair of windlasses decorated with colourful vine roses by Paul's father.

Up two steps the boatman's cabin at the stern is a stunning classic. An Epping boatman's stove nestles exactly where it should: at the back doors beside the feet of the boatman or boatwoman standing in its heat when driving the boat in winter.

The cabin is festooned with traditional brass, ribbon plates, decorative bedknobs, copper kettles on the stove, ladles above, lace-edged curtains tied back and rag rugs on the floor. Narrowboat enthusiasts Rosie and Jim and some boaty friends have taken up residence on the side bed.

The rounded top, drop-down table cupboard has a beautiful painting of castle and canal surrounded by flowered decoration. Traditionally, built in beside this, would have been a 'bed 'ole', or large cross-cabin fold-down bed, behind an ornamented panel. In this refined version we find a tall cabinet acting as an extension to Eileen's wardrobe.

Historically, from the mid-nineteenth century onwards, the boatman's cabin on a traditional working boat would have housed an entire family, and would have been a place to cook, eat, sleep, relax and store everyone's personal possessions. In contrast Paul and Eileen's beautifully crafted narrowboat demonstrates how far we have taken that early lifestyle afloat and made it modern and luxurious while remaining true to its traditions.

How SAFE is it?

2

This is not a question about how safe it is to OPERATE LOCK GATES and mechanical paddles, manoeuvre a 15-ton steel boat through a gap with an inch to spare either side, or CLIMB OFF A BOAT using a gangplank slick with MORNING DEW. Although it should be. Instead it is usually a question inspired by unarticulated fears of attack in the night on lost, LONELY BENDS of canal by unknown marauders. Or being robbed of all possessions in broad daylight. The question, 'HOW SAFE IS IT?' represents our instinctive fear of the unknown.

ABOVE: *Peaceful end to one family's long day of cruising, West Mills, Kennet & Avon Canal.*

'Like barrels at sea, boaters tend to float together. It's often a loose relationship, held together by social gravity.'

The NARROWBOAT community

The first thing to realise is that out on the cut or riverbank you are rarely alone. Like barrels at sea, boaters tend to float together. It's often a loose relationship, held together by social gravity. Narrowboaters usually gather at good moorings with easy access to the 'outside world', such as shops, pubs, bank machines and railway stations, as well as around useful boating facilities, such as water points and pump-out stations.

It is easiest to moor at the purpose-built public moorings that are scattered throughout the system. Here, you can normally secure your boat in reasonably deep water against a straight, vertical-sided, timbered-edged wall by tying up to handy rings or bollards. There will probably be a bridge a stone's throw away that leads to a nearby town, suburb or village.

Public moorings on the inland waterways are regulated through a variety of posted time limits, largely set according to their popularity. Public moorings not in great demand may allow you a stay of up to 14 days. Well-used, short-term public moorings restrict your visit to 24, 48 or 72 hours. If you want to stay longer near the short-term moorings you will need to get out your mooring stakes and move a little further down the towpath, where you can stay for up to two weeks. This is where you will often find a couple of other liveaboards tied up a few yards apart and going about their business. Spend more than a day or two in the vicinity and you will probably get to know them. In this curious way you become part of the boating neighbourhood.

My experience is that most liveaboards are essentially private individuals, but friendly, especially towards other boaters. So, despite keeping to themselves once tied up, boaters also waylay each other with interesting conversation at opportune moments, and it is absolutely standard that the briefest 'hello' in passing can lead to a lengthy discussion about practically anything.

Here's a typical experience. You decide to get an early start to the day and plan to walk into town to pick up some milk, bread and cheese, perhaps stop by the hardware shop, and

PREVIOUS PAGE *Patriotism and skulduggery afloat – bunting decorating a narrowbaot roof.*

BELOW *Sign over the canal of the former Horse & Barge pub at Harefield, Grand Union Canal.*

RIGHT AND BELOW: *Night starts to draw in on lonely towpaths beside the Kennet & Avon Canal, Wiltshire and West Berkshire.*

then pause for a coffee. Just before you leave the towpath you say 'hello' to a fellow boater and comment on the level of the canal, or the kingfisher you just saw fly by. Your new friend has some witty retort to make, or kernel of arcane knowledge to share about canal levels (or kingfishers) and you stop to chat. After about 20 minutes their partner comes out on deck, attracted by the banter, and jokes about some tangential issue concerning canals or birds or cheese, and suddenly an hour and a half has passed.

ABOVE *Not taking any chances! This end-of-garden narrowboat is sited just below Woolhampton Lock, where the full force of the River Kennet joins the canal at the mouth of the lock.*

Boaters might be a loosely affiliated group, cruising at differing rates and moving in different directions, but it is through these casual conversations that it becomes a genuine community. Naturally, you can pick up a lot of knowledge about the waterways' system and local cruising conditions, but you also discover a good deal about each other's interests and outlooks and different ways of living. Like members of all true communities, boaters also talk about each other, so that a loose network of knowledge about who's doing what, when and where begins to develop. This is the boating grapevine, and you will be astonished by how quickly news can travel across canal systems and up and down rivers. At a much greater speed than any narrowboat!

You'll start to find that people recommend other boaters to you. Someone might say, 'Looks like you're having trouble with that smokey engine. You should talk to Jason down by the bridge on *Meander*. He's great with BMCs.'

Also, like good neighbours on land, liveaboard boaters tend to keep an eye out for each other and their boats – usually not in any overt way, but quietly and even anonymously. If you need to be wary of something there's every chance someone will let you know about it. For example, 'Watch out for these two guys walking along the towpath asking if you have any old batteries you don't need. They're looking for things worth pinching when you're not around.'

If you are a little worried about security on a boat, it's good to know that this community exists and that it is more self-aware than its dreamy, life-in-the-slow-lane character suggests.

There is also a very extensive, lively and helpful online community of boaters on the inland waterways. The most popular gathering can be found at www.canalworld.net/forums/.

What about MOORING in the MIDDLE OF NOWHERE?

Of course you *can* moor in the middle of nowhere: on a lost, overgrown bend with views over the rolling fields of Cheshire; against an uninhabited island on the Thames; nestled within the wooded cut of the Tring summit. Being out on your own in nature is one of the great joys of boating.

The inherent character of rural canals and rivers, and even many urban waterways, is that they are quiet and out of the way. After dark, canal and riverside paths are usually pitch black and uninviting. They often have low branches overhanging them, a slippery root or awkward depression underfoot, and towpaths are punctuated at locks with unusual machinery. These low-level obstacles tend to dissuade casual passers-by. In my experience rowdies, drunks or troublemakers rarely have the energy to make it out to 'the middle of nowhere' in daylight, let alone at night. You usually have to *work* at being this far out under the stars. Of course you, being a boater, will have a small but powerful LED torch in your pocket, a reasonable knowledge of the towpath and a nice cosy cabin awaiting you at the end of your walk.

If you did feel a threat from people hanging about in the dark nearby on a canal, I suppose you could untie your ropes and shove your boat to the opposite side, which is usually inaccessible from the towpath, and tie up to a tree or the bank until morning. Nobody willingly climbs into a canal at night. But I've never heard of an instance when this sort of evasive action was necessary.

In the middle of nowhere in daylight, anyone passing by will almost invariably be a dog-walker (having parked their car nearby), a cyclist (commuting or touring), or a rambler. If you do have concerns, tie up at a spot where there are a couple of other boats nearby.

ABOVE *Two bows – of a modern leisure and traditional working narrowboat – viewed through a porthole at Cowley Peachey, Grand Union Canal.*

BELOW Morning Mist *on a golden day.*

'Being out on your own in nature is one of the great joys of boating.'

ABOVE *Bulls Bridge Junction, where the Paddington Arm from central London joins the Grand Union Canal Main Line.*

RIGHT *A narrowboat travelling in the early morning mist below Hartslock Wood on the River Thames.*

AMELIA

LOCKS and alarms

'... liveaboard boaters, generally and by necessity, have fewer possessions worth stealing than their suburban counterparts. We tend to "pack light".'

RIGHT *Boating with heart. Another quiet mooring on the Kennet & Avon Canal.*

BELOW *Padlocked hatch on a converted working boat.*

Crime can happen anywhere: on land, on a canal or in the open sea. Premeditated, waterborne crime usually requires more effort and time than land-based activity, for reasons of accessibility. It's relatively rare for someone to be able to drive up to the door of a boat, discreetly break in to perform their dirty deed, then make a quick get-away.

It is also a simple fact that liveaboard boaters, generally and by necessity, have fewer possessions worth stealing than their suburban counterparts. We tend to 'pack light'. There simply isn't the space on a boat to store a lot of possessions, and anything that doesn't get regular use (or isn't too beautiful for words) is usually chucked out or recycled.

Canal crime is remarkably uncommon. When serious theft does occur it is usually in urban areas by people who watch boat movements, perceive boaters' habits and come to know when a particular boat is likely to be unoccupied. The message here is: don't hang around the same place for months on end following the same predictable patterns.

Also, make sure your boat has decent, security-level locks on its doors and hatches, and don't leave £1,000 generators or expensive mountain bikes in the open protected solely by cheap cable locks. A rule-of-thumb is that you should spend 10 per cent of an exposed object's value on a lock to secure it.

There are various ways of locking narrowboat hatches and doors. Many use padlocks. If you go this route, make sure they are of the quality you'd find on a shopfront or lock-up. Pair them with good-quality, hardened-steel hasps. An alternative when securing sliding hatches is to padlock the steel rails behind them. Note, though, that exterior padlocks signal that no one is at home.

You can also have good, home-style deadlocks fitted to your doors, but ensure that they are internally secured and with bolts passing through doors and frames – preferably through steel. Lock fittings simply screwed into wooden frames are not very secure.

There are also some great, shackleless 'garage bolt'-type locks available. Their bolts are of hardened steel that can extend 3in behind or into a steel frame, and they can be positioned in a variety of ways to secure side hatches, doors and overhead hatches. Some have unique 'star' profile keys and can be operated from within the boat as well as outside through neat, chrome-plated escutcheons. For various exterior boat lockers you can also buy handy sets of padlocks that use the same key. At the top end of the market are those armoured, high-security locks you see on the doors of some commercial vans and trucks. Seemingly indestructible, they are perhaps a bit ugly. Paint a rose on them.

Further options are electronic boat alarms, strobes and immobilisers triggered by a variety of motion detectors and sensors. Keep your batteries topped up! There are also mobile phone or tablet app-based security packages that will monitor various systems aboard your boat, warn of tampering, set off different types of alarms, GPS-track its location and so on.

'It is an unspoken etiquette that you don't board a boat uninvited... It would be like walking into a stranger's home because they happened to have left their front door open or unlocked.'

KNOCK and ROCK around the CLOCK

It is an unspoken etiquette that you don't board a boat uninvited. You call out or knock on the cabin side. Ignore this and, at the very least, you will be thought gauche and probably regarded with some suspicion. Do it on the wrong boat and you may end up in the canal or river. It would be like walking into a stranger's home because they happened to have left their front door open or unlocked.

While on board, the most basic but reliable signal that someone has stepped on to your boat is a rocking motion. You will become so attuned to how your boat sits in the water that the slightest shift will draw your attention. We have a wind chime hanging in the galley, charmingly tuned to the 'Chimes of Pluto', which also happens to tinkle lightly when someone steps on board.

To be honest, these unbidden visits are rare among boaters. We have had only one uninvited person step on board while we were at home in six years of cruising. This was a fellow at Pangbourne trying to attach a leaflet to the front door, inviting us to his church's Sunday service the next morning. Although unintentional (he didn't think anyone was on board), him being there was a real shock to us, calmly puttering about inside, and we instinctively leaped to the door and confronted the poor guy with a robust verbal response. After apologies all around he returned to his mission, confessing that he was unlikely to climb aboard another boat without an invitation!

RIGHT *Only a camera's long exposure can 'see' these public (left) and private moorings in the night at West Mills on the Kennet & Avon Canal. To the human eye this scene appears nearly black, marked only by a few pinpricks of light from distant lamp posts and a dim glow through narrowboat curtains.*

SAFETY of stuff OUTSIDE your boat

'The boating community is essentially a trusting one in which you find a healthy respect for one another and the variety of floating lifestyles that form it.'

When we first moved on board I was worried about people stealing items from the cabin roof: boat poles, an aluminium gangplank, a fine collection of planters full of herbs and flowers. I was going to drill the poles and thread the other things with cable locks, but never got around to it. I justified the criminally exposed nature of our planters by the fact that each one was weighted down with 20lb of gravel as drainage and ballast. It would take real dedication and muscle to run off with any of these!

I quickly began to notice how much stuff, useful and ornamental, other boaters displayed on their roofs and around their decks. None of this was bolted down and most of it was within easy reach of the towpath, so I began to relax. The boating community is essentially a trusting one in which you find a healthy respect for one another and the variety of floating lifestyles that form it. And part of this ethic appears to embrace a good, old-fashioned respect for each other's property.

I don't want to paint too angelic a picture of waterways folk; there is the occasional inland pirate. But I'm sure one natural restraint to thieving a neighbour's big Buddha from his cabin roof is the knowledge that any getaway narrowboat won't be travelling much quicker than 6mph!

Another factor that ensures the relative safety of some outdoor possessions is that non-boaters usually have little use for boating equipment. What are you going to do with a steel-plate Danforth anchor and length of heavy chain? Display it in your garden? How about a 7-foot barge pole? Fly a flag from it? What would you do with a 25kg sack of coal, or a rusty Workmate?

We have had three small solar lights (worth about £2 each) plucked out of our rooftop planters over the years. I imagine these beacons attracted drunken lads on the towpath wending their way home after last call at the pub. No doubt the lights end up in the canal when the culprits reached the welcoming sodium lamps of suburbia.

LEFT *Well-used watering can decorated with roses and castles on a cabin roof, Grand Union Canal.*

ABOVE RIGHT *Well serviced moorings at Apsley, Grand Union Canal.*

BELOW RIGHT *An unguarded container of flowers set provocatively on the bow of a narrowboat. The 20lb of gravel in the bottom – for drainage and ballast – would prevent most people from running away too far with it.*

Registered at Watford No. 505357
DREAM CATCHER
HUNGERFORD

SAFETY of stuff INSIDE your boat

Towpaths can be very public places. Be sensible and don't put anything of real value on display. Like many boaters, we tend to close the curtains on the towpath side and open those on the canal or river side when tied up. No need to show off expensive laptops, flat-screen TVs, mobile phones or jewellery to passers-by. I tend to close and sometimes lock the bow door if I am deeply engaged working in the stern.

Having a dog on board is popular with many boaters. A friendly greeting is nice to come home to at the end of a day, and your best friend can be good security for your floating home while you are out.

You should already have third-party liability insurance and basic marine cover for your vessel itself, which will probably also cover a small number of personal effects. If you live aboard, add residential boat contents' cover to insure all your possessions properly. Some plans will protect things like bicycles, laptops and cameras off the boat as well as on it.

LEFT *Away with the fairies. A dreamy narrowboat tied up on a quiet stretch of the Kennet & Avon Canal.*

BELOW *Deep autumn in the Goring Gap: Lone narrowboat tied up on the public moorings at Goring, River Thames.*

Is it COLD in the WINTER?

3

This is *the* question most often asked of a LIVEABOARD NARROWBOATER. It's probably a question in the minds of 50 per cent of gongoozlers (a boating term for non-boating people attracted to CANALS and boats). It is not an issue I troubled myself with until we actually moved on board. Now I am asked 'Is it cold in the winter?' a COUPLE OF TIMES a week – by DOG-WALKERS, ramblers, kids on bicycles, work colleagues and gongoozlers peering down at me in locks. In one sense I suppose it is a primal question based on our INSTINCTS OF SURVIVAL. Just as we must feed ourselves, we must also keep warm. But surely there is more to it than that. There must be a good reason for the deep-seated fear that living in a narrowboat in the DEAD OF WINTER might be the most miserable of experiences: damp, bone-cold and utterly lost.

ABOVE *Canal and River Trust working barge* Snowdrop *in a blizzard, Cowroast, Grand Union Canal.*

PREVIOUS PAGE *Moored on a curve of the Thames at dusk near Dorchester, River Thames.*

BELOW *Heat from the inside of a narrowboat making its mark on the cabin roof through brass mushroom vents.*

BOTTOM *Frosty rope on a cabin roof thawing in the early March sunshine.*

It's not like CAMPING when you were A KID

Here's my first theory. One huge mistake people make is to equate living on a narrowboat with camping. I don't mean 21st-century camping, with all its clever, compact, lightweight, sophisticated conveniences, but a sort of malevolently nostalgic memory of camping from childhood. Most people cherish one early experience of camping out in a wet field crammed into a leaking tent. Cheap and forlorn sleeping bags become sopping wet and cold in the night. Tripping over other inmates in unfamiliar tents ensues, often culminating in stumble-tumbles outside in the pitch dark.

Delve a little further into these accounts and you will discover cooking plays a large role, usually dinners that take hours to prepare in battered aluminium camping pots on inconvenient gas rings or over campfires, their contents ultimately and invariably burned. Tents are remembered as being over-complex to pitch, often with poles or pegs missing. Slipping in mud, losing (or never packing) warm or waterproof clothing, and mislaying critical bits of personal equipment (such as torches, knives or toilet paper) also feature regularly in these reminiscences.

People love recounting these youthful, tragi-comic experiences of camping – wonderful disasters from beginning to end. And I couldn't count the number of people (it must be dozens) who experienced one such childhood or adolescent adventure and now proudly report that they have *never* gone camping since.

If it isn't this, almost patented, British camping experience that puts people off boating, it could easily be a similar holiday staying in a caravan or beach 'chalet'. Chilly Easter or May Day vacations spent wrapped up in woollen jumpers watching a 12in black-and-white TV as four stovetop gas rings hiss dangerously in the background supplying meagre heat, with condensation streaming down the windows.

Of course narrowboating is nothing like this. Camping and caravanning today are nothing like this either, but I'll leave that to one side.

'You are more likely to find a rogue spider scuttling about in a layer of dust in your cabin bilges than water.'

RIGHT *Snowy towpath, with a smoking narrowboat keeping warm outside Kings Langley, Grand Union Canal.*

BELOW *Liveaboard narrowboats frozen in during the particularly cold January of 2010, Tring Summit on the Grand Union Canal.*

NARROWBOATS are damp on the OUTSIDE, dry on the INSIDE

I think another misconception, especially about narrowboats, is that they are somehow akin to rowing boats or open dinghies, with water sloshing about in their bilges making everything damp. Any half-decent or reasonably maintained narrowboat, barge or cruiser keeps water on the outside. You are more likely to find a rogue spider scuttling about in a layer of dust in your cabin bilges than water. These are hand-built, customised cottages afloat, not life rafts.

You *may* find a bit of water in the bilges of a neglected or poorly designed boat, usually rain that has crept through the rusted frame of a window or hatch, or condensation that has formed on hidden uninsulated surfaces and trickled down the inside of the superstructure. Often this is something that can easily be repaired with sealants and paint, or by insulating behind a cooker or the back of a closet, or opening up a floor panel to aerate the bilge.

NARROWBOATS are INSULATED

ABOVE *Cacti and eagle under snow on narrowboat* Azteca *during the big Christmas snowfall of 2010, Uxbridge, Grand Union Canal.*

RIGHT: *Liveaboard boat warming up nicely before school, Hanwell Flight, Grand Union Canal.*

The fundamentals of insulation and heating can be applied to any boat designed for living aboard. Even some originally designed for seasonal excursions, such as small plastic cruisers. The secret behind all insulation is that it forms a static, intermediary temperature layer between a cosy interior and a colder, less comfortable outside. Without getting too technical, the basic types are worth knowing about.

Narrowboat builders and fitters have a variety of insulations to choose from to keep a boat's interior warm: spun fibreglass or rock wool, microfibre batting, sprayed foam, or cut and fitted foam panels. These various materials not only help keep heat in but also control condensation and, to some extent, suppress outside sound.

1) SPRAY FOAM is exactly that, a porous, polyurethane foam that is sprayed with specialist equipment on to the inside of the raw steel hull, cabin walls and roof to a depth of about 2–3in. Usually some type of battens, or longitudinal supports, for mounting a boat's interior panelling are installed before spraying. It is more expensive than other forms of insulation, but the advantages of spray foam are that it adheres to all interior steel surfaces, leaving no air gaps in which condensation can form, and it fills every nook and cranny (of which there are many).

2) RIGID FOAM PANELS, or foam boards, come in large sheets in a variety of thicknesses. Many have facings that act as air and vapour barriers and some are also flame-resistant. The better polyisocyanurate and polyurethane panels have dense closed cells, allowing thinner boards to be used. The panels are cut to fit between wall and ceiling battens and hull-stiffeners – with thinner strips of insulation placed over protrusions so there are no 'cold spots' of contact between the interior and exterior.

Foam-panel insulation is popular because it is reasonably affordable and can be installed with tools no more sophisticated than a tape measure and a bread knife in combination with a keen eye.

3) FIBREGLASS OR ROCK WOOL BATTING is placed on the inside of the hull and cabin sides and ceiling between stiffeners or battens, not unlike its positioning in the walls of houses. This method of insulation is relatively inexpensive. The downsides are that it needs to be about twice as thick as foam-type insulations – thicker walls mean slightly smaller cabins – and batting will absorb water if given the chance.

4) MICROFIBRE BATTING is similar to fibreglass insulation but with fibres up to 10 times finer. As a result, more air is trapped within the insulation and thinner layers can be used to keep the boat warm. Microfibre insulation is lightweight and fairly flexible to install and 'tuck' into corners and gaps. It is also a highly efficient acoustic insulation, making for a very quiet boat. The downsides are that it is expensive, a bit obscure and you must be careful not to catch and pull it when drilling walls.

'There is nothing finer in winter than sitting around the fire of a solid fuel stove and enjoying its flames – with good friends or family, listening to the radio, reading a book or enjoying a meal.'

NARROWBOATS have central heating

Given reasonably good insulation, all that remains for a comfortable winter afloat is to heat up the air inside your boat. Here's how.

There is a wide variety of heating systems installed in narrowboats, and many boats will incorporate two or more of them. Pride of place, though, must go to the traditional solid fuel stove.

1) SOLID FUEL STOVES are the centrepiece of a great many narrowboat lounges, and some are real sculptural beauties formed of cast iron or worked steel. Rather handily, they can run on a variety of fuel, either bought or found. You can burn coal, split logs, tree deadfall and eco logs as well as chopped-up bits of packing case and pallet. They are simple to operate and difficult to break. There is nothing finer in winter than sitting around the fire of a solid fuel stove and enjoying its flames – with good friends or family, listening to the radio, reading a book or enjoying a meal. Lazing about beside a fire on a Sunday morning with mugs of tea and muffins warming on the stovetop rates pretty highly too!

A sophistication of the solid fuel stove is to have a back boiler built into it, which is essentially a metal-box heat exchanger through which water is piped and fed to a series of ordinary heat radiators. Cleverly installed back boilers simply rely on gravity, inclined pipework and the fact that hot water rises to spread heat throughout the boat. Other systems incorporate a small pump to circulate the heated water.

Traditional narrowboats with a boatman's cabin at the stern will also have a small boatman's stove mounted beside the rear hatch. Not only does this miniature solid fuel stove heat the back cabin, it also allows the helmsman standing immediately beside it to stay warm while cruising in winter.

Some people complement a solid fuel stove, usually installed at one end of their boat, with one of the more sophisticated heating systems described below to cover the other half. What's nice about having the solid fuel stove is that if your technologically advanced central-heating system suddenly runs out of diesel or propane, or breaks down, you can always find *something* to burn in the lo-tech fire grate to keep warm.

ABOVE *Tracks in the snow.*

LEFT *Traditional water cans under a fresh blanket of snow.*

OPPOSITE TOP *Frosty morning. This was the first day of a two-week-long freeze.*

OPPOSITE BOTTOM *Catching up on some reading in the winter sun, River Thames, Oxford.*

OVERLEAF *Bronze morning sun raising mist on the Grand Union Canal at Hanwell.*

2) GAS CENTRAL HEATING is also popular on boats – again, often in addition to a solid fuel stove. Gas central heating operates in much the same way as land-based systems: an LPG- (Liquid Propane Gas) fired boiler heats water and circulates it through a series of radiators or finrads (thin metal 'fins' surrounding a pipe that 'radiate' heat.) The joy of propane is its 'instant' on-off nature. Turn up the heat when you want it; turn it down when you don't; or set it on a timer and regulate it with a thermostat. Central-heating boilers also usually supply hot water to the separate domestic system that feeds taps and showers.

The downside of GCH is the ever-increasing cost of propane. Propane is also volatile, so systems using it must be installed and regularly serviced by experts. Some people prefer gas-free boats, while others enjoy the convenience and clean heat gas offers. The vast majority of boaters will at least use LPG to fuel their cooker and hob.

3) DIESEL CENTRAL HEATING operates similarly to GCH systems except its boiler is fired by diesel, the same fuel that drives the narrowboat's engine, and is usually drawn out of the same tank. As long as you regularly top up with diesel your central-heating system will be ready to go. Diesel is also inherently safer to use than propane.

Diesel boiler types can be broadly distinguished by how they are powered. Some require 12 volts to operate, others run on 230 volts, and gravity-fed boilers use no electrical power at all. Style-wise, some diesel boilers look like small industrial boilers and are hidden away in cabinets or cupboards. Other units are designed to look like solid fuel stoves and can take centre stage in the lounge. Like gas central heating, timers and thermostats will allow you to control your environment with relative precision.

4) ELECTRIC SPACE HEATERS can be used if you have access to good 230-volt shore power and are wired appropriately. Obviously you must be *very* careful with electrical radiant heaters in the confined spaces of a boat.

ABOVE *Slabs of inch-thick ice on the canal after a working coal boat has broken through. It is possible to cruise in sub-zero conditions in winter in the wake of a working boat, but progress is slow and it is likely to ruin your blacking at waterline.*

RIGHT *Visiting neighbours while frozen in on the Tring Summit, Grand Union Canal.*

Other WAYS of keeping a narrowboat COSY in WINTER

OPPOSITE TOP *A snowy wonderland that has descended on boats tied up at Apsley, Grand Union Canal.*

OPPOSITE BOTTOM *A philosopher's cat keeping warm by a solid fuel stove.*

BELOW: *A serious supply of cut logs to see this pair of boats through the winter, The Grove, Grand Union Canal.*

Given decent insulation and a reasonable heating system, there are further ways of making a boat cosy in the winter. How about laying some nice carpets over bare floors? We invested in some Persian carpets for the lounge and galley; not antique ones with pedigree and subtle drape, but newly made ones that are thick and cushy, brightly patterned and reasonably priced.

We were lucky to have large, double-glazed windows installed in the second-hand boat we bought. A bit swish, but not rocket science, and they do make a big difference when it comes to retaining heat. They are also condensation-free and block out a surprising amount of noise when we are tied up beside a railway line. If I were commissioning a new boat today, I would specify double-glazing. Good, thick curtains will also help retain heat.

A Christmas present to ourselves during our first winter aboard was an Ecofan. This small, self-propelled fan sits on the solid fuel stove and gently wafts heated air to distant corners of the boat without the aid of electricity or batteries. Other boaters redirect heat by installing low-voltage computer fans in strategic places.

During a particularly extreme cold snap, accompanied by snow and -10°C temperatures, we discovered that leaving our closet door open across the passage in the middle of the boat contained the heat in the main living areas.

Having a nice warm bed at night makes for a cosy winter as well. We buy an inexpensive duvet in late autumn for extra night-time warmth, and chuck it out come springtime to save space.

I usually wear a favourite fleece and a pair of big woolly socks when lounging around inside in winter. We automatically trade mucky outdoor boots for slippers at the front door. Karen swears by a pair of Nordic-type slipper boots. I like ordinary padded ones with rubber waterproof soles, so that I can step out on to the deck or bank to inspect the weather, spy on birds, chop some kindling or chase the muse, without changing back into the outdoor winter boots.

'If I were commissioning a new boat today, I would specify double-glazing. Good, thick curtains will also help retain heat.'

A RECYCLED, REPURPOSED NARROWBOAT

This remarkable narrowboat's interior has been hand-built and assembled from repurposed and recycled materials by its owner Dave Godwin. It is based on a 72-foot iron-sided hull from a 1930 'Joey boat'. Originally designed for transporting steel rods across the Birmingham Canal Navigations, it had no engine and would have been poled between wharfs.

Dave is a highly creative craftsman, former musicians' tour-bus driver, and independent spirit with a deep interest in the countryside he passes through and its history. He continuously cruises at a snail's pace – the boat has an unusual hydraulic propulsion system that occasionally relies on the original boatman's pole for manoeuvring – and runs a bicycle and canoe in parallel for local errands and collecting deadfall wood. He also has an old Alfa Romeo sports car that is occasionally used to journey further afield. He says that everyone likes his or her own space on a boat, and when his girlfriend Samantha visits from London she has her own special retreat: another small boat!

This narrowboat retains a hint of its original working profile with a large wooden back cabin and a suggestion of angled tarpaulin top cloths over a forward hold. But the analogy ends where recycled and modern materials take over to produce a delightful and spacious liveaboard craft.

Unusually, you enter the boat in the middle, through one of its angled wooden hatch doors on either side. A couple of steps take you down into a vestibule where you are faced with two different worlds. To stern is an antique, intimate, wood-panelled den, lounge and sleeping cabin. Towards the bow is a series of bright, airy cabins with the light and atmosphere of a tall rustic conservatory.

The galley is well equipped for preparing and cooking meals, with large wooden countertops, a Belfast sink and a curious collection of Dave's own handmade floor-

A RECYCLED, REPURPOSED NARROWBOAT

and wall-mounted cabinets. Even his various tea kettles are recycled vintage items. The propane gas cooker is mounted on gimbals so is always on the level, even when the canal level occasionally drops to leave this large boat temporarily tilting to one side. Fruit and vegetables are stored in open baskets on low, deep shelves, while mugs and kitchen utensils gently sway out of the way on dedicated hooks.

The walls at this end of the narrowboat, above the gunwales, are made of double-skinned canvas filled with expanded foam-board insulation. The walls, sourced from a second-hand marquee, are kept taut over a wooden frame by a neat system of ropes attached to a wide 'top plank' that runs the length of the boat to the bow. In a traditional working boat this top plank acted as an aerial walkway used by the boatman to pass over a hold full of cargo. Leaded windows mounted in the canvas walls give views of the surrounding landscape. Most light, though, enters through the translucent, reinforced plastic material directly overhead. It is this Monotex sheeting that ensures the quality of light inside the boat changes with every passing cloud, and keeps it extraordinarily bright even under rainy skies. Indeed, some of the accompanying photographs were taken during a downpour.

Throughout the boat the variety of natural materials and textures give its interior a warm glow and organic coherence. Dave has treated all the reclaimed wooden floors, doors, wall panels and worktops gently – lightly sanding them and applying oil or wax – to proudly retain the dents, stains and bruises accrued during previous lives.

Next door to the galley and dining area is Dave's workshop. It is well appointed with a large workbench, table saw, planing machine, bench drill press and a host of tools arrayed in dedicated slots, with a remarkable collection of fittings in drawers and cabinets and a store of wood piled neatly on shelves. In addition to the translucent roof there is a good variety of 12-volt and 230-volt directional lighting, with candle power held in reserve. Stained-glass windows through to the galley bring in more light and allow you to keep an eye on a boiling kettle.

Through a pair of glazed wooden doors towards the bow is what can perhaps best be described as a conservatory bathroom retreat. Here, the translucent walls extend down to gunwale level and are punctuated by ornamental turned wood columns. With its tangerine-coloured bulkheads, waving green plants and sun filtering through the ceiling and side walls, it's easy to feel that you have not just reached the end of the boat, but have stepped into the dawn of time. Stars applied to the ceiling, hanging candles and strings of fairy lights must supply an equally enchanting atmosphere come dusk.

Pride of place here, let into the stone-tile floor, is a tapered metal bathtub supplied with hot water from an enormous tea urn. While Dave is normally frugal with water, he admits that a full hot bath is one luxury in which he indulges. Once poured, the water can take up to an hour and a half to cool to bathing temperature, but it is

well worth the wait. Opposite is an inspired piece of boating furniture: a hybrid bench storage seat and table, fitted with the ornamental backrest of an Edwardian Thames rowing boat. In another corner is a raised enamel washbasin with a large, galvanised ship's light hanging beside it on a chain.

Right at the bow is a large plank door on iron strap hinges. Dave cheerfully explains that it is made of elm coffin boards that, rather conveniently, are the height of a man. Behind this facade is a shallow, wide room with a simple portable toilet. The chamber is well ventilated with a swing-open stained-glass window overlooking the small bow deck, and it contains a full-height wardrobe and small library.

Books are found throughout the boat: on isolated shelves, in bookcases and tucked into mesh-fronted cabinets mounted high in out-of-the-way corners. It is a holistic collection, with varying subjects stored in different parts of the boat, and helps sustain a unique liveaboard lifestyle.

If we return to the middle vestibule of the boat, a pair of tall wooden doors opens into the back cabin: a secret, warm and cosy world of antiques gathered round an enamelled French solid fuel stove. Coloured light peeps in through small stained-glass panels that cast curious patches of light on the carpets and worn pitch-pine floors. Discreet light also filters in through a 'bullseye' in the ceiling – a small porthole fitted with a thick convex lens – as well as the periscope of a Challenger tank! The latter also allows covert views across the roof to the towpath. In bright weather, this cabin can be transformed by throwing open its huge side hatch, a smaller hatch beside the desk and the stern deck doors with sliding hatch above. This floods the space with sunlight and reveals the surrounding fields and trees and sky above. Magic.

The back cabin's framing is left exposed and its graceful lines contrast with the upper cabin walls and ceiling panelled in white tongue-and-groove. Below the gunwales are recycled dark wood panels, some applied with Yves Saint Laurent leopard-print fabric.

A French Bergère armchair with carved serpent arms faces the stove across a silk carpet. This is the sort of encompassing chair in which you could spend an entire winter's day curled up reading. A stereo system, a shelf of music and more books are close to hand.

Opposite, a triangular desk fashioned from an antique bank filing cabinet is paired with an equally remodelled swivelling cane-back chair on castors. These sit perfectly positioned for study: you gain the natural light of two Gothic windows to your left, with the heat of the fire by your feet. Overhead, Dave has crafted a wooden ceiling fan to circulate heat or create a soft breeze, depending on the season.

At the stern is a large cross-cabin bed. Storage drawers are built in beneath, swing-out candle-holders and LED lamps are available for reading, and a video monitor appears at its foot. No incentives here to get up and light a fire on a chilly morning.

Perhaps a reminder of cooler days to come, mounted on hooks along one wall is a collection of hats and tucked behind the copper back boiler pipes is a bevy of slippers. An old Aga kettle perched on top of the stove will keep water on simmer indefinitely. Dave admits that in deepest winter he spends most of his time at this end of the narrowboat. That said, with the fire going, hot water circulates by gravity to a series of recycled cast-iron radiators strategically placed throughout the boat.

'Samantha's boat' is a salvaged 19-foot Isle of Wight Day Boat that he has restored and turned into a pretty, miniature ark. With its ogee-arched side hatches, stained-glass panels, tiny oval and square portholes and carved wooden tiller, it attracts a lot of attention. Not only is it cute, though, it is a fully functioning liveaboard vessel.

The single cabin contains a large double bed that extends beneath the small foredeck, a boatman's stove to keep it comfortably warm, and a pew bench seat. A recycled hardwood counter features a brass sink and taps, with a solid gas ring for cooking set at one end. There is good storage in the cabinets beneath, on shelves and in drawers under the bed. This is a real Tardis, seemingly twice as large inside as it looks from the towpath. And there's even room for a couple of people to hang out on deck.

The interiors of both boats are elemental and sit naturally within the waterways' environment. They express a playful sense of style and offer pleasing home comfort – the result of fine craftsmanship that has brought recycled and repurposed materials back to life.

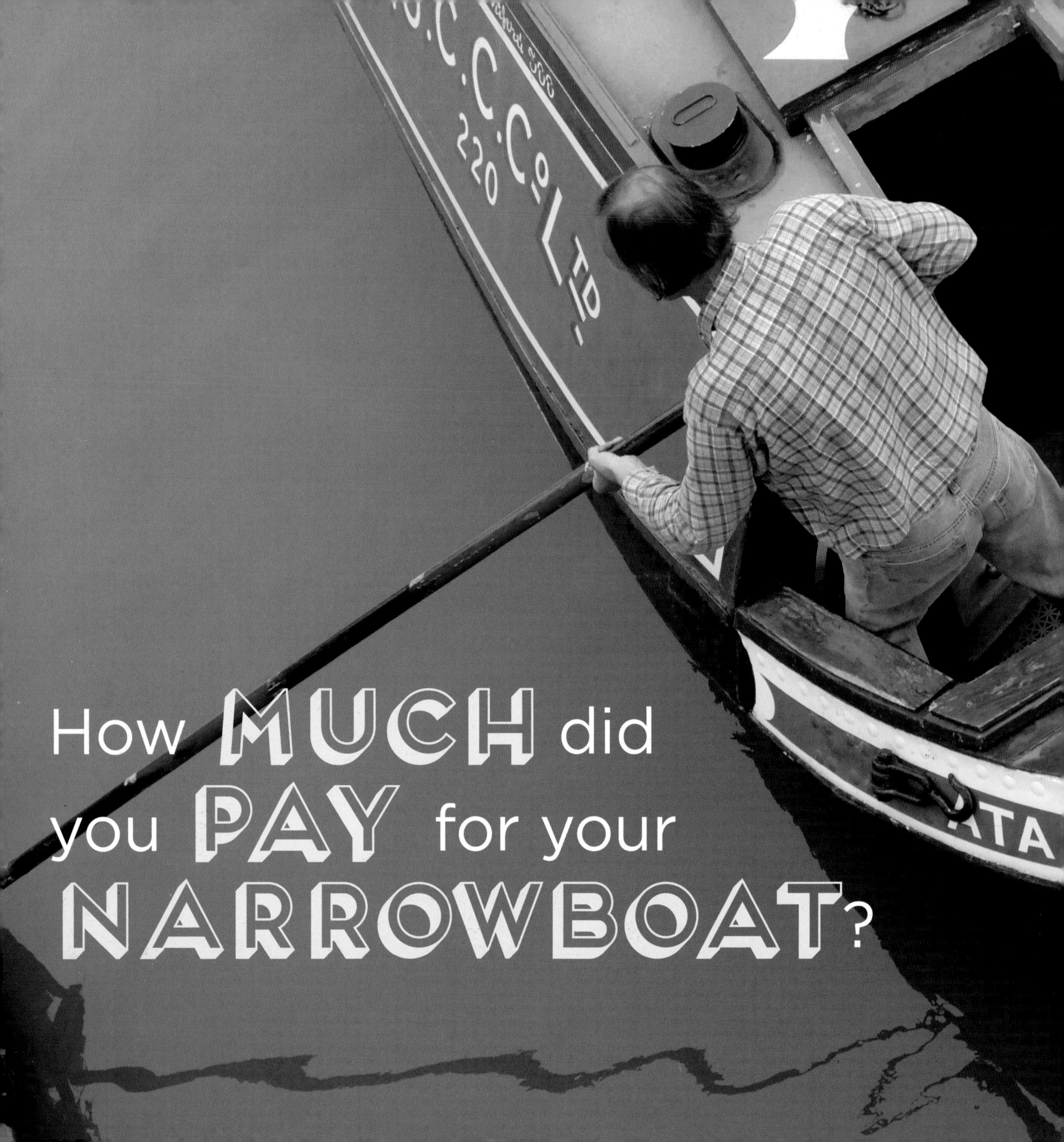

How MUCH did you PAY for your NARROWBOAT?

4

This popular, if tactless, question is an HONEST ONE and the first many people think of when seeing an attractive narrowboat. We pride ourselves on knowing how much DIFFERENT THINGS COST: cars, houses, designer toasters, a decent bottle of Bordeaux. Because narrowboats stand outside the orbit of most people's experience, NON-BOATERS have no idea how much they are worth – just as anyone but a farmer would scratch their head over the VALUE of a combine harvester, for instance. (About the same as a narrowboat, as it turns out.) What people really want to know is, 'How much does a NICE NARROWBOAT cost ... and could I afford to buy one?' Of course, this is the classic, 'How long is a piece of string?'-type question.

ABOVE: *A procession of flowerpots along the roof of a clean-lined narrowboat overnighting on the Thames near Sonning.*

'Subtle curves of the cabin roofline, sweeping upwards and inwards towards the stern, and graceful bow curves indicate skill in forming steel... Really skilful curves look like they were sculpted with a butter knife.'

PREVIOUS PAGE *Pushing the boat out: boatman manoeuvring the stern of a towed butty with a bargepole, Braunston, Grand Union Canal.*

BELOW *Decorated Buckby can and traditional triple cabin string on the roof of a beautifully signwritten narrowboat.*

QUALITY of build is an INTRINSIC VALUE

The quick and unqualified answer to 'how much does a narrowboat cost?' is, 'Between about £6,000 and £160,000.' (For widebeams and smaller Dutch barges, think £20,000 to £300,000.) This tells you a lot and, at the same time, very little about the value of boats.

There are four main factors that affect the value of a boat: the quality of its build (the steelwork); the quality and specification of its fit-out (the inside); how old the boat is; and how well it has been looked after.

Boats built by acknowledged masters of steelwork tend to retain their value over many years, while poorly constructed craft lose their worth quickly. A well-built, stylish hull of any age can always have its interior beautifully refitted, its coachwork professionally repainted and become the envy of the cut. Whereas a rough-and-ready hull with 'boxy' lines and exposed welds, even fitted with granite kitchen worktops and the finest hardwoods, will always be regarded as something of a gilded skip. Boat-owners, canal magazines and online boating forums can give you a good idea of who the respected builders are. But you can usually tell by looking. Here's how.

Consider a boat's hull and cabin top. Narrowboat shells are constructed of steel plates welded together over internal steel frames. On a good build you won't see the joins – the welded joints will be ground back and finished level with the surrounding faces. If you look down the length of the cabin sides or roof there should be minimal waviness. The smoother the plating, the better the build. That said, fresh and highly reflective paintwork can emphasise small imperfections in large surfaces that are not worth worrying about. Narrowboats are rather special in that they are built by hand, not banged out by machines.

Subtle curves of the cabin roofline, sweeping upwards and inwards towards the stern, and graceful bow curves indicate skill in forming steel. Pleasing ornamental scrolls of steel on the cants – the flat, upper edges around a bow deck and stern counter – and incorporated into the handrails are difficult to fabricate and signal fine craftsmanship. Really skilful curves look like they were sculpted with a butter knife.

Look for boats specified with 10/6/4 or greater steelwork – which means 10mm-steel plate is used on the hull bottom, 6mm-steel plate on the hull sides and 4mm-steel plate on the cabin sides and roof. You may also see boats specified 10/6/5/4, which means 10mm-steel plate hull bottom, 6mm-steel plate hull sides, 5mm-steel plate cabin sides and a 4mm-steel plate cabin roof. Up until the mid-1980s it was standard practice to use 6mm- even 5mm-steel plate on the bottom of leisure narrowboats, whereas today quality boatbuilders use 10mm- or 12mm-steel plate.

Well-built boats will manoeuvre better in the water. Unfortunately this aspect is hidden to the casual observer, so only driving a boat combined with experience will reveal how it handles.

LEFT *A group of finely restored Fellows, Morton & Clayton working narrowboats at the Braunston Historic Narrowboat Rally, Grand Union Canal. Narrowboat* Dove *was built in 1925, while the originally steam-powered* Monarch *was built in 1908.*

BELOW: *An interesting mixture of hand-crafted styles that can be found in narrowboats: Indian, Persian and English.*

QUALITY of fit-out is a shifting VALUE

A well-crafted and imaginatively fitted-out interior is a joy to look at, smooth your fingers over and explore. Most people love the natural tones of wood panelling, curvaceous cabinetry, thick wood or stone worktops and artistic fabrics found in a beautifully put-together modern narrowboat. They appreciate how quality joinery fits into all the odd corners. The installation of Belfast sinks, Rayburn cookers, hidden freezers, glazed showers and oak-lined wine beds in the bilges elicit giggles of delight.

Equally impressive is the clever use of space, such as a 6in-wide, full-height larder hidden in a galley wall that smoothly rolls out to reveal a month's worth of dry and tinned goods. Or a shelf of cooking pans automatically 'presented' to you: swinging out from under a hidden back corner when a cupboard door is opened. A king-sized bed on rollers that appears from under a tug deck. A calorifier (hot water tank) tucked neatly into the back of an airing closet so that its heat dries damp clothing out of sight. A raised Pullman table that offers a clear view of the world by day and a sumptuous, memory-foam sleep by night.

As at least 60–70 per cent of a boat's initial price is based on its fit-out, it is important to consider closely the quality of its carpentry and furnishings, how state-of-the-art its appliances and electronic goods are, and the cleverness of its layout.

Notice, though, that I have called the quality of a narrowboat's fit-out a *shifting* value, because it is so easily subject to change – unlike a boat's metal superstructure. For example, whatever the original quality of a narrowboat's interior, it will physically age and degrade at a rate dependent on how it has been used. Has it enjoyed life as a liveaboard, or has it been lightly used on occasional weekends as a leisure craft? Has it been continuously cruised in all weathers, or statically moored for long periods in one place? Has it been lovingly tended or left to the elements? The electronics of a boat can also date quickly and affect its value.

Just like land-based homes, a boat's fit-out can age stylistically as well. Not too long ago, yellow pine tongue-and-groove diagonal panelling was the fashion; today, light and airy American white ash and oak are on trend.

As well as value-for-money, part of a second-hand narrowboat's attraction is that its interior can be rejuvenated, reworked or completely replaced. Its style can be changed to suit a new owner's tastes.

Evaluating a boat's fit-out can be tricky because much of its interior is hidden from view. For example, you can only glimpse bits of its plumbing, insulation, electrics and underfloor support. Here you must infer the quality of what you can't see from that you can.

Ultimately, the value of any boat's fit-out is going to be more subjective than its steelwork. To help quantify this to yourself, think about how much you would enjoy owning and living on a particular boat (taking into account its layout, style and overall quality), then calculate how much you would want to spend changing or improving its fit-out. How much is the joy of the former worth the cost of the latter?

A good pedigree fit-out will hold its value for as long as you and others cherish it. That said, traditionally styled narrowboats with standard layouts tend to be most widely cherished, so hold their values longer than highly personalised boats with offbeat interiors. Personally, I tend towards the quirky.

LEFT *Traditional narrowboat* Troubadour *making its way down the Crofton flight of locks, Kennet & Avon Canal.*

The COST of BRAND-NEW narrowboats

'... part of a second-hand narrowboat's attraction is that its interior can be rejuvenated, reworked or completely replaced.'

OK, let's get to the nitty gritty of boat prices. To understand what boats are worth in pounds and pence let us start at the top end, with shiny new narrowboats. The cost of a new build will depend on the boat's length and the quality of the builder and materials, components and appliances used.

A basic-specification narrowboat by a competent builder and fitter will cost at least £1,000 per foot. A well-specified boat based on a shell made by a good boat builder and completed by a good boat fitter should cost from about £1,500 per foot. A narrowboat with a sophisticated specification (lots of bells and whistles, electronics and fancy paintwork) on a shell by a highly regarded builder and a fitter known for the quality of his or her craftsmanship will set you back in the region of £2,000 per foot upwards.

If these figures give you vertigo, savour the thought that the same boats can sell for up to 40 per cent less within a few years of being launched – *if* they come up for sale. There are enough people out there who commission boats and sell up within a couple of years, either because boating is not for them or for financial reasons, to make seeking out one of these second-hand deals an option.

ABOVE *Automatic satellite-seeking dish on a whimsically-painted Art Nouveau narrowboat.*

RIGHT *Panoramic view of a narrowboat awaiting repairs at a marine boatyard – beached at low tide at the confluence of the River Thames, Grand Union Canal and River Brent.*

The COST of SECOND-HAND narrowboats

What's a second-hand narrowboat worth? Note that in this context 'worth' (or 'value') are not to be confused with 'asking price'. Some sellers, especially sentimental private sellers, wildly overestimate the value of their boats. When buying, either privately or through a broker, you should always negotiate.

Overall, the second-hand narrowboat market has remained relatively stable over the last decade. There was a gradual dip in boat prices during the economic downturn from 2008 but they slowly returned to previous levels by 2013. Since 2014, interest in narrowboats has greatly picked up. Today, curiously, many basic-specification second-hand boats, of any age, are available for prices similar to those of a few years ago. Good news for those who simply want a good, functional boat to live on. At the high end of the market inflation has had a greater effect, especially on boats under five years old. Fairly new, quality crafted and highly specified second-hand narrowboats can fetch 10–20 per cent more than their equivalents a couple of years ago.

What follows is, broadly, what you can expect to pay for your perfect second-hand narrowboat. The figures reflect boat values at the beginning of 2016.

ABOVE *A well-preserved liveaboard narrowboat sporting a variety of custom-built storage boxes on the roof and stern deck on the Kennet & Avon Canal in deepest Wiltshire.*

Registered at Tamworth 5050
JOSEPHI

'... almost every narrowboat is unique and originally was someone's pride and joy. In addition to market forces, its value will also depend on how closely it matches your vision of the ideal boat and how much you would like to own it.'

Boats less than five years old

If a professionally built and fitted-out narrowboat is less than five years old it should still look in good shape outside and in. If you stand back half a boat's length the paintwork should still appear intact and have some shine. From this distance you shouldn't see any rust.

Inside, if the boat has been used for leisure purposes – cruised, say, for four weeks plus half a dozen weekends each year – the woodwork, appliances, soft furnishings and loo equipment should still be in good order. If the boat has been used as a liveaboard, expect to find some wear on counter-top and cabinet edges and surfaces, partially soiled carpets, well-used kitchen and shower-room appliances and perhaps a little staining from condensation on window ledges and beneath hatches. These are all things that are generally easy to replace or repair.

The engine, if regularly serviced, should still be running smoothly, with no smoke issuing a minute or two after start-up from cold. Very generally, if the engine has less than 1,500 hours on it within this time-frame, it's probably had sporadic leisure use. If over 2,000 hours, then it's probably been used for extended cruising or following a liveaboard lifestyle.

A basic-specification narrowboat under five years old would cost you anywhere from £700 to £1,000 per foot. A well-specified boat of the same age is worth about £1,000 to £1,250 per foot; and a beautifully crafted, top-end boat would set you back in the region of £1,250 to £1,800 per foot and upwards.

Of course, almost every narrowboat is unique and originally was someone's pride and joy. In addition to market forces, its value will also depend on how closely it matches your vision of the ideal boat and how much you would like to own it.

LEFT *The mirror-bright paintwork of narrowboat* Josephine *reflecting its neighbours at the Canalway Cavalcade in Little Venice, London.*

Five- to ten-year-old narrowboats

OPPOSITE *Hot and cool colours of narrowboats reflected in calm waters.*

BELOW Upsy Daisy, *Abingdon, River Thames.*

Some boats of this age really look weather-beaten and down-at-heel, while others look remarkably fresh and bright. After five to ten years' weathering and use, it is apparent how well or not a boat has been looked after.

Cared-for narrowboats hold their value quite well and for one of this age in good condition you can expect to pay between £600 per foot at the basic end and £1,000 per foot at the premium end.

If you start getting serious about boats it is important that any narrowboat that is more than a couple of years old is bought 'subject to survey'. Under these terms, after you have made an offer and had it accepted (and probably put down a deposit), you need to organise a marine surveyor of your choice (not the seller's) to perform a pre-purchase condition survey, including a full out-of-water hull survey. You will also have to pay to have the boat craned or pulled out of the water, but it will be worth every penny. A hull's condition is critical and something you simply cannot appraise without professional advice and ultrasonic measurement. The cut is full of stories about seemingly immaculate boats whose hulls had corroded to credit-card thinness.

HAMPSHIRE
ROSE

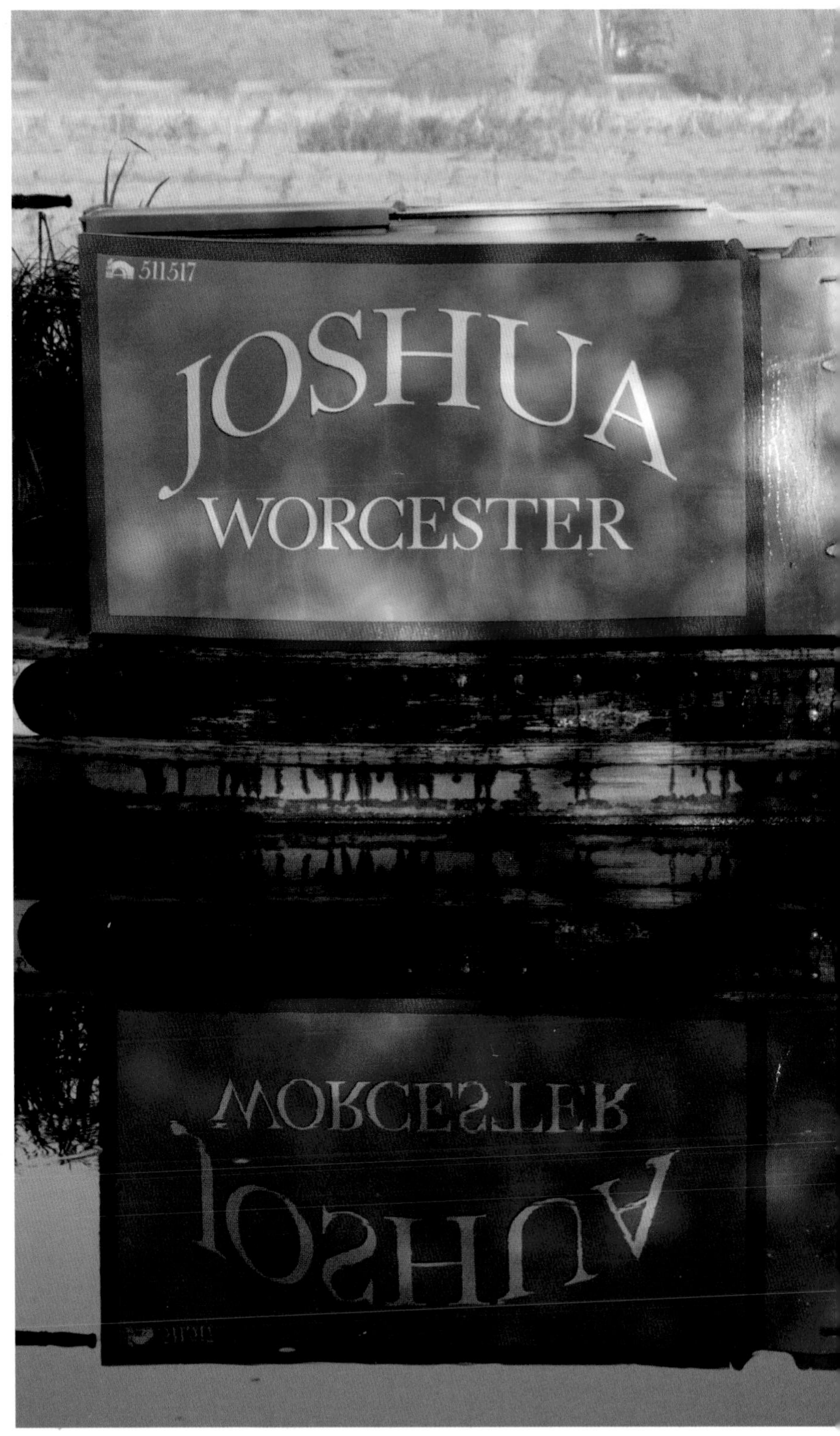
511517
JOSHUA
WORCESTER

Ten- to twenty-year-old narrowboats

All of the above applies to boats over 10 years old. Just more so!

When considering an older boat, and trying to decide whether it is worth the time and expense of surveying, look at how the inside of the hull has weathered: the bilges should be dry. After 10 years, any water that has collected under the floorboards (through condensation or rain ingression) can have caused serious rusting. Open up any floor inspection hatches, often found under mats towards the stern, and look at the steelwork's interior condition using a torch. Get down on the floor to feel areas you can't see. What you don't want to find are expanses of thickly flaking rust. Also have a good look for rust in the engine compartment – on the counters (the 'shelf' part either side at the stern) as well as the bottom plate. Multiple layers of thick, flaking rust in any of these places suggest neglect and the value of the boat is probably at least £10,000 less than might otherwise have been expected.

How old is the engine? Is it the original plant or has it been recently replaced? Is there a record of servicing you can see? If you think you might want to replace the engine in the next couple of years, value the boat accordingly.

For narrowboats that are between 10 and 20 years old expect to pay about £500 per foot for clean and functional standard builds, and up to £900 per foot for quality top-end examples. If you can afford it, there are some particularly good deals to be found on boats of this age put together by some highly respected builders.

ABOVE *Baby on board. And a great pile of toys too!*

RIGHT: *Some liveaboards will tell you, 'Oh, I can never throw away anything', and it usually shows. Beautifully crafted, but weighed down, narrowboat on the fringes of Hungerford, Kennet & Avon Canal.*

ABOVE *A beautiful old GUCCC working boat converted into a full liveaboard craft.*

Twenty-year-old and over narrowboats

There are lots of good, cosy, well-appointed narrowboats out on the canals and rivers that are over 20 years old. Boats with classic lines and quality fit-outs age particularly well from an aesthetic point of view. I like the darkened woodwork and heavy brass of many old boats, which make them look 'boaty' or 'nautical'. On the other hand, many older narrowboats' interiors have been reworked over the years, either by their owners or professionals, and contain modern kitchens and shower rooms and updated furnishings. Some old craft have been completely and utterly refitted and updated – with varying degrees of success.

While an older boat's fit-out is comparatively easy to evaluate, caution is still required when it comes to its hull. Although overplating a hull isn't especially difficult, it is expensive, disruptive to cruising, not something your average boater can do for him- or herself, and not nearly as interesting as installing new galley worktops, choosing new curtains or even laying recycled oak floorboards.

When valuing a narrowboat that is more than 20 years old, and especially one manufactured with an 8mm (or 6mm) base plate, my starting position would be to assume it needs some overplating. I would inquire about whether, when and how much plate work had already been done. If the owner or broker swore that the hull was fine, I would ask to see a relatively recent hull survey (no more than a couple of years old) that showed spot readings of plate thickness. Failing that, and if I really liked the boat, I would assume I'd need to spend between £5,000 and £15,000 (depending on the size of the narrowboat) to have it overplated. Again, do your homework and value a boat accordingly.

Narrowboats with reasonable hulls that are over 20 years old are worth between £400 per foot for a good, basic build and up to about £700 per foot for a particularly well-crafted classic.

'GOSH, I think I can AFFORD a narrowboat!' – some QUICK checks

If you are beginning to think seriously about buying a liveaboard boat here are some tips for quickly spotting good second-hand value. You can apply these checks even before entering a boat, so you needn't waste time considering duds.

Quick check 1: condition of the paintwork

Look at a boat's paintwork. Is the surface reasonably intact, or are there patches of rust that have been left to spread? Pay particular attention to deck corners, around hatches and the inside edges of handrails. Look for signs of rust where fixtures meet with, or protrude through, the shell: mushroom vents, pigeon boxes, fairleads (rope guides), stove pipes, as well as windows and portholes. Check around fender eyes, hose outlets and grilles in the hull – anywhere water might collect and sit.

Some boat-owners will typically touch up bits of rust on a regular or annual basis – perhaps with a bit of spot sanding and a dab of rust inhibitor before painting over to seal. Others will leave it for a couple of years, allowing penny-sized rust patches to percolate through the paint's surface before tackling them. Some boaters simply ignore their craft to the point that saucer-sized sheets of rust develop and begin to flake off.

If considering a boat in the latter condition, ask yourself how much it would cost to get its finish as smart as you'd like it to be. Could you do the work yourself, or would you want to pay a professional a few thousand pounds to do the job? More importantly, ask yourself what *other* problems, possibly hidden from view, have also been ignored for so many years.

Finally, be wary of the 'cover-all-evils' coat of paint, usually applied quickly and without much finesse just before a boat is offered for sale.

Safety first

Never put your hands or fingers between a boat's hull and the bank or dock if there is any chance of them becoming trapped or crushed, for example if another boat passes by or a strong wind picks up. Narrowboats weigh 10–35 tons and can do serious damage to limbs. I have usually checked hulls from raised pontoons that are open below the waterline, such as you find in marinas.

Quick check 2: condition of the hull

It is very difficult to perceive the state of the hull without a full out-of-water survey made by a professional marine surveyor, which I would consider mandatory before buying any second-hand boat. Luckily, there are a couple of checks you can make in about 10 minutes to get an initial impression of a hull's condition, to see if it is worth surveying. To do this you will need to lie down and get your hands wet.

HULL SIDE CHECK The greatest amount of corrosion usually occurs just below the waterline, where oxygen in the water is richest. Rub your fingertips gently against the hull, a couple of inches beneath the water's surface, at various points along the boat's length. Can you feel any indentations? Rub off any growth if necessary. You may very well feel nothing. If you do, how deep do these depressions

LEFT *Imagine the craftsmanship and time that has gone into forming the graceful bow curves from raw plates of steel on* Grey Hare.

BELOW *You can see how the hull of this project boat has risen in the water after its interior was stripped out for re-fitting, revealing extensive and active rusting. The rust was removed and the hull re-blacked the following week.*

RIGHT *A pretty, short narrowboat on the Grand Union Canal at Rickmansworth. All you need, really, to get afloat.*

BELOW *A wooden cruiser liveaboard tied up on the River Thames below Wittenham Clumps, near Dorchester.*

feel – 1mm, 2mm, 3mm, more? How large do they seem – tiny circular indentations, 50-pence sized patches, or semi-continuous horizontal stretches? Do they seem to flake at the edges?

If you do feel indentations – this is pitting – try and have a look at them through the water. Do they seem lighter, even orangey or rust-coloured, against the blacking? If so, the hull is actively rusting at those points and needs blacking. If they appear black it may represent previous corrosion now sealed with paint.

Most modern narrowboat hulls have 6mm-thick plate sides when new. If you feel 3mm-deep pitting, for example, then there is half the hull thickness remaining at that point. This is only a general indicator of the hull's condition and the chances are good that there will be other places on the hull pitted to at least the same extent. There may also be corrosion inside the hull, which is much more difficult to check.

BOTTOM PLATE CHECK While you are down there, and if you can do it safely, reach down under the boat to feel the bottom plate. It should protrude about half an inch, to protect the hull edge from abrasion against banks in shallow water. It will probably be worn along the edges, but you can confirm its thickness. Any waviness or curling of this edge indicates a particularly thin baseplate and a cheaper build. Value the boat accordingly.

If you really like a boat that seems to have substantial pitting (say to a depth of 2–3mm or more), talk to a marine surveyor about your findings and what the implications might be. This will help you decide whether the boat is worth the expense of pulling it out of the water for a professional ultrasonic survey.

SACRIFICIAL ANODES CHECK Finally, have a look at the bow and stern sides to see how much is left of the sacrificial anodes. These are protective 'lozenges' of raw metal welded below the waterline and designed to galvanically corrode in advance of the steel hull around them. Compare the anodes to the size and shape of similar new ones for sale in chandlers. If they are eaten away and nearly gone they will need replacing and the hull blacking. If they are absent, be suspicious.

ABOVE *Christmas wreath on the prow of a Canal & River Trust working barge, Cowroast, Grand Union Canal.*

LEFT The Beach Hut. *A light, bright, airy handmade boat spotted on the Thames.*

TEA, the OFFER and a SURVEY

For some of us, finding a good layout we can live with in a second-hand narrowboat poses the greatest challenge. Others are happy to adapt themselves to a layout if the price is right; they just need to be realistic about what they can live without. Try to spend an hour or two alone, without the owner or broker, on any boat you are seriously considering living on. Sit in it. Walk about in it. Take a Thermos of tea and relax with it. Can you imagine being happy living on that boat?

Before making an offer, again, try to understand the quality of its steelwork. Also, drive the boat to see if it steers well and seems responsive. Listen to whether the engine runs smoothly.

Having discovered and agreed a price on the boat of your dreams there is one final hurdle: a pre-purchase condition survey. A professional surveyor should help confirm much of what you've already discovered about the boat, but can tell you more about what you cannot see. They are your hired expert and forensic detective, so guide them towards anything in the boat you're not sure of or don't understand. Ask for their opinions.

As a nice bonus, most surveys usually offer you some leverage in negotiating any repairs required or modifying your offer.

LEFT ABOVE AND BELOW *Dining room and galley of a narrowboat at dusk.*

RIGHT: *An older but well-looked-after narrowboat on private moorings.*

TOPSY
TOPSY

WHY do WOMEN do all the WORK?

5

When this question of women doing all the work pops up it is always in PLAYFUL JEST, based on light-hearted observations of narrowboaters working their way through A LOCK. It is usually asked of women winding the paddle gears of a lock gate, or leaning into its massive BALANCE BEAM to swing it open or closed. Or it is asked of men stood relaxed at the TILLER seemingly staring off into middle distance waiting for all this work to be COMPLETED.

ABOVE *Raising a gate paddle with a windlass.*

'Between locks, people often walk the towpath, rather than cruise on the boat.'

PREVIOUS PAGE *Boatwoman wearing a traditional bonnet and clothing sitting on the stern hatch of a working narrowboat.*

BELOW *Controlling a single narrowboat in a double lock as it rises.*

Indeed, it is very often women who *do* engage in the heavy physical work involved in raising or lowering a boat from one pound to the next. This is not usually due to any overt sexism or unfair division of labour; many simply choose to do so because they enjoy the routine, which when going uphill on a wide canal with double gates (for those of you who don't know) involves...

First, empty the lock of water by cranking open the left and right gate paddles at the lower end of the lock. When the water inside has equalised with that below, open the gates by pushing on the long balance beams. As gates can weigh 1, 2 or more tons each, it is usually most easily and safely done with your back positioned against the beam and pushing with your feet. Once open, the boat can enter.

After the boat has been driven into the lock, close both lock gates and wind down both gate paddles. Then walk to the opposite, upper end of the lock and open those paddles. Depending on the type of lock, this may involve a ground paddle, a gate paddle, or a combination of the two at each gate. Opening these must be done in a controlled fashion so that the bow of the boat is not swamped with a flume of water, and to ensure the boat isn't violently flung about inside the lock.

When the lock has filled and the water levels have equalised at the upper end, the left and right gates can then be pushed open. After the boat has been driven out, the two gates must be closed and all the paddles dropped. On some locks, for conservation reasons, you must return to the lower gates and open their paddles again to drain the lock.

Taking a boat downhill through a lock involves roughly the same motions but in reverse.

Between locks, people often walk the towpath, rather than cruise on the boat. If they get to the next lock before the boat arrives they can begin to prepare it in the same manner, to speed progress.

EXERCISE?

ABOVE *Leaning against the beam of a lock gate waiting for it to 'give' – a subtle signal that the water levels have equalised on both sides of the gate and it can be pushed open, Oxford Canal.*

A fair number of people, including some women, view working the locks as a good opportunity for getting some exercise. Unless you do a lot of heavy lifting, this type of workout isn't easily found in the everyday flow of life. And most liveaboard boaters, in my experience, are allergic to rowing machines and weight-training equipment.

So, are women more energetic and health-conscious than men? Not really. Energy and lethargy seem pretty evenly distributed among the sexes. And walking between locks – say up to half a mile – is usually enjoyed by everyone: women, children and men. It is another way of admiring the countryside, listening to the birds, breathing fresh air and having a little time to yourself.

'Operating a lock ... allows you to joke, swap witticisms, complain about the state of the canal, point out where the blackberries and free firewood are, or compare recipes for sloe gin.'

SOCIABILITY?

Operating a lock, as opposed to driving the boat and controlling it within a lock, can be a much more sociable affair. There's lots of time to talk to other boaters, walkers or gongoozlers who have gathered while the lock empties or fills. It's a great opportunity to discover what's up ahead – the best pubs, restaurants, mooring spots, tricky bits of navigation, dicey neighbourhoods etc. It allows you to joke, swap witticisms, complain about the state of the canal, point out where the blackberries and free firewood are, or compare recipes for sloe gin. Or talk about the weather.

So, are women more sociable creatures? Do they martyr themselves to the toil of operating locks in order to brush up against fellow humans and raise their spirits? Probably not. Even male skippers at the helm, deep within the shadows of a dank, slime-coated lock, can be heard bellowing over their fuming engines about the merits of diesel bug additives, hull designs and methods for capturing the best broadband reception. We all like to talk about what we know. And the weather.

RIGHT *Two women with windlasses walk to the next lock as their partners navigate their narrowboats alongside, Braunston Flight, Grand Union Canal.*

SOCIAL conditioning?

My partner Karen says that women do all the lock work for the same reason that they may be the ones to clean the floors and toilets while men take out the rubbish and mend leaky taps: out of social conditioning and habit. The fact that so many women work the locks, do the shopping, cook the meals and clean the inside of the boat, while the majority of men drive the boat, service its engine, repair the internal 'life-support' systems and keep its exterior rust-free (or not) suggests we are socially conditioned to some extent. We're raised that way or it's what's expected, so they are easy habits to fall into. At a recent liveaboard boater's party I heard this segregation of tasks referred to as 'pink work' and 'blue work'.

There's no right or wrong way to allocate tasks, and of course in many cases these generalised observations don't, ahem, hold water, but perhaps the conditioned division of labour becomes more polarised when living on a boat simply because *more* labour is required. Narrowboats are more complex than most flats or houses, so there are more things to know about, attend to and occasionally fix.

You *can* do both 'domestic' and 'boaty' chores solo, and there are hundreds of single-handers out there, both women and men, who will attest to this. But you need to be very dedicated to the lifestyle and expect to put much more time into it than if you were living on land. Two people sharing this variety of tasks, however divvied up, undoubtedly makes boating life much easier.

RIGHT *Jules' Fuels: Jules and Richard sell solid fuel and diesel throughout the year from their coal boat and butty on the Grand Union Canal.*

TOWCESTER
(Reg'd at Rickmansworth № 144)
J.E.COOK
07740 487222
STOKE BRUERNE

LEFT Apple Queen *cruising up the Thames near Dorchester.*

ABOVE *Teamwork can be key to navigating a narrowboat around the inland waterways.*

ZEN and the ART of diesel MAINTENANCE

The role of diesel engines in boating appears to loom larger than we might wish when considering why women 'do all the work', notably all the paddle gear cranking when locking. Generally speaking, and of course there are exceptions, more men than women are interested in understanding the intricacies of diesel engines. Given that all marine engines require regular attention or they will seize up – from the daily oil/water/belt checks, through regular oil changes and filter replacements to long-term servicing – *somebody* has to take an interest in this. Otherwise you end up with an expensive lump of scrap in the bowels of your boat.

Those people who do take an interest in their engines are also prone to noticing the regular sounds and vibrations they send out when driven. These noises signal the state of an engine's health and allow the listener to keep it running smoothly and free of trouble.

It seems little wonder, then, that whoever looks after the engine will want to be close to it when it's running. Literally 'keeping on top of it' in the case of many narrowboats. If an odd note or a rough shudder should arise, they will be keen to work out why, and decide what, if anything, needs to be done about it. This 'engine-love' theory may explain why men do most of the driving and women the locking.

A SPANNER in the WORKS

I am conscious that we have slipped into what is widely considered a male mode of thought. Understanding engines is part of the joy of boat-ownership because there is an intrinsic pleasure in understanding how their various parts work in harmony. Is this social conditioning? Could love of machinery be genetic? This is a pretty big, non-boaty topic, and probably worth steering clear of here.

Many people feel that relationships are held between people and not towards machinery, and it is certainly true that engines are incapable of returning any attention lavished on them. Furthermore, they believe engines should just work if they are any good. This view is difficult to argue with, but if you find that you're not that keen on understanding diesels and their maintenance then you'd better make sure your engine is well serviced on a regular basis by a professional.

RIGHT *Manoeuvring two boats to a waterpoint in the early morning mist, Crofton Pumping Station, Kennet & Avon Canal.*

'Understanding engines is part of the joy of boat-ownership because there is an intrinsic pleasure in understanding how their various parts work in harmony.'

CONCLUSION

Clearly no part of physically driving a narrowboat (steering with a tiller, putting a Morse control lever into forward or reverse gear at differing levels of propulsion), and no part of engine maintenance is beyond the capabilities of any woman or man. It is all a matter of practice.

Ultimately, whether you are male or female, I suspect that if you have even the smallest inclination towards understanding your boat's engine, then there is a better-than-even chance you will end up driving the boat. Rather than 'doing all the work' operating the locks.

STEP ABOARD...

A ROVING CANAL TRADER

This traditional, 70-foot narrowboat has a bright, open interior that is brought to life with hand-crafted objects of beauty and function, many made by the owners themselves. It is a modern working boat: sustaining a self-sufficient, work-from-home lifestyle that remains true to the traditional spirit and rhythms of the inland waterways.

Gillie and Dave Rhodes and their lurcher Sophie live aboard full-time and continuously cruise, tending to travel close to family in southern England during the slow winter months, and exploring the rest of the waterways system from springtime to autumn. Both work from the boat, but in quite different ways. Gillie specialises in hand-crafting a variety of traditional narrowboat rope work, such as tiller tassels and cabin strings, as well as smaller items like knotted hatch handles, key rings and bracelets. She can also produce overnight a made-to-measure Turk's Head for your tiller or stripy broom handle!

The boat has a Roving Trader business licence and Gillie sells her work straight from the boat as well as through mail order. As they are also members of the Roving Canal Traders Association part of their cruising

pattern is guided by visits to some of the Association's floating market events around the country, to show and sell her work.

Dave is an engineer and associate consultant specialising in vehicle sound and vibration issues. He is one of those lucky people able to create and communicate his work from the helm of his laptop, via a rooftop Wi-Fi connection, comfortably seated with a view of the world through a side hatch.

The exterior of the boat declares its working credentials with traditional signage hand-painted across its stern cabin sides. There is the stubby stern deck of a 'trad' narrowboat, with a line of portholes down both sides and a large, open deck at the bow. Here you enter a pair of doors decorated with castle scenes and step down into a lounge that runs open-plan all the way through the dining and work area to the galley.

The cabin walls and ceiling are lined with light ash panels trimmed with marsh-green beading. Against this clean-lined and surprisingly modern backdrop are hung selections of special craft pieces and mobiles that add patches of unexpected colour – and that gently sway with the motion of the boat. Art Nouveau tiling reflects heat from over the stove, while more traditional brass lamps sprout from the walls for night-time illumination. The varnished floors are of a durable red hardwood that reflects patches of dark and light.

Given its traditional design, this is an uncommonly bright boat, the result of seven side hatches interspersed between the portholes. A side hatch beside the front doors casts light across a sofa-bed draped with hand-knitted and mirror-studded throws. Cabinets and display shelving flank either side of the front doors and the 'flip-top' steps offer yet more storage. Behind those steps, under the front deck, is a massive 1,000-litre water tank that allows weeks to pass between fillings. Beside the tank is a low-down storage cupboard that Dave says makes a good 'second fridge' for veg and beer.

Opposite the sofa in the lounge is a modern solid fuel stove with a large window for enjoying the fire: the best narrowboat TV. This stove replaces an antique Stratford range that until recently sat here – a cast-iron wonder the size of a pirate chest – that unfortunately put out more fumes than heat. Lots of fuel is to hand, presented in a great coal scuttle on a pedestal that shares the hearth.

In the middle of the lounge across from the stove is another side hatch. Suspended from its curtain rail is a range of Gillie's tiller tassels – ornamental rope work designed to hang beneath a narrowboat's tiller and secure its tiller pin. They are playful objects and light streams around them and heightens their textures. Conveniently, some side hatches double as 'shop windows', displaying Gillie's craftwork to towpath passers-by. Dave has also mounted some very discreet brass rails along the lounge ceiling so that when stock is especially abundant it can be hung on hooks there: decorative yet out of the way.

There is a large freestanding table and chairs in the area between the stove and galley that serves as both a dining and working area. Natural light floods in through the side hatch over it – also hung with knotted rope work and decorations on display. On the opposite wall is a handy bookcase.

The galley seems enormous, with expanses of hardwood worktops on three sides illuminated by two further side hatches. There is a freestanding gas cooker to one side, with a marine fridge-freezer and washing machine installed under the other counters. Overhead are cabinets with underside lighting that match cupboards and drawers below. In the centre of the galley ceiling is a 'pigeon box' – a raised vent with a pitched roof and small portholes – that Gillie has painted with traditional rose motifs. As well as offering a glimpse of the

sky it also helps to control temperature and steam in the cooking area.

Between the galley and side passage leading to the stern of the boat is a neat, half-height gate that safely restricts Sophie when needed, such as when Gillie and Dave are working the boat though locks. This stretch of the boat and its cabins are fitted with portholes, which suggest a quieter, more secluded living space. The first cabin off the passage is the loo, with a shower, built-in vanity unit and pump-out toilet. Following this is a sleeping cabin fully open to the corridor, which makes for a large and cosy retreat, which would explain why Sophie has claimed it for herself! It's also a comfortable place in which to kick back and read.

Further along, the corridor makes a dog-leg (no pun intended) around a full-height storage closet to the opposite side of the boat and enters the engine room. This is a neat, green industrial space with a Beta JD3 tug engine at its heart. Despite the gleam of copper piping and brass fittings, this is a modern powerhouse built in the tradition of classic narrowboat engines, with lots of low-rev, high-torque 'oomph' to move and control a 24-ton boat. The engine room contains two more side hatches that allow its plant to be displayed to the outside world and fresh air to blow through and cool it. Gillie and Dave discovered an unexpected bonus of this cabin shortly after moving aboard: it's the perfect place in which to hang up cloths after a wash, where they dry especially quickly if the engine is running.

PETTER UNIVERSAL AIR COOLED PETROL ENGINES
2, 3, 4, 5 AND 6-8 B.H.P.
BRASSO
BRASSO
METAL
Polish

A step up takes you into the traditional boatman's cabin at the stern. This is a masterpiece of narrowboat decoration, where every square inch is scumbled, save for where magnificent castle scenes are depicted on the drop-down table and stern door panels. There is also a genuine 'bed 'ole' here: an ingenious, traditional piece of engineering that sees a double bed fold out from what appears to be a wall cabinet, to extend across the width of the cabin. In the daytime it is folded back completely out of sight to allow easy passage. There is an upholstered bench, or side bed, alongside that offers another place in which to relax during the day. By the back steps is a low boatman's stove for winter warmth, a cluster of cabinets and open storage slots. A row of traditional brass 'bed knobs' reflects light into the cabin from the sliding hatch above when it is open.

This is an unusually flexible boat that offers the attractive 'port hole style' and evening privacy of an enclosed traditional narrowboat. At the same time it has many side hatches that bring in loads of daylight and open it up to the outside world, which also happens to be perfect for trading. It is beautifully decorated and manages to combine craft style, modern convenience and traditional character to fully support a self-contained cruising life afloat.

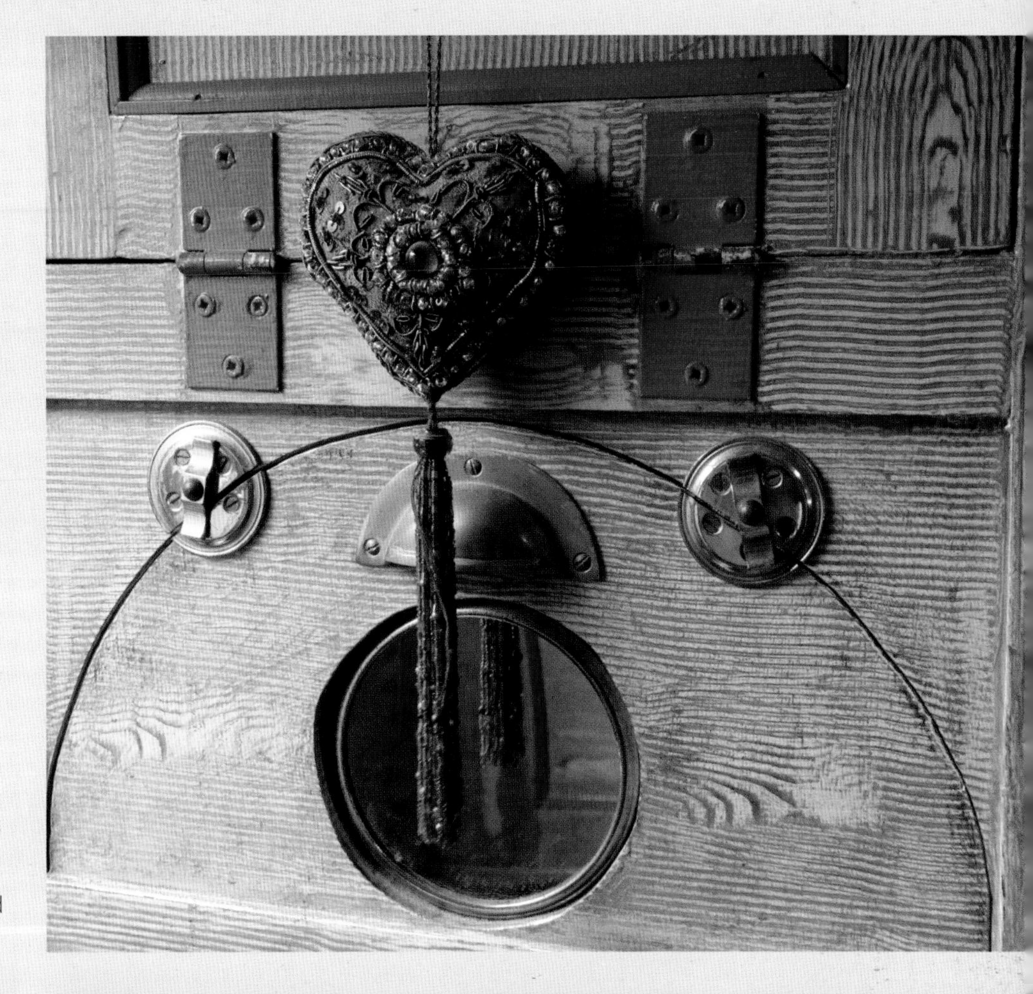

DID you PAINT it yourself?

6

When regularly asked if I have PAINTED OUR BOAT myself, I am very flattered. If only I had the skills... The paintwork on a traditional-style narrowboat is usually the HANDIWORK of a craftsperson with years of experience in the trade, and is usually the last in a series of professionals to make their mark on your boat. A steel boat will usually be built by an EXPERT BUILDER and welder, then passed on to another specialist or team for fitting out, and finally conveyed to the PAINTER. Even then, after a boat is painted, a signwriter or canal artist may be drafted in to complete the decoration. These PROFESSIONALS become renowned (or not) for the quality of their work and a good painter, in effect, places the CROWN on a truly great boat.

ABOVE The Rose of Hungerford *revived: blocking in some diamonds, Hungerford, Kennet & Avon Canal.*

'The paintwork on a traditional-style narrowboat is usually the handiwork of a craftsperson with years of experience in the trade ... and a good painter, in effect, places the crown on a truly great boat.'

The FORTH Bridge

There *is* a sense, a sort of Forth Bridge sense, that I have painted our boat myself. Each year in about March I pull out from beneath the bow a variety of tins of original paint and begin to touch up those parts of the boat that have degraded during the course of the previous year. It might be the handrails, forecabin wall and stern deck one year; scuffed bow decoration and pitted roof spots the next. These touch-ups take place sporadically over the spring and summer. Come autumn a few strokes of gloss black are usually applied to various scrapes and gouges we've picked up along the hull sides over the year.

PREVIOUS PAGE *Freshly painted roses and castles. This cruiser stern narrowboat belongs to the artist and is something of a practice ground and showpiece of his work, Grand Union Canal.*

RIGHT *Spectacular stern paintwork of a traditional narrowboat.*

DIY narrowboat-painting – the IMPOSSIBLE DREAM

Painting and touching up a steel boat involves a curious process that requires the alignment of myriad factors that will almost never coincide.

First, the temperature has to be right. If it's too cold the paint will go on like mud. Too hot and it will dry between strokes and build up ugly scars of overlap. Early spring and dry Septembers are usually best. So is autumn, but it can be a bit of a gamble. Come October the season can suddenly shut down into a horrible wet sleaze and that's it: your window of painting opportunity has slammed shut.

Second, you cannot paint while it is raining, unless you have a monster motorway overpass to tie up beneath, which is a pretty depressing place to be in the rain. Similarly, it will be too moist to paint in mist and fog. If it is snowing you know it is too cold to paint!

Almost as important is the need for a relatively calm day, as the smallest puff of wind will stir up tiny cyclones of dust, no matter how thoroughly you have swept your decks, and speckle your beautiful paintwork. Even worse is dust and grit raised from the towpath. A couple of cyclists race by and suddenly your fine gloss handiwork has taken on a matt finish. A rogue dirt-biker can destroy a day's work in a single pass. So, if possible, moor up against turf or find somewhere rural where you're not likely to be much disturbed for a few days. Alternatively, it doesn't hurt to damp down the towpath beside your boat with a few buckets of canal water; walkers and cyclists tend to avoid the damp patches.

The time of day must also be right for painting. Early-ish on a nice day, just after any overnight condensation has lifted, is a good time to start. If it takes, say, three hours for your paint to become tack-dry after application, you must complete painting three hours before you expect the dew of evening to descend, otherwise your finish will be cloudy and mottled and you'll have to do it again.

In warm weather, a canopy of overhanging leaves can offer dappled shade that will condition the temperature of your steel boat and modulate the rate at which the paint dries. Just be mindful of birds roosting and making deposits overnight. In spring be on the lookout for petals, willow catkins and other 'tree fluff' that will be on the fly and that can gently float down and bed into your fresh paintwork. In summer, keep your boat away from lime and

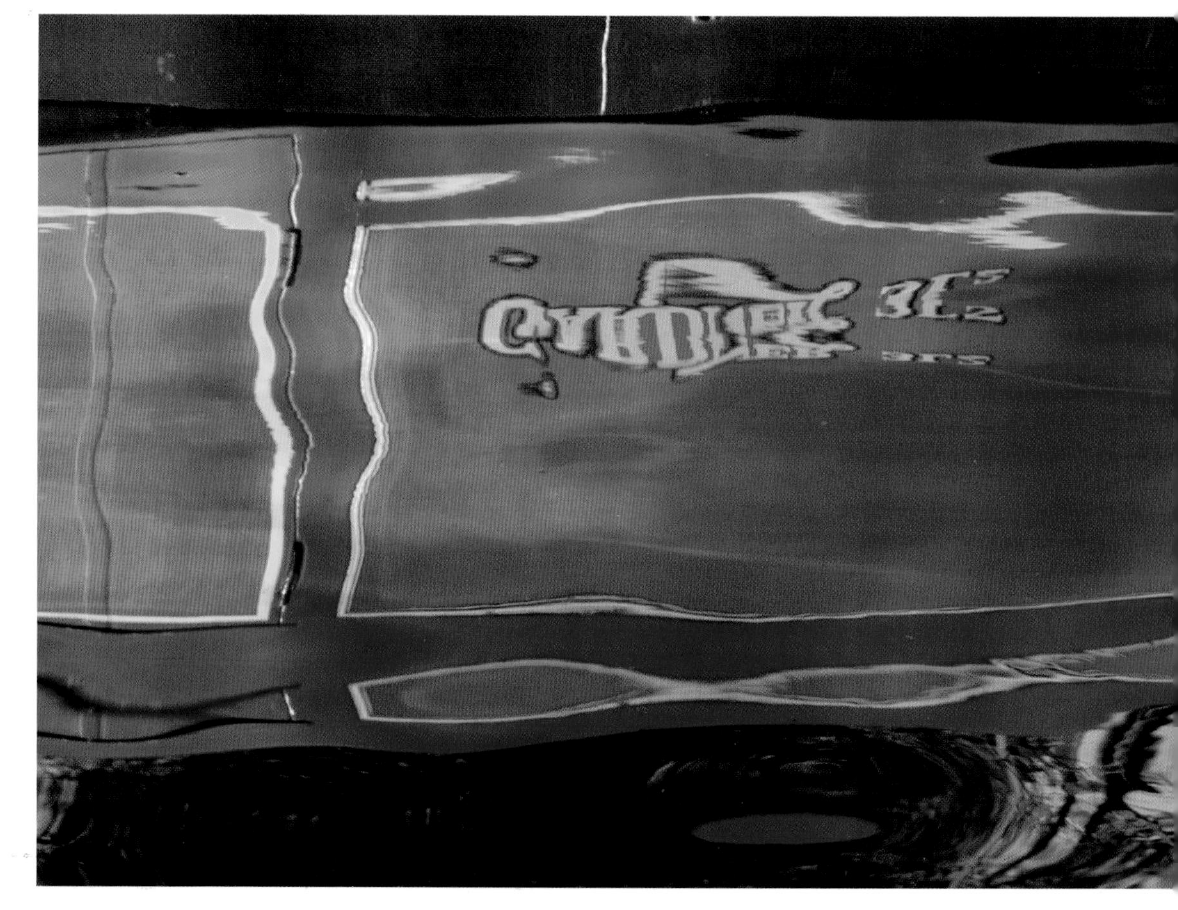

'As with life, luck plays an important role in painting your narrowboat, along with a bit of skill and timing.'

LEFT *Preserving the past: original roses and daisies painted on a cabin side.*

RIGHT *Beautiful bow paintwork, hand decorated barrels and a host of horse (and swan!) brasses.*

BELOW *Traditional narrowboat, with Gardner engine badge painted on the cabin side, reflected in calm waters.*

Regd at Gloucester № 505136
M.&M. PINNOCK
ENFIELD
Registered at Uxbridge №589
MORTON

'There is nothing more joyful to the eye than traditional narrowboat coachwork and signwriting.'

LEFT *A collection of beautifully painted working and ex-working boats, Little Venice, London.*

ABOVE *Some fine, freehand block lettering on narrowboat* Quince.

sycamore trees, whose resident aphids will coat your work with sticky 'honeydew'.

Depending on the season and your environment, be wary of bugs, flies, mosquitoes and other insects attracted to your shiny wet surfaces. Contrary to what I've already said, this is when a little fresh breeze can help keep them away while you are painting. If airborne critters do descend, just leave them until the paint is dry and then brush them off.

It will be easiest to paint your gunwales if your boat sits proud of the edge of an accessible mooring. Look for a sealed stretch of towpath edge, avoiding tall grass and scrub. Finally, on canals, it's a good idea to secure these near-perfect conditions close to a winding hole so that you can easily turn the boat around to paint the other side. Alternatively have a dinghy or inflatable boat handy.

As with life, luck plays an important role in painting your narrowboat, along with a bit of skill and timing. There's no need to become depressed if a completed job is not spot perfect – in the beginning all narrowboats and barges were working vessels and seriously knocked about.

Given all of the above, it is not surprising that a common reply to the question, 'Did you paint the boat yourself?' is, 'Yes, but I wish I'd had a professional do it!'

LETTING the PROS paint it

BELOW *A variety of hand-painted canalia on display at the annual Canalway Cavalcade, Little Venice, on the Paddington Arm of the Grand Union Canal.*

There is a lot of paint on a narrowboat: a 60-footer will probably have two 45-feet-long cabin sides and two 6-feet-wide bulkheads fore and aft. At about 5-feet high, we can estimate coverage at 510 square feet. The cabin roof adds another 270 square feet. The stretches of hull between gunwales and rubbing strake, and inside the bow and stern decks, will add about another 240 square feet. Forgetting for a moment about the 'special paint' on the hull below the waterline, the total exterior coverage is just over 1,000 square feet. Pretty sobering when you consider that the average car door panel requires about 10 square feet of paint.

Of course no vehicle relies on a single coat of paint. Besides the coat of primer that goes on the bare metal of a new or shot-blasted narrowboat, a proper job will see two full applications of undercoat and at least two (often more) finished gloss coats on top – usually hand brushed, but sometimes sprayed. So quadrupling the above, we have 4,000 square feet of coverage. Now we can start adding coach lines, scumbling and fine decoration.

There is nothing more joyful to the eye than traditional narrowboat coachwork and signwriting. Admire the deeply shaded, blocked-out lettering hand-painted in contrasting colours and feathered tones on a cabin side, perhaps set in a graceful arc over a brass porthole. Enjoy the bold white text set over bright red that shouts out a boat's former coal-carrying credentials. Oddly-shaped visual spaces are often filled with twisting floral patterns. Scumbling may frame side panels or cover entire rear cabin rooftops.

Then there are the beautiful roses and castles painted on the insides of hatches and doors: *the* traditional narrowboat embellishment. Each swag and cluster of roses, indeed every petal, is as unique as the fingerprints of the artist who painted it, as are the playful towers and winding rivers of each castle scene. Displays of diamonds are also traditional, in all colours and patterns, laid out along roof panels, across hatches, bulkheads and cratch boards, or strung end-to-end across bows like chains of good luck.

If you are looking for a traditional painter, the Waterways Craft Guild oversees, accredits and lists different levels of practitioners. Of course there is nothing like looking at boats you admire and asking their owners who painted them.

A traditional, professional narrowboat paint job with some signwriting and a modest amount of castle and rose decoration can easily cost you £6,000 and upwards for a 50-feet-long boat. Widebeams and Dutch barges, usually without the traditional decoration, will cost proportionally more. All of which, by now, should not come as any surprise.

TOP *Artistic camouflage. When the owner of narrowboat* Arbuthnot Jones *realised he had some inheritance money left over he commissioned artists Jim McCarthy and Ruta to paint this naturalistic canalside masterpiece on what must be one of the system's most unique boats.*

RIGHT *Traditional roses and castles freshly painted on the seating of a cruiser stern narrowboat. This is the artist's own boat – his paints are on the deck – that acts as a portfolio of his work. A good artist is able to reproduce all of these motifs from any angle, including upside down!*

How GREEN is LIVING on a BOAT really?

7

The quick answer is that few NARROWBOAT ENGINES are green, but MANY narrowboaters are. The more COMPLEX AND TECHNICAL answer I will come to in a moment.

ABOVE *A morning of wonder: a heron fishes under a bridge at dawn as sunlight is reflected off the rippled surface of the Kennet & Avon Canal and captured in the rising mist.*

'The outdoors has also become our garden. Its blackberries and apples fill our crumbles. Field flowers brighten the tabletop. Rooftop planters supply chives and oreganos, mints and thymes to enliven our meals.'

PREVIOUS PAGE *Note the turf roof, solar panel and spectacular plants festooning beautifully green narrowboat* The Hedge, *moored among wild flowers near All Cannings, Kennet & Avon Canal. The owner is a landscape gardener.*

BELOW *Canalside willows flowering in April sunlight, Tyle Mill, Kennet & Avon Canal.*

BOTTOM *A family of Canada Geese come for a visit.*

Knee-deep in NATURE

One of the first things land-living visitors to our narrowboat comment upon when looking out of the windows is that we are standing below the waterline. It is a curious source of wonder that the rippled surface of the canal or river is so close to view. With the side hatches open you can easily lean out and trail your hand in the water, or sprinkle breadcrumbs for sun-dazed fish hovering just below its surface.

On a boat you are immersed in an intimate world and very close to your wildlife neighbours. In the morning we often find swans attempting to nod through the side hatch to nip toast off our breakfast table. Throughout the day local geese, mallards, coots or moorhens will come by asking for a handout. (Feeding a few chunks of grainy bread to swans and other waterfowl is unlikely to do them any harm in the long term, but it is no substitute for the diet they seek out for themselves when you're not around!) Occasionally a duck will flap up on to the cabin roof to tap a merry dance. And I once interrupted a heron standing quietly, fishing off our bow. You are never alone on a boat.

Otherwise, most birds in the neighbourhood happily ignore us: the robins and magpies and blackbirds and thrushes. As do the wagtails and wood pigeons and great crested grebes. The swallows and house martins, as a group, keep their distance, while lone buzzards and red kites usually keep to the heights. Shy kingfishers and great spotted woodpeckers occasionally appear in nearby trees, and it is not unknown for a barn owl to make a mystical fly past. It can be a poetical existence.

On the towpath side of the boat we might find three cows staring vacantly down into the lounge from behind a wire fence, or a lone horse idling ... before suddenly galloping off. From the bank, wild flowers press at the windows. Reeds and yellow flag iris sprout around the bow. Willows, oaks, alders all lean in to offer their filtered green shade. Or ashes, beeches, or a poplar stand nearby.

The outdoors has also become our garden. Its blackberries and apples fill our crumbles. Field flowers brighten the table top. Rooftop planters supply chives and oreganos, mints and thymes to enliven our meals.

The sky, too, is always very close. Its clouds and sun and wind-blown leaves greet us on the deck. Its canopy of stars twinkle through the Houdini hatch at night. Its rain thrums a song on the steel roof and sends us to sleep.

OK, there's that romance of the inland waterways again. But it is difficult to think of a more intimate way of living in the countryside than on a boat. This close to nature, immersed in its seasons and textures, colours and scents, it becomes easy to marvel at, enjoy and come to respect its many different elements. In this way you start to become part of your environment. You begin to harmonise with nature whether you are tied up on a lost rural bend or within an urban cut. Through a sort of environmental osmosis you become 'green'.

TOP *Green energy: solar panels and snapdragons on a narrowboat roof.*

ABOVE *Spring has sprung.*

RIGHT *Tied up in rural Wiltshire near Honeystreet on the Kennet & Avon Canal, a very green part of the world that attracts not only boaters but other visitors from afar. This is crop-circle country and unexplained lights have been reported hovering over the nearby fields to the night.*

MINIMAL consumption, MAXIMUM pleasure

The notion that life aboard a boat is living the 'simple life' is a bit tongue-in-cheek. I have already outlined how advanced technology, clever fitting-out and modern appliances can make life aboard a boat pretty luxurious.

What you don't have is the luxury of mass consumption: there simply isn't space to store stuff. You will quickly reach a point at which any new item brought on board requires the removal of something of equal size, and you will probably think long and hard about which treasures go to a charity shop, to another boater or take their place on eBay. So, your reduced shopping habits and newfound ethic of recycling conspire to greatly reduce your environmental footprint.

Even better, given this zero-sum game, for us it makes sense to follow the aesthetic rule set by William Morris: 'Have nothing in your houses that you do not know to be useful, or believe to be beautiful.' Or, on boats, preferably both. So, own the most beautifully designed or crafted carpets and bedspreads, kettles and cabinets, curtains and candleholders that you can afford. If you have room for loose furniture, acquire pleasing tables and comfortable chairs. (Of course, making sure beforehand that you can get them *into* your boat through at least one aperture!) Cook with good pots and pans, drink from hand-thrown mugs and fine china, dry yourself on the best loomed towels and sleep under beautifully woven blankets and goose-down duvets. Rejoice in some decorated water cans, designer dog beds or sparkly solar lights. Compact living means green by default. Why not celebrate it?

'Rejoice in some decorated water cans, designer dog beds or sparkly solar lights. Compact living means green by default. Why not celebrate it?'

ABOVE *Greener than most: horse-drawn trip boat on the Kennet & Avon Canal.*

WHERE do YOU GO to the toilet?

'... living on a boat is not akin to perpetual childhood camping'

This is a surprisingly common question, so I can't really laugh it off. Clearly, there is a suspicion in the back of some gongoozlers' minds that the skills of a woodsman are called for here. Or some expertise with hedgerows. Or buckets. Or endless chains of pubs.

The subject of boat loos, and boaters' opinionated battles over the best system, could easily merit its own chapter. I have buried it here for lack of illustrations. That's my excuse and I'm sticking to it!

For those who have twigged that living on a boat is not akin to perpetual childhood camping, another surprisingly frequent question is, 'Does it go into the canal?'

To which the answer is, 'No, of course not. It only goes into the canal in France!' Well, it does all over Europe, which has canal and river systems built to a *much* larger scale than ours. And in boats at sea, it goes into the sea. Here in Britain, our inland waterways craft have sealed and contained toilet systems, usually designed in one of two basic types: pump-out or portable. That said, a recent, evolving and very green alternative starting to gain momentum is the composting loo.

ABOVE *On a narrowboat you become intimate with the reeds.*

Pump-out loo systems

Pump-out boats will have a poo tank built into them, either welded into the steelwork of the hull or installed separately as a sanitary plastic or stainless-steel holding tank and cleverly hidden during the fit-out.

Pump-out toilet bowls are made of ceramic or solid plastic and can look exactly like land-based loos. When the tank is full it requires emptying at a dedicated pump-out station, which are dotted all over the inland waterways as card-operated DIY machines or found as a service in many marinas and boatyards. Charges vary. Depending on the size of your tank and use, you might need to pump out every couple of weeks or every few months.

The beauty of pump-outs is that you can forget about this task for the weeks in between. Another bonus is that the process pretty much remains sealed from beginning to end, so there is less exposure to odour and content. Also, if you are so inclined, you can get other people to pump out your tank for you while you doddle about their chandlery looking at new cruising guides and funky tiller pins.

Portable loo systems

Portable toilet systems range from sophisticated cassette styles to very simple Porta Potti© types. Most portables are built of sturdy plastic, look a bit 'boxier' than land-based toilets, and have two parts: the loo top with a seat and water reservoir for flushing; and the bottom waste-holding tank.

The waste tank must be detached and emptied about every two or three days, depending on use, at a sanitary disposal (or 'elsan') point. Elsans are distributed more generously around the system than pump-out stations and are usually free of charge. With a bit of care, portables can also be emptied into regular toilets.

ABOVE *A combination of wind and solar power support life aboard this steel Caribbean cruiser on long-term moorings in West Mills on the Kennet & Avon Canal.*

LEFT *Family of swans insistent at the sidehatch.*

GREAT BEAR

LEFT *A quick start: Dutch barge burning oil (and ejecting river water circulated to cool its engine) pulling out from Henley public moorings on the River Thames. Most diesel engines will 'smoke' a little on start-up for anywhere between 20 seconds and five minutes, depending on their age and type.*

RIGHT *Meadow flowers on a River Thames bank.*

Cassettes are sealed waste-holding units designed to be transported like small but heavy suitcases. Spare cassettes can be stored separately for 'emergencies' or used on a rotational basis. Top-end systems have ceramic bowls, plumbed-in water, with waste electrically flushed to remotely located cassettes.

One advantage of portable systems is that they are usually less expensive to install than pump-out ones. Also, you don't necessarily need to take the boat anywhere to empty them, which is handy if you are frozen in, have engine failure, don't mind a bit of a walk down the towpath with a cassette in tow, or run a vehicle in parallel with your boat. The downside for some is that you must deal with toilet waste every few days rather than every few weeks.

Some continuously cruising liveaboards rely on a pump-out system but keep a small, inexpensive portable toilet as a backup.

Compost systems

Composting toilets on inland waterways craft are fairly rare, but their use is increasing. They are moulded in robust plastic and tend towards 'throne size', although this is changing. The best units separate liquid and solid waste to be dealt with separately, and the whole process is waterless.

On the solid waste side of the system, a handful of sawdust is sprinkled down the bowl after each use. Composting takes place in a drum or chamber below, which is vented/aerated by a 'chimney'. Options might include a 12-volt fan to encourage the drying process and even electric heating. Natural microbial action (*not* bugs and worms!) also contributes to the composting process, bolstered by periodic application of commercial peat and microbe mixes. The result is that waste is reduced by about 80 per cent and transformed into a black, earthy loam. Perfect for gardens. For two-person liveaboard use, expect to empty the compost between four and eight times a year.

On the liquid waste side of the system, urine is collected in a container and disposed of separately, as you would with cassettes, but much less frequently.

Most users swear that their composting toilets do not smell at all, or perhaps occasionally give off a subtle 'earthy' scent, because odours simply go up the chimney. Talk with other users before opting for this system, if only to confirm where the latest eco-loo technology stands.

The best loo?

Arguments about the best toilet system for a boat, which thoughtfully weigh up all the pros and cons, always seem to lose out to personal preferences. So follow your instincts.

By the way, the water in your sink and shower *does* go into the canal, so as a green boater you might want to use biodegradable washing-up liquids and soaps that have a minimum impact on our aquatic environment and wildlife friends.

'The main reason you do your utmost to preserve water, electricity and fuel on a boat is because they require work, time and inconvenience to replenish.'

NATURAL RESOURCES:
water, electricity and heating fuel

In a very functional way, living on a boat immediately focuses the mind on finite resources. You will soon find yourself automatically wondering, 'How much water do we have left in the tank?', 'How much electricity is stored in the batteries?' and 'How much coal or wood (or diesel, or LPG) do we have on hand to keep us warm?'

Boating also makes you think about waste. Not just how much space is left in the loo tank before it needs emptying, but also about where you can next get rid of domestic rubbish and where you will keep it until you reach a suitable waste disposal point or bin.

If you don't think about these things you quickly find yourself up the proverbial creek without a paddle. The main reason you do your utmost to preserve water, electricity and fuel on a boat is because they require work, time and inconvenience to replenish.

ABOVE *Rainbow colours of a sun brolly reflected in a polished stove chimney.*

RIGHT: *Solar panel aimed directly at the sun on the Grand Union Canal near Blissworth.*

Water

When your water tank is getting low you must stop at a water point and spend about half an hour filling up – if you are cruising. If you have stopped in a beautiful spot for a week and you run low on water, you will need to make a special journey, probably half a day's cruise, to fill up at the nearest water point.

Few experienced liveaboards will run taps while brushing their teeth or take long showers without turning off the water between rinses, unless they have a permanent water source to hand or are moving daily. Showers and washing machines use substantial amounts of water, and human nature is such that we will often forgo such water-intensive 'luxuries' in order to gain a few extra days of relaxation in a particularly pleasant or convenient spot. If you take your repose time seriously you might even decide to wash Victorian-style, standing over a basin, saving even more water. And remember, it is environmentally sound to postpone washing up until there is a decent load of dishes!

Electricity

Electricity is also a precious commodity. When you generate it yourself and realise that storage is limited by the size of your battery bank you naturally take care using it. Turning out lights becomes a habit, as does setting the fridge thermostat lower, keeping an eye on laptop surfing and eschewing 1700-watt hairdryers.

You also quickly learn that electrical appliances draw different amounts of energy, and seek ways of reducing the load. LED cabin lights, for example, use one-tenth the energy of halogen bulbs, so you can light up for ten times longer. Microwave ovens and washing machines notoriously draw a lot of power. Some liveaboards use energy-hungry devices only when running the engine, and often while cruising. Or they do without them.

Of course, running a diesel engine isn't the only way to produce off-grid energy. Boaters in particular are pioneers in alternative energy generation. Any portable technology that helps keep batteries topped up is extremely valuable

CANOPUS
GB

'Like those who habituate Scottish castles and historic homes, you'll probably develop a close relationship with a favourite jumper or fleece during the frosty months of winter.'

and explains the sometimes-obsessive interest in the evolution and use of solar panels and wind generators. After an initial investment, the energy these systems produce is essentially free and green. They can radically reduce the amount of time your 'big diesel engine' (or small petrol generator) needs to chug away recharging batteries.

Heating fuel

Whether you heat your boat with logs, coal, diesel or LPG, you become aware that these fuels too are precious and limited resources. Precious in that they are not cheap when buying them by the bag, tankful or canister. And limited in that you can run out of them if you don't manage their use. Only so much fuel can be stored on a boat, even precariously piled on the roof. Like water, heating fuels involve work and hassle to replace, such as cruising to a supplier, hauling them back to the boat along the towpath or organising delivery to an obscure public mooring with vehicle access. That is why fuel-trading boats are so valuable and popular, especially if they pass by your boat in winter.

Even scavenging deadfall wood requires a good deal of time and physical effort in order that you can transport it to your boat in usable chunks. If you use a chainsaw, you are dependent on managing yet another fuel: petrol. Petrol, by the way, requires very special storage to keep it safe on a boat, should only be poured into equipment *on the bank or towpath*, and usually entails a journey with jerrycan in hand somewhere off-cut to collect it.

Given the precious nature and storage challenges of heating fuel, boaters tend to use only what they need and when it is needed. Like those who habituate Scottish castles and historic homes, you'll probably develop a close relationship with a favourite jumper or fleece during the frosty months of winter.

Happily, compared with a flat or house, a boat requires much less fuel to keep it warm as there is much less space to heat. The volume of space inside the living quarters of a standard 57-foot narrowboat, for example, is roughly equivalent to that of a 15 square-feet lounge with an 8-feet-high ceiling: 1,800 cubic feet. Admittedly a boat is a bit more challenging to heat because of its separate cabins, but you get the ecological drift.

RIGHT *Swivel-and-tilt solar panels amid a rooftop garden of flowers, Henley, River Thames.*

518326
GEORGINA

DIESEL engines

Let us now speak of engines. There is no getting away from the fact that most inland waterways boats are dependent on large diesel (occasionally petrol) engines for their propulsion. This is always noted by those sceptical about the greenness of residential boating.

Furthermore, a good number of liveaboards run their engines for an hour or two or four on days when they aren't even cruising – to top up the charge of their batteries. Given that these engines emit a variety of pollutants, such as carbon monoxide, nitrogen oxides and various particulates, this is not great.

We might feel better when we consider that a diesel automobile may burn four or five times as much fuel as a diesel-driven narrowboat over the same period of time. The car would pollute the atmosphere four or five times as much.

On the other hand, we might feel a bit worse if we thought about covering distance. To travel from Birmingham to London, say, we'd need to run our boat engine for about a week, rather than using the car for a day. So the boat would pollute much more than the car. Then again, boating on the inland waterways is rarely simply a matter of getting from A to B; it accomplishes much more than that. As a result the comparison isn't quite fair.

Consider the amount of *work* a boat engine can accomplish. It can easily shift half a dozen people and somewhere between 10 and 35 tons of living quarters and self-sustaining equipment (a home, in fact) from one place to the next. In comparison, a car burns an extravagant amount of fuel to move a few passengers and a picnic basket the same distance. Or to get an individual to work.

Also consider that a traditional working narrowboat pair (motor and butty) can transport 70 tons of cargo. How many polluting car journeys would it take to transport 70 tons of flour or coal from Birmingham to London? Quite a few.

Unfortunately, engine comparisons get even more complicated. Modern car and boat engines have stringent and sophisticated emission controls built into them, so newer models pollute less than older ones. But this doesn't necessarily mean new engines are environmentally greener than vintage engines. Take, at random, a 1930s Gardner diesel, lovingly tended over the years and still powering a narrowboat up and down the waterways, which is reasonably common. How many times would a modern engine be junked and replaced

BELOW *A classic Bolinder single-cylinder engine, on display at The Canal Museum, Stoke Bruerne, on the Grand Union Canal. Occasionally it is still possible to hear these semi-diesel engines fill a valley with their ponderous, rhythmic 'thunk... thunk... thunk'.*

over the same 80-year period, incurring the extra environmental manufacturing costs? Six times perhaps? Eight times?

Where boat engines have an environmental advantage over automobile engines is in routinely multitasking. Like cars, they take you from A to B, often in beautiful comfort. But most narrowboat engines will also heat and supply free hot water to your taps, shower and/or central-heating system. They will also have a second alternator to generate and store useful amounts of electricity in a battery bank, to sustain your domestic electrical needs. Given a good set of batteries and a smart recharging routine, this stored energy will run cabin lights for the evening, keep miscellaneous water pumps active, ensure a 12-volt fridge stays cool, power a music system and even deliver a couple of hours' TV viewing. Not many cars, or even camper vans, will do that.

Given the dependence of boats on engines, probably the best we can do environmentally is to make sure our diesels are well serviced and maintained. And look forward to the day when biofuels (chip fat and vegetable oils) are easily available in good quantity along the cut.

ABOVE *Coal, diesel and smokeless fuels. Coal and fuel boats can make life much easier when living on the cut in winter. Most will drop off coal even if you are not on your boat when they pass by, and payment can be as simple as leaving cash in an appropriate outdoor place or electronic transfer. Talk with your local supplier!*

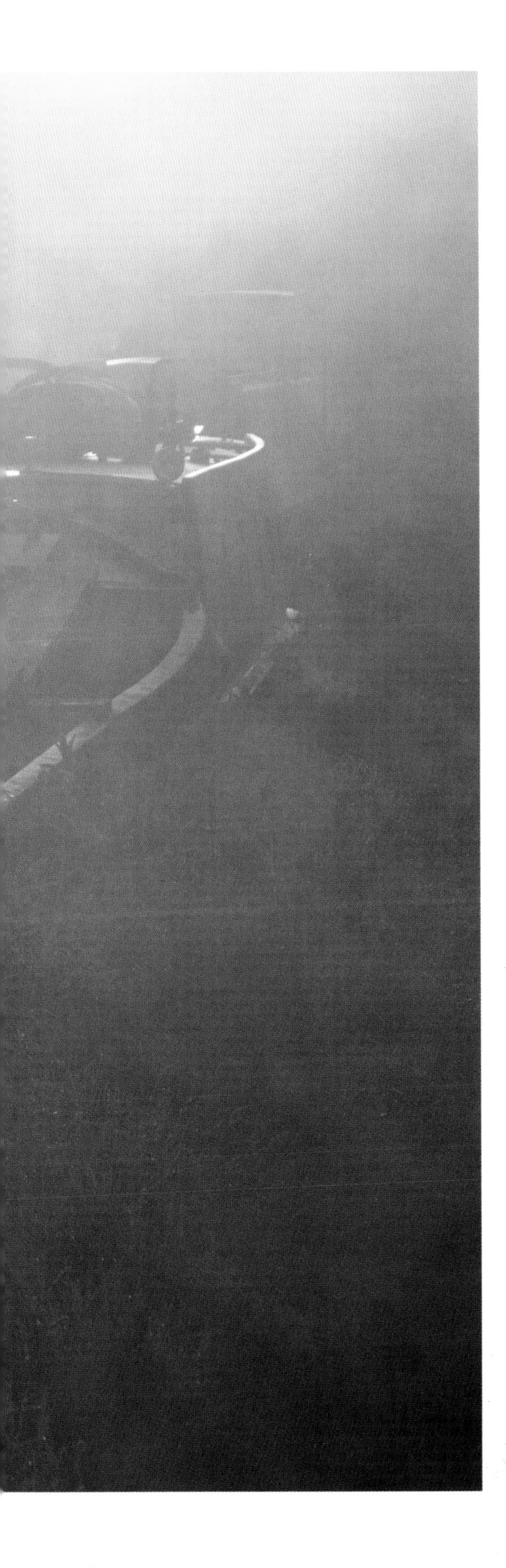

HYBRID diesel-electric ENGINES

Interestingly green, but not cheap, are the hybrid diesel-electric engines that have begun to appear on a handful of inland waterways craft. Under normal canal conditions, propulsion is delivered by an electric motor component of the engine. The length of time it will operate depends on the size of the battery bank: somewhere between three and ten hours. With this set-up a boat only draws power when it is actually moving and not, for example, while sitting waiting for a lock to fill. In this 'electric motor mode' you are not burning fuel, so you are not polluting your environment. And cruising becomes beautifully smooth and whisper quiet!

When the batteries get low, or you need some real oomph navigating a river, you switch to 'diesel engine mode' by firing up the engine and driving the boat in the regular way. In diesel mode the electric motor becomes a powerful generator that quickly recharges your battery bank.

I read an article a couple of years ago about a videographer who commissioned a narrowboat with a hybrid diesel-electric engine. The boat could be used as a near-silent and vibration-free platform from which to make cruising videos of the inland waterways. 'Hybrid cruising' and 'slow TV' certainly offer one antidote to a hyperactive digital age.

LEFT *An empty working narrowboat in the morning mist opposite Hungerford Marsh, Kennet & Avon Canal.*

ABOVE *Sheep at Cleeve Lock, River Thames.*

GREEN footprints

By living knee-deep in nature you will almost automatically reduce your carbon footprint simply because of storage restrictions and the need to think more about natural resources and waste. More interestingly 'nature' becomes the place you inhabit rather than visit, and this network of green inland passageways becomes your back garden and its wild creatures your neighbours.

RIGHT *Swans and newly born cygnets like this family are your neighbours, and you will get to know them intimately!*

BELOW *Pretty flowers keeping company with a tunnel lamp.*

'... "nature" becomes the place you inhabit rather than visit, and this network of green inland passageways becomes your back garden and its wild creatures your neighbours.'

LEFT *Spot the widebeam boat. A picturesque rural mooring with views of wide-open spaces. Hungerford Marsh Lock and ancient right-of-way swing bridge is to the left, near Hungerford, Kennet & Avon Canal.*

BELOW *Tea for two: celebrating the Queen's Diamond Jubilee at the Henley-on-Thames Coronation River Pageant.*

STEP ABOARD...

A WELL-READ ARK

At 53 feet long this is the shortest boat presented here, but is ideal as a two-person liveaboard because of its unusual layout and space-saving features.

Jim Batty, Karen Chester and their cat Hobbes continuously cruise their semi-trad in all seasons: sometimes short distances, sometimes long, tending to slow down in the winter. They were recently offered a private winter mooring at the end of a jetty, with an electricity outlet and water tap, which made a pleasant change to full self-sufficiency during the chilly months.

Both work from the boat in different ways. Karen is an historian with a talent for popularising history through her illustrated lectures and personalised tours. All of her communication with clients, organisation of 'gigs' and research is carried out from the boat – through laptop, mobile phone and a website – with occasional broadband Wi-Fi support from coffee shops and public libraries along the way. She also designs and creates beaded jewellery.

Jim researches and writes from the boat but also holds permanent, part-time work as a graphic and photographic designer. They are both prepared to travel by public transportation from their floating home to anywhere in the country and have been known to make some very lengthy commutes from far-flung moorings!

At the bow of the boat is a shallow well deck long enough to hold two bicycles, and an anchor when they are cruising rivers. Two folding chairs easily fit out here and the flat top of the forward locker can support a full tea service and cakes, or the obligatory chilled cider and bar snacks after a full day's cruising. During the winter months, the locker below can hold five 25kg sacks of coal for stoking the stove. Beneath the deck, accessible from inside, is room to store half a dozen plastic storage crates and a deflated inflatable kayak on top of the 380-litre water tank.

You enter the boat through glazed Dutch doors and step down into a large forward cabin that extends half the vessel's interior length. This unusual room has the lounge at the front, followed by an open sitting area by day and roll-out bed by night. The ceiling and walls are lined with light ash panelling neatly framed in warm cherry wood, and the feeling of space is emphasised by the 6½-feet-high ceilings and four large double-glazed windows.

The decor is a curious combination of English Arts and Crafts, handmade ethnic and animal representation. Quirky beasts inspired by children's books populate the boat, as well as bison, rams and wild cats sculpted by Karen's artist father.

The entrance steps are beautifully crafted in contrasting hardwoods and have drawers built into them, useful for storing maps and fire-lighters. Beside them sits a blue enamelled solid fuel stove with a big 'screen', accompanied by a fluted brass coal scuttle. Warm Persian carpets appear throughout the boat. Because they are handmade, almost any shape can be found to fit the odd proportions of a narrowboat cabin. Sitting on them are two leather reclining chairs, a hand-painted Indian cabinet, a crafted metalwork magazine rack and a pair of speakers – driven by a car-type music system installed in the galley. The William Morris 'Strawberry Thief' print curtains – in two colourways as they couldn't decide which they liked best – are held up by woven toggles and can be rolled down over the windows when needed. Overhead is a glazed Houdini hatch that gives satisfying glimpses of the sky and mystical views of the heavens at night.

To one side, along the full length of the lounge, is a series of bookcases and a repurposed display cabinet. Jim and Karen love books and it is a habit they will never lose despite the availability of e-books and e-readers. Building a library on a boat, though, is a zero-sum game and they seem to go through phases of acquiring one collection only to get rid of another to make room. As books are not light, their weight is counterbalanced by a couple of 56lb coal weights in the bow locker to keep the boat in trim.

At the furthest end of the cabin is what looks like a large built-in sofa. In the daytime you can relax against its full-length backrest under the window, or recline against the far cabin wall chaise longue-style.

At night it takes about three minutes to convert this unit into a full double bed: the base rolls out partway into the passage; the backrest drops down into place; the thick padded quilt is removed to reveal a duvet and pillows at the end, which are unfolded and tucked into place. Simple. In the base are three deep drawers. As it is easy to heat this long cabin with the solid fuel stove, half the boat remains warm and dry throughout the winter. No climbing into an icy back-cabin bed here.

The side passage at the far end leads to the stern half of the boat. First off the passage is a walk-in closet with two doors that open outwards either side to form a changing room. A full-length mirror is framed on the inside of one door and a map of the inland waterways' system lives on the other. The closet is 3 feet wide and has 50 hangers of clothing on the rail that runs across it. There's full-height hanging space on one side and half-height on the other plus various hooks, so boaty and business clothing can be kept separate and fresh. This was one of the features the owners found lacking in so many second-hand boats for sale and that has helped make this one so easily liveable. Below the clothing is a laundry basket and seasonal storage, so the closet is no longer 'walk-in'.

Next off the passage is the wet room. Its toilet is a porcelain, electronic flush, pump-out model and beside it is a small sink and vanity unit. On the opposite wall is a thermostatic mixer shower. A clever, minimalist feature is the stainless vertical strip attached to the wall beside the door. At a touch the thin housing, hinged at the top, slowly rises on a gas strut to extend a narrow accordion shower curtain across the width of the room. Look closely at the floor edges along three sides and you will see the gaps where shower water disappears into the custom-built tray beneath – to be automatically pumped overboard. Brilliant!

The end of the passage opens into the dining area and galley. There is an intimate, 'boaty' feel to this end,

with wood-rimmed portholes, a swinging brass lamp overhead, a pigeon box with tiny light portals let into the ceiling and lots of varnished woodwork.

The dining area is cosy, with a built-in table flanked by bench seats. Various flaps, doors and drawers in the seat bases reveal more storage and one houses the inverter – key to the boat's 230-volt electrical system. What transforms this end of the boat are two large side hatches at either end of the table. When these are swung open the great outdoors and the whole spectacle of canal- and river-life floods in. Suddenly you notice fish splash, waterfowl squawk, trees wave, people and boats pass by, and a breeze brush your cheek. This area makes for great al-fresco dining and is the perfect bright and airy place in which to spread out and work. If it is too windy or chilly, Plexiglas panels, stored in the passage, can be quickly slipped into place.

Just over a narrow counter is the short galley. All of the cabinetry here is made of solid ash that is complemented by brushed stainless worktops. The working area is wider than usual and has another thick Persian carpet underfoot. A line of shiny cooking utensils hangs over a four-ring gas hob and stainless-steel sink with drainer. Beneath the counter is a bank of drawers, a marine larder fridge and a gas oven and grill. Against the back wall is the ultimate off-grid luxury: a hand-cranked coffee grinder.

On the other side of the galley are counter-to-ceiling cabinets. Their shelves decrease in depth the higher they are positioned because of the 'tumblehome', or angle, of the cabin sides. So egg cups and spice jars are stored at the top and serving dishes and sacks of flour reside at the bottom. In the cupboards below the counter are housed the boat's diesel central-heating boiler, which feeds two radiators and the towel rail in the loo and heats water, as well as an electrical cabinet, solar controller and tool store.

Against the back wall of the galley is an ingenious set of mahogany steps that access the semi-trad stern deck. They are designed to slide upwards and hang vertically out of the way when not cruising, offering an extra 2 feet of floor space. Another good trick lies beneath your feet. Roll back the carpet and you will find a long floor hatch that opens to reveal a naturally chilled cabinet against the boat's base plate. Perfect for storing a dozen boxes of juice.

It is the flexibility of its layout that makes this boat so eminently liveable. The large multi-purpose fore cabin means that it can be used and enjoyed in a variety of ways during the day, and it makes a generous, cosy space in which to sleep at night. Similarly, the separate dining area and galley are multi-functional, used for eating, working and – with the side hatches open – simply lazing about in an extremely pleasant environment.

Of course Karen and Jim say that flexibility of *attitude* is also important when sharing a narrowboat. And having two distinct, workable ends to the boat supports this extremely well. It gives them their own separate space when they want it, as well as comfortable room to enjoy life afloat together with their books and animals.

DOES he
(the cat, dog, parrot)
LIVE on the BOAT?

8

ABOVE *A cat's eye view of the Kingston-upon-Thames' waterfront.*

'... for every cat on board a boat there is a different cat-way they live on it. And they will quickly let you know what suits them best.'

PREVIOUS PAGE *Keeping an eye out on a traditional narrowboat.*

BELOW *An illustration of canalside humour.*

BOTTOM *Toad in the grass.*

CATS

We have a cat, named Hobbes, who lives on board with us. As far as he's concerned it's his boat and we, his people, look after it for him so that he can live a quiet and comfortable life. That's him in the photograph doing what he does best, sunning on the bow and gazing at the world. He's also pretty good at sleeping in an armchair, or wherever a patch of sunlight falls.

People, and especially children, are just thrilled when they see Hobbes living on his boat. You can't imagine the cries of glee we have heard drift in from the towpath when he is sitting out on the roof or bow. Locals who regularly walk their towpaths (people we have never met) greet him like an old friend and ask him how he is doing and whether he has had fish for tea. Or they exclaim how much he looks like Poppy or Wilson or another cat they have known and cherished in the past. If I happen to be out on deck at the same time, children and adults alike will smile and point and excitedly call out to me, 'Does he live on the boat too?'

I think this astonishment at cats on boats has something to do with a common belief that felines and water don't mix. True, on the few occasions Hobbes has fallen in – misjudging a leap from the side hatch or losing his footing on the slippery steel roof – he is clearly not thrilled about bathing. But he does have some innate ability to 'cat paddle' long enough to get to shore or, more often than not, until I pull him out. What he *does* enjoy is being towelled dry afterwards. Mmmmmm. We usually hang a rope fender over the downstream side of the boat to help him climb out if needed, but this is probably more for our own peace of mind than anything else.

People are amazed he doesn't wander off. But that's just Hobbes and his upbringing. We've never had to resort to ringing a bell whenever his breakfast is served, a trick many boaters use to develop their pet's Pavlovian homing responses. Nor have we had to worry about him leaping off the boat when passing through locks, as the instant the engine starts chugging he curls up in his cat bed and goes to sleep.

LEFT *Morning walk beside the Thames opposite the public moorings at Christ Church Meadow, Oxford.*

ABOVE *Beautiful painting of a cat on* Spirit of Marmalade. *A surprising number of boats are named after favourite pets.*

Every wandering boat cat we have met or heard of has always returned home ... eventually. They just might take anywhere from a couple of hours to a couple of days to do it. Cats do know their boat and seem to remember their route taken from it.

When I was a child our family tabby once escaped from our car and disappeared about 6 miles from home. He turned up at the front door a week later, having traversed woods, fields, a river, a motorway and suburbia. So it seems cats have a type of innate 'GPS' to help guide them home.

Unlike many other boaters' cats, Hobbes is thankfully uninterested in bringing back mice to the boat, stalking songbirds, or even collecting fluffy ducklings as they parade by. The bell on his collar remains nothing more than a fashion accessory. He has an alternative nasty habit though: eating fresh grass on the bank and coming in to regurgitate it on to the carpets.

Our main worry is Hobbes' stupid fearlessness of dogs, but only when he is on his boat. He is all raised hair and spit if a dog noses up to the bow, and he simply doesn't back down. For this reason we keep an eye and ear out for him when he's outside by a busy towpath and leave the door ajar. If he meets a wandering dog on the towpath he races for the boat or runs up a tree. Perhaps of greater concern are fast-paced bicycles. For him they seem to appear out of nowhere and have quirky movements that are impossible to anticipate. Actually, that's exactly how they appear to me, too!

Ultimately, I think that for every cat on board a boat there is a different cat-way they live on it. And they will quickly let you know what suits them best.

DOGS

'Who can resist the notion of cruising the inland waterways with a canine friend at your side sharing in the great adventure?'

I have never owned a dog, but Karen has regaled me for years with the antics of her family's boxers Sinbad and Nikki. Every year we seem to say that we would have a dog if work commitments didn't take us away from the boat so often or we could take a dog to work ... and it would have to be a terrier ... and probably a border ... but possibly a cairn or scottie. Then again, it is usually pets that find *us*.

There is a strong tradition of dogs living on boats; Dutch barge dogs and schipperkes are famous for it. Perhaps as a result, few people seem surprised to see a dog sitting in the bow of a narrowboat, or peering down from the rail of a barge, or flopped across the cockpit of a cruiser. But many are charmed. Who can resist the notion of cruising the inland waterways with a canine friend at your side sharing in the great adventure?

Boating seems the perfect life for a dog. There is an abundance of safe and pleasant walking a couple of steps from home. Cruising offers plenty of fresh air and exercise, new smells, a variety of landscapes to explore and the society of other dogs and their walkers.

The big question always seems to be, 'What's the best kind of dog to have on a boat?' I know people are looking for a particular breed here, but I really think the best dog is the one you are prepared to love and welcome aboard; the companion you are willing to look out for, clean up after, train and enjoy spending time

BELOW *Comfortable cruising with a playful dog on board, Shropshire Union Canal near Nantwich.*

with. We have seen everything from dachshunds and whippets to huskies and bullmastiffs very happily living aboard boats.

If pushed a little further, logic might suggest the best dog for boating is a small or medium-sized one that can be carried over an arm, with relatively short hair that doesn't shed much, that is nimble on its feet, not averse to swimming, who barks only at intruders ... and likes boats. I'm not sure, though, how far logic will take you in selecting the perfect companion. How about a reasonably portable, sweet-natured mongrel from a rescue centre?

It seems obvious that smaller dogs are going to demand less of your confined boaty space than larger ones. But what about psychological space? A rambunctious Jack Russell will probably seem to 'take up more space' than a mature Labrador. This is because temperament, age, breed and training also enter into the equation. Dogs have their own sense of space, whatever their size, and while one might be happy with a bed on the floor by the fire, for example, another will do best with its own private bunk. Everyone who lives aboard a boat (or camper van, bus, railway carriage, or indeed a house) must decide for themselves the personal space they need to enjoy their lifestyle and the extent to which they wish to share it with others, including dogs.

Size and breed will affect the ease with which your dog can get on board and off, and different boats offer different types of access. Stepping on and off the stern of a narrowboat is fairly easy for most dogs, whereas climbing out of a deep bow deck is much more difficult. Consider which end of the narrowboat *you* will be using. The gunwales of some cruisers and wire railings of small sailboats can prove difficult barriers for some dogs. Gangplanks can also be awkward things to traverse (even for humans), depending on their surface and incline, and spook some dogs. You may have to carry your dog across.

Are you physically and safely able to carry your dog ashore? On tidal rivers, high banks and steep moorings can sometimes be tricky or impossible for dogs to negotiate on their own. Tied up beside a looming quayside, your sole access to the fields of gold or urban parkland above may be a tall slippery ladder. If you regularly cruise tidal rivers it's probably a good idea for your dog to wear a life jacket, and if you get one with a handle fastened to the back you will have less trouble helping it ashore. If your canine friend is a true heavyweight you may want to train them to use a patch of artificial turf on board when tied up to difficult river moorings.

By the way, if you do have a large dog (or a couple of dogs) living aboard, think about where you are going to store their food. Rooftop boxes may help, or a nice big deck, or you may need to run a vehicle and make regular trips to the pet superstore.

When cruising, some dogs like to perch on the cabin roof to evaluate the world from a high, blanketed position. Others prefer to sit by your feet, transfixed by the propeller wash. Whatever their habits, be sure to establish a safe place in which your dog can wait while locking (either on board or on shore) and when passing through canal tunnels.

A final word on etiquette. The towpath is your garden path. You will only have to tread dog poo through your boat once to realise how disgusting and irresponsible it is to not clean up after your animal. They can't do it themselves. If you don't, there's a good chance your liveaboard neighbours will let you know what they think. This characteristic straightforwardness of the boating community is one of its many attractions!

Having decided for yourself the best kind of dog to have on a boat, you should then be in a good position to answer the second most popular doggy question of liveaboard boaters, 'Can he swim?'

ABOVE AND BELOW: *Friendly terrier enjoying passers-by on the bow of his narrowboat, Great Bedwyn, Kennet & Avon Canal.*

PINEAPPLE

'EXOTICS'

There is a surprising number of other pets that successfully live on board boats, including: cockatiels, parrots (keep away from draughts and windows), rats, ferrets (block up small hidey-holes), rabbits (train to not eat dangling electrical cables and dig up carpets), fish, birds of prey (preferably with their own butty), guinea pigs (separate males and females) and humble chickens (usually with a coop on the bow, but a chicken run on the roof is probably going a bit far).

LEFT *A friendly welcome (and a watchful eye).*

RIGHT *Portrait of a dog worked into the decoration of a cabin side panel, Abingdon, River Thames.*

BELOW *African grey parrot taking the air on a stern hatch while cruising.*

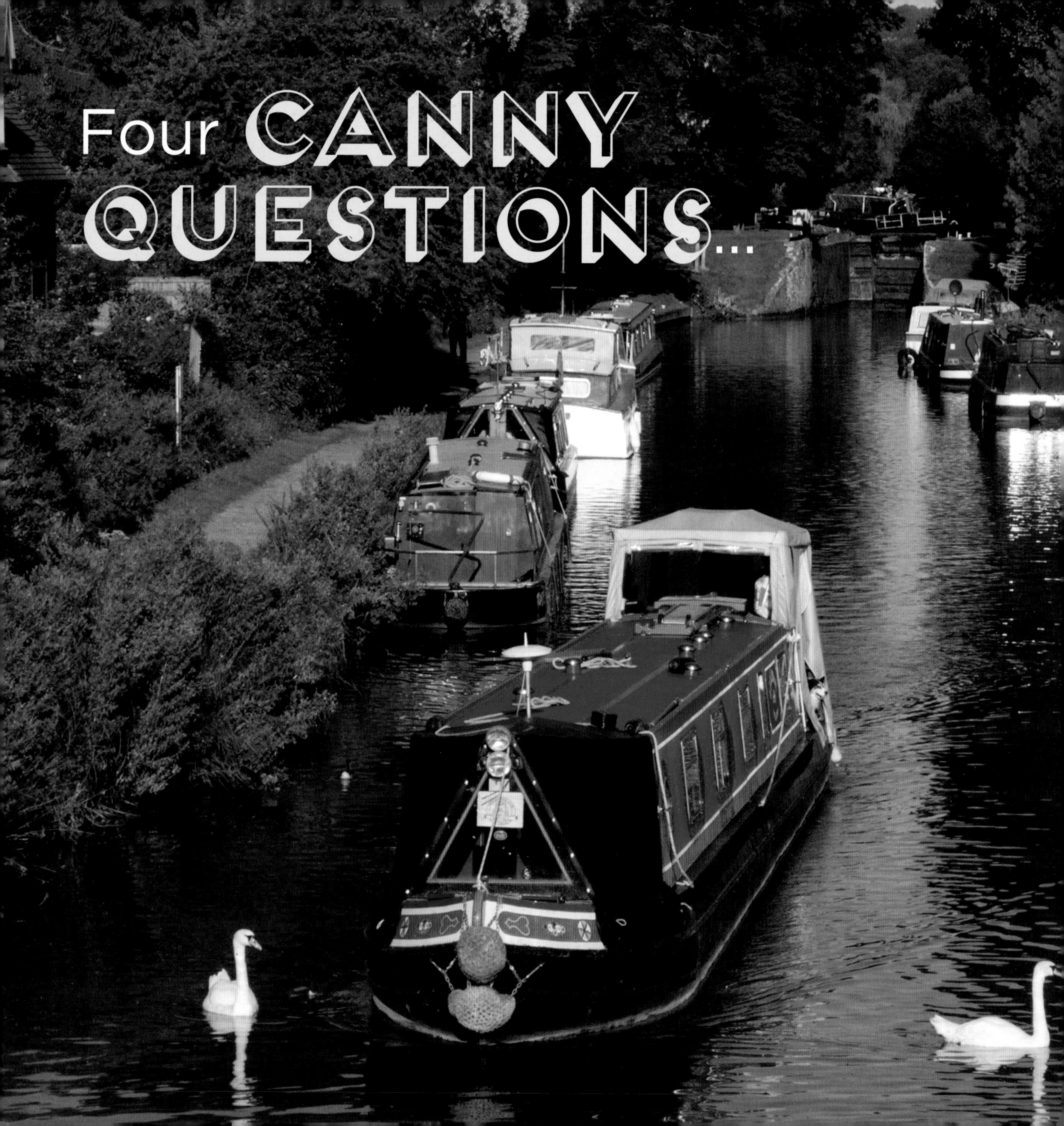
Four CANNY
QUESTIONS...

9

about continuously CRUISING

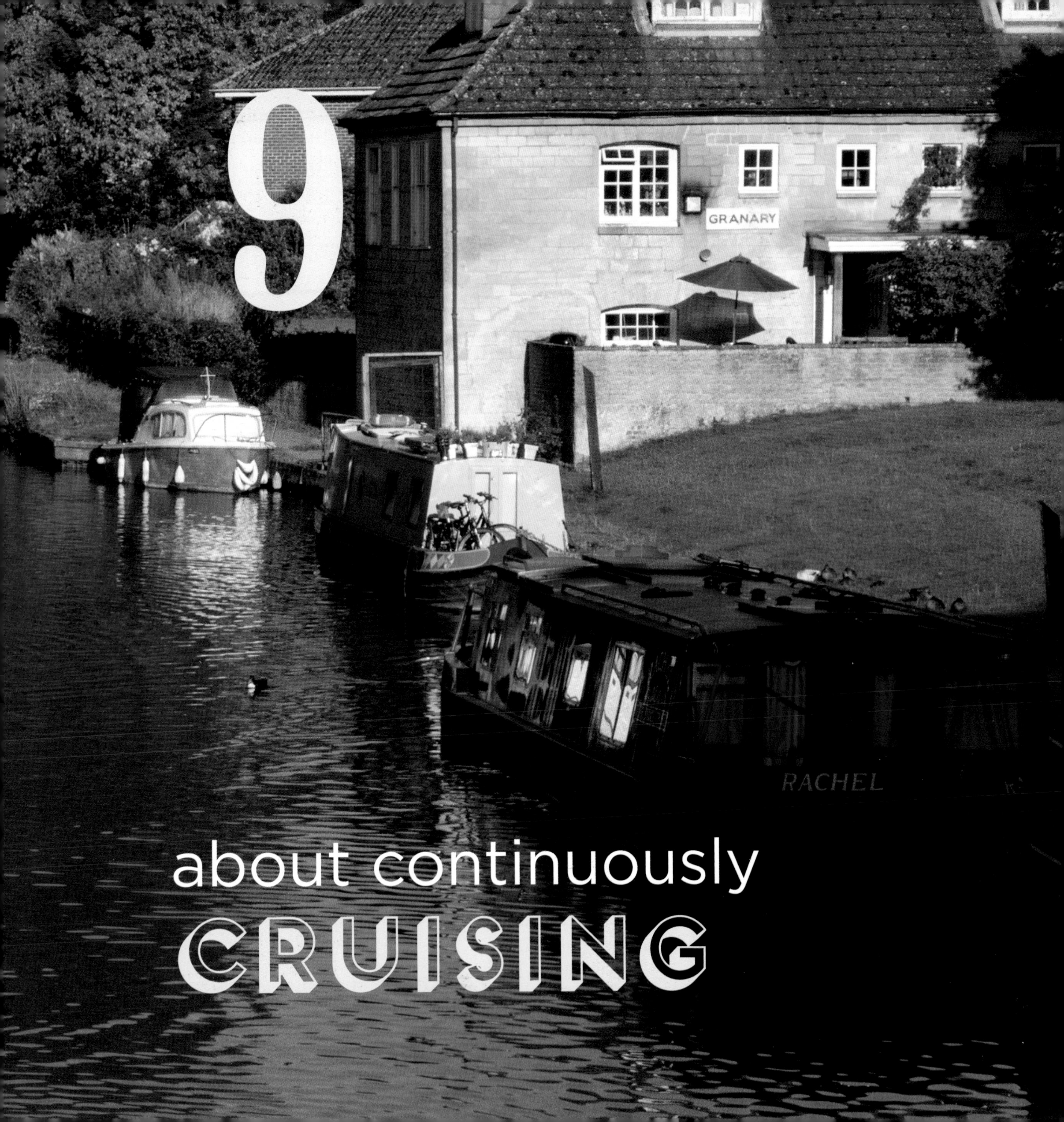

These are the **SAVVY QUESTIONS** I regularly hear from people curious about how you can actually **LIVE** on a continuously cruising boat and remain **SOCIALLY** plugged in.

ABOVE *Barges, static houseboats, cruisers, a small ship and narrowboats huddled together at low tide on the River Thames at Kew Bridge, London.*

'... it seems remarkably easy to get online and stay in touch, even if it sometimes means running a modem up to the top of a gardening stake on the roof to catch a signal...'

PREVIOUS PAGE *Cruising through Hungerford Basin, Kennet & Avon Canal.*

TOP *Rosie and Jim – probably the most famous narrowboat liveaboards.*

BOTTOM *Fully committed to a wandering lifestyle.*

If you have a bona-fide residential mooring all of the things discussed in this chapter except, perhaps, internet access are accomplished in the same way they are from a flat or house. Your post is delivered to either a mailbox near your boat or to the marina where you moor – sometimes to a shelf or pigeon box in a facilities block. You register with a local doctor and dentist in the usual way, your children go to a local school and you commute to work either by public transport or a vehicle parked handily nearby. Depending on the local authority, you may also be required to pay lowest-band council tax. Permanent residential moorings (and especially good ones), though, are difficult to find and most are oversubscribed.

Many other types of residential moorings are set up on an ad-hoc or temporary basis, usually dependent on the goodwill, flexibility or canniness of a marina manager or riparian landowner. They will offer a few basic facilities for living aboard, but generally expect you to have your own postal or forwarding address elsewhere and to be self-contained.

HOW do you receive POST?

1) RELY ON FAMILY OR FRIENDS. Most continuous cruisers and those on temporary moorings use the address of a family member or friend for mail contact. Having people you trust means that important-looking mail can be opened and read to you over the phone if required.

2) HIRE A MAILBOX. This is a good alternative to friends and family. Mailbox companies are found in cities and towns across the country, often located close to universities and colleges as they are popular with students. You generally rent a mailbox within the shop and access it with your own key. The rental fee depends on the size of your box and length of the hire period. Post is addressed to you by name at an ordinary address – the company's address – and your mailbox number may be incorporated into it as 'Suite 37' or 'Flat 37' or 'Studio 37' or whatever is appropriate.

RIGHT *Widebeam on Canal & River Trust mooring beside St Mary's Church in Great Bedwyn, Kennet & Avon Canal.*

BELOW *Narrowboat tied up on the River Kennet in the heart of Reading during the winter floods of 2014. In the background stands The Blade office building.*

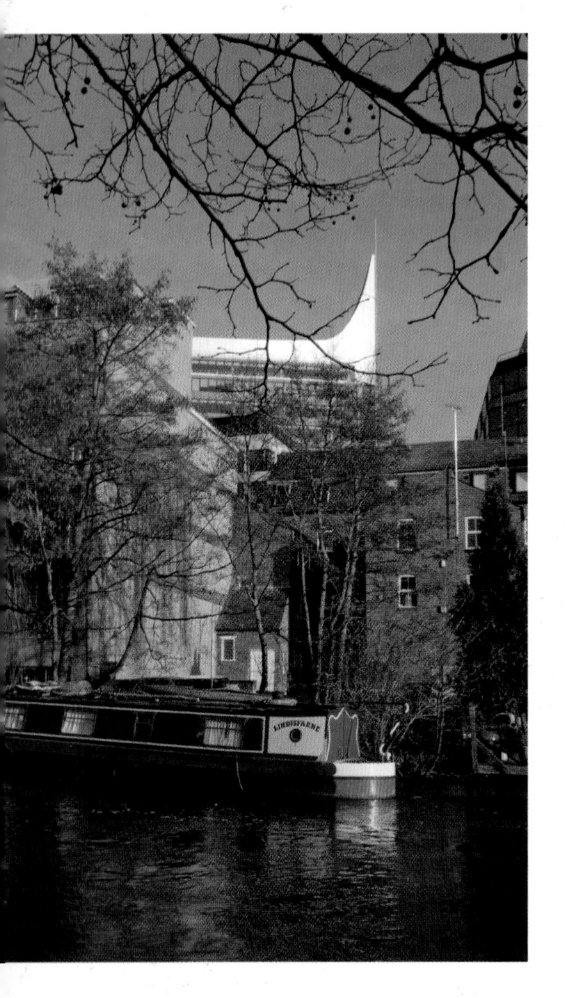

Mailbox companies usually offer a variety of useful services, such as: forwarding post to a destination of your choice either at set regular intervals or following phone and email requests; remote mail-checking or email alerts; and accepting, signing for and holding parcels. Our mailbox service holds packages for five days without charge and will forward anything anywhere for the price of postage.

Some services can offer you the ultimate virtual existence. They will open, scan and email you letters, provide hot-desk office space and meeting rooms, even rent self-storage lockers for the stuff you can't fit on to your boat.

3) POSTE RESTANTE still works as well as it ever did and is available at most, but not all, Post Offices. Go to the branch where you'd like to receive mail and ask for their full address (or search for it online), then pass this on to your contacts. Mail should be addressed as:

Your Name
POSTE RESTANTE
Post Office Name
Full address of the Post Office
Postcode of the Post Office

Remind senders that they are required to put a return address on anything sent, and you should take some form of ID with you when collecting it. Post from the UK will be held for 14 days and from overseas for one month. The poste restante system is meant to be a temporary way of receiving mail for people travelling around. 'Temporary' is going to be open to interpretation by individual branches, so it's probably a good idea to present your 'sunny side' when collecting mail and not abuse this valuable system.

HOW do you see a DOCTOR?

ABOVE *Late moon rising over calm waters. View from the public moorings at West Mills, Kennet & Avon Canal.*

TOP RIGHT *Serious bow fender on a serious boat.*

BOTTOM RIGHT *Narrowboat passing Stoke Lock lockkeepers cottage, River Wey Navigation, Surrey.*

1) KEEP YOUR LAND-BASED DOCTOR. Many new continuously cruising boaters retain the doctor they had while living on land, making the journey from wherever they happen to be whenever an appointment or check-up is required. Although potentially costly in travel fares and time-consuming, this makes sense if you have built up a good relationship with a trusted GP. After all, they know the history and state of your health better than anyone else.

I think it's best to be upfront with your doctor and tell them about your new lifestyle, and how you would like to retain them. Most people, including doctors, find the idea of living on a boat fascinating. And your GP has probably come across more patients living in unusual circumstances than you suspect: homeless people, real travellers, other boaters, caravan-dwellers and a host of temporary visitors. GPs are also more aware than most of how some individuals can easily fall through the bureaucratic cracks of the NHS, the world's largest health bureaucracy.

2) REGISTER WITH A DOCTOR in a place that you regularly visit. Counter to a persistent myth, you do not need to have an address to register with a GP. You can legitimately register using a surgery's address. (This is what homeless people do.) If you already have a forwarding address, you can also register a local address, something like:

Name of Your Boat
The Wharf
Local Town or Village
Local postcode

Just make it very clear to the surgery that they must use your forwarding address (*not* the 'Wharf' address) if they need to contact you by post. This is especially important for hospital appointments.

Dave and Gillie Rhodes, whose boat is featured in one of the *Step Aboard....* sections, have written about finding and retaining a doctor while continuously cruising and some of their excellent suggestions include: try and register with a doctor who is familiar with boaters; check out rural practices, which are often friendlier than urban ones; when you do find a doctor you like, it is a good idea to visit the practice at least once or twice a year to keep yourself familiar; and to renew prescriptions while cruising find a local chemist that will accept a fax from your registered GP, then contact your home surgery to set up the fax transfer.

3) VISIT A LOCAL GP on a temporary basis while cruising. If you become ill or need medical attention while cruising you can receive emergency treatment at any GP surgery in the country for up to 14 days. After this you would need to register as a temporary resident.

You can register as a temporary resident with a GP if you are in an area for more than 24 hours but less than three months. You remain registered with your usual 'home' doctor, but you can see your temporary GP for the duration of that three-month period.

If you are unfortunate enough to need extended medical or hospital attention while cruising, it's a good idea to let the local canal or river authority – such as the Canal & River Trust or Environment Agency – know about your situation. They are usually very sympathetic and will allow you to keep your boat in one place for as long as necessary.

'... it's best to be upfront with your doctor and tell them about your new lifestyle, and how you would like to retain them. Most people, including doctors, find the idea of living on a boat fascinating.'

NEWBURY
LOCK

HOW do you USE the INTERNET?

Cruising liveaboard boaters link to the cyber hive through wireless mobile technology. Very generally speaking (for it is never certain), wherever you can get a mobile phone signal you can get an internet connection from the same network. The strength of that connection is dependent on myriad factors, ranging from weather conditions, looming nearby obstacles and local levels of broadband use, to the politics of shared telecoms masts. Given these challenges it seems remarkably easy to get online and stay in touch, even if it sometimes means running a modem up to the top of a gardening stake on the roof to catch a signal.

Not surprisingly urban areas have better coverage than rural ones. In the countryside, if you can actually see a mast poking up from behind a village or beside a hillside wood, all the better. Indeed, for some boaters mooring position is dictated by signal strength.

Computing on board

Because of limited space and regulated amounts of 230-volt power, laptop computers are usually king on boats. They will be relied upon to accomplish all the workaday tasks normally demanded of a PC on land, such as web-surfing, writing emails, using social media, doing research, entertainment, as well as running hefty office, hobby and professional software packages. Curiously, a similar shift in device use often sees tablets act as laptops and mobile phones stand in for tablets. Sort of.

We have friends who live on a small sailboat on the Thames who stream and watch videos on a mobile phone Velcro-attached to the low ceiling over their bunk. For another, their full set of cruising guides only exists on their tablet. We also know a number of people who run businesses with a global reach solely through their laptops. And this book was written and all the images post-produced on a laptop ... sitting in an armchair ... before a fire ... steaming mug of tea to hand!

Most laptops connect via a dongle (mobile USB device), or a wireless Wi-Fi hotspot router (MiFi), or through mobile phone tethering (either physically linked with a lead, or with the phone acting as a Wi-Fi hotspot.) If you plan on tethering make sure this is acceptable on your phone contract. An external aerial is another option that helps you reach out and connect. Tablets usually have their own SIM card and connect directly.

Don't forget that all these devices will need to be recharged regularly, so it will be important to keep those leisure batteries fully topped up. One good idea is to install a 12-volt car 'cigarette lighter' socket somewhere convenient and use adaptors to run and recharge your devices. Solar panels will be your saviour in producing energy for storage.

LEFT *Wide-lock banter.*

HOW do you HOLD down A JOB?

'If you work for yourself and can contract out your services then you are in a fine position to support a continuously cruising lifestyle.'

There is a variety of ways in which people work while continuously cruising. Here are the main methods they use to support themselves.

Self-employment

If you work for yourself and can contract out your services then you are in a fine position to support a continuously cruising lifestyle. Similarly, if you can practice a skill or trade and promote it from the lounge, dining table or back cabin of your meandering boat, you are ahead of the game. A few examples of people who successfully work from a continuously cruising boat are software engineers, web designers, writers, researchers, photographers, some types of craft workers and artists, consultants, accountants, visiting hairdressers, visiting masseurs and alternative therapists, tour guides and lecturers, and musicians.

The main challenge for most self-employed pursuits is attracting and securing enough customers to make the business viable. If you have successfully run a business from a flat or spare bedroom, for example, and are prepared to be flexible, you stand a good chance of transferring your business to a boat. No doubt you will (continue to) rely heavily on mobile communication and meeting clients in cafes or pubs or at their workplaces.

Some professions, trades or crafts require more support than others. You may need to run a vehicle in parallel with your boat (see below), or require regular supplies, or indeed travel with a workshop butty in tow. All of which will strongly influence how and where you cruise.

Many self-employed boaters supplement their income with temporary or seasonal work. The flexibility and mobility of liveaboard boating can act in your favour, and may surprise you with some unusual and interesting opportunities.

Self-employed boaty work

Boaty trades are a popular source of income for liveaboards. All boaters are likely to need the services of a marine electrician, carpenter and fit-out person, diesel mechanic and a plumber/gas-fitter at some point. Or they may want to commission someone to make rope fenders to protect their boat, or hire a traditional canal artist to decorate it.

One couple we met very slowly explored the inland waterways while designing, making and fitting cratch covers and pram hoods for other boaters. Another woman, who made all of our curtains, cruises a large regional circuit and from her floating workshop expertly designs and sews any soft furnishings a boat could possibly need, while her husband handles the initial measuring up and final installation.

What successful, cruising, boaty business people seem to have in common is a reputation for high-quality work at prices markedly lower than those of their land-based or canalside competition. And that reputation precedes them through the waterways' grapevine. Few of them are looking to make a fortune, but simply want to support their cruising lifestyle doing something they are good at and enjoy.

LEFT *Hi ho, hi ho, it's off to work we go.*

OPPOSITE: *What's in a name?*

BELOW *Signwriting and fuel supplies: a matching pair of boats that work the western end of the Kennet & Avon Canal throughout the winter months.*

ABOVE *Ultimate mobility? A motorcycle tension-strapped to the short tug deck of a narrowboat.*

ABOVE *This unusual, converted narrowboat with its distinctive 'stepped' full-length cabin, easily finds room for a range of two-wheeled transport.*

ABOVE *Another clever way of transporting a motorcycle: rotating, extendable bow ramp.*

Working for other people

It is possible to work for an employer and continuously cruise, but doing so depends on a unique combination of factors: your job's location and its relationship to surrounding waterways; access to a wide network of public transportation (if you don't run a vehicle); and a dedication to cruising and replenishing your floating home on days off.

The reason for dedication is that as a continuous cruiser you are expected (it is a legal requirement) to move at least every 14 days in a 'progressive' fashion, not simply back and forth between a few bridges or locales. As I have inferred in previous chapters, cruising, watering-up, visiting sanitation points and general maintenance can easily eat up a weekend, so part-time or very flexible working conditions, if you can secure them, make life much easier and more pleasurable.

Geographically speaking, it is usually easiest to work in a city or town surrounded by, at the junction of, or criss-crossed with at least two inland waterway routes. This ensures that you can cruise widely and experience an interesting range of environments – which is surely the *raison d'être* of a cruising life.

Commuting from the inland waterways

1) RUN A VEHICLE alongside your boat. Some continuous cruisers run a vehicle in parallel with their boat, usually a car or van. This makes commuting to a workplace from wherever they are tied up a doddle. On the down side, it is less of a doddle when cruising, as it effectively doubles the time needed to move from one place to the next. After moving to a new location you must return to the vehicle (by foot, bicycle, bus, train) and move *it* to the new mooring spot. Where you tie up is also likely to be dictated by proximity to relatively safe parking. That said, some people view the freedom and comfort to get around by car and continuously cruise as the best of all worlds. It's probably a good idea, though, to drive something not-too-bright-and-shiny if you plan to take it down muddy lanes in winter and park it in lonely lay-bys beside remote stone bridges.

Of course some vehicles can ride with you on your boat. Bicycles are great if you can find room to stow them, and are relatively inexpensive to run. Some boaters swear by folding bikes. Motor scooters sometimes find a place to stand on a tug deck, cruiser stern, or even semi-protected between the panels of a semi-trad deck. Proper motorcycles, because of their size and weight, really require dedicated mountings – balanced to retain boat trim. A removable or articulated boarding ramp would also help you get them on board and off without busting a gut.

2) COMMUTE BY TRAIN OR BUS – all aboard the 07.14. Canals and railways are often found together. This is because, historically, their routing and construction faced the same basic geological and topographical challenges, and their economics dictated similar paths: follow ground contour as much as possible to avoid expensive deep cuttings and high embankments.

Despite this, the canals and railways have made odd bedfellows over the years. After the heyday of canal-building in the 1790s, some of the canals began to go into decline as early as the 1820s, outpaced by advances in metal-track and steam-engine technology. By 1845, nearly a quarter of canals had sold their assets to railway companies, and it was not unknown for some railway owners to deliberately run down their canal stock in favour of rail. What followed over the next century was a steady

decline of commercial life on the canals and near abandonment of the waterways' system itself. Much of the network would have been filled in and built over had it not been for a couple of pioneering canal campaigners and their followers in the late 1950s, who turned the fate of the inland waterways on its head – to be reborn as the vast leisure network we see today.

So it is indeed great, if ironic, luck that modern cruising boaters are able to tie up at such a variety of moorings across the network and catch a convenient train to work. Be thankful and make good use of it.

Commuting from a different station or stop every couple of days or weeks is odd in that you must consciously note where you need to come home *to* at the end of each day. That said, I have only ever once stepped out at a platform and wandered over to the canal ... only to remember that our boat was tied up at the next town.

Another commuting oddity is that the time your train departs in the morning will change from place to place as you cruise, and you will want to re-set your wake-up alarm accordingly. Fares will change for different journeys, as will the way you buy your tickets. You might purchase a ticket from a booking office, a platform machine, from a conductor on the train (in which case you need to remember where you got on!), or occasionally at your destination. If you move from one rail company's territory to another, ticket details and discounts will also change.

There's no such thing as a 'typical commute' and how far you travel to work is partly down to the thickness of your wallet and personal stamina. Consider the distance some land-based commuters are prepared to journey to the big city. It is possible to commute 50, 60,

ABOVE *Home aboard a traditional working boat. Three abreast at the Braunston Historic Narrowboat Rally, Grand Union Canal.*

'What successful, cruising, boaty business people seem to have in common is a reputation for high-quality work at prices markedly lower than those of their land-based or canalside competition.'

'... it is indeed great, if ironic, luck that modern cruising boaters are able to tie up at such a variety of moorings across the network and catch a convenient train to work. Be thankful and make good use of it.'

70 miles to a particular workplace from remote waterways. We travelled from five different counties into London for a few years. Mind you, we commuted to part-time jobs with off-peak rail fares. It would have been unmanageable (for us) otherwise. A long commute can greatly depend on the flexibility of your work and employer. Journey times for these sorts of commutes can easily be one to three hours each way, so you must be up for it. The pay-off, of course, is your time spent 'knee-deep in nature' on your boat during time off.

Over the months and years, as cruising brings you closer to and further from your workplace, the time and money invested in longer commutes tends to be offset by the shorter journeys. Like many, we have tended to cruise closest to workplaces in the winter and furthest afield in the summer.

Of course most of what relates to commuting by train equally applies to bus and coach. One niggle is that some buses only accept exact cash payment, so you need to be armed with a small sack of coins for each trip. Obviously the more changes required during a commute the more exacting the logistics become.

I like good, old-fashioned, printed rail and regional bus schedules illustrated with maps. They are great for planning commutes, but also suggest possibilities for exploring an area. Alternatively, you can often track down timetables online or on-phone, download an app, or make specific A-to-B route-finder searches through a transport company's website.

LEFT *Tied up on the visitor moorings at Abbey Meadow, Abingdon, River Thames.*

ABOVE *Chilling out after a full day's work, above Rushey Lock, River Thames.*

OPPOSITE: *Railway line and the Kennet & Avon Canal in close quarters, Little Bedwyn.*

3) CYCLE TO WORK. Many cruising liveaboards rely on and enjoy using their bicycles to get to work, often cycling the full distance on towpaths and back roads while they are within comfortable cycling range, and using them to reach railway or bus stations when they are far flung. I rarely cycle more than 5 miles each way, although I know some keen cyclists who will cover 20 miles or more going to work and the same distance back to the boat. There is nothing more invigorating and pleasurable than cycling an empty, well-metalled towpath in the dewy freshness of an early summer morning. There are also few things worse than cycling down a humpy, mucky towpath at night in blowing winter rain.

Most intercity trains restrict the conveyance of ordinary bicycles during rush hours, and few buses carry them at all, but both allow you to carry a folding bike. This might be a good investment if you regularly need to cycle at either end of a rail or bus commute. In addition, folding bicycles are easy to store on a boat. Otherwise buy a second-hand knock-about bike for exclusive use at the workplace-end of your journey, and lock it up at the station or somewhere safe nearby on days off.

The fact that you live on a boat almost ensures you will become the subject of interest, sometimes envy, and occasionally awe within any workplace. At least until the novelty wears off after a couple of years. Or when you come in smelling of coal smoke. If your colleagues can get used to this, they will quickly get used to your curious commuting habits involving towpath walks, train travel and bicycles.

'The fact that you live on a boat almost ensures you will become the subject of interest, sometimes envy, and occasionally awe within any workplace.'

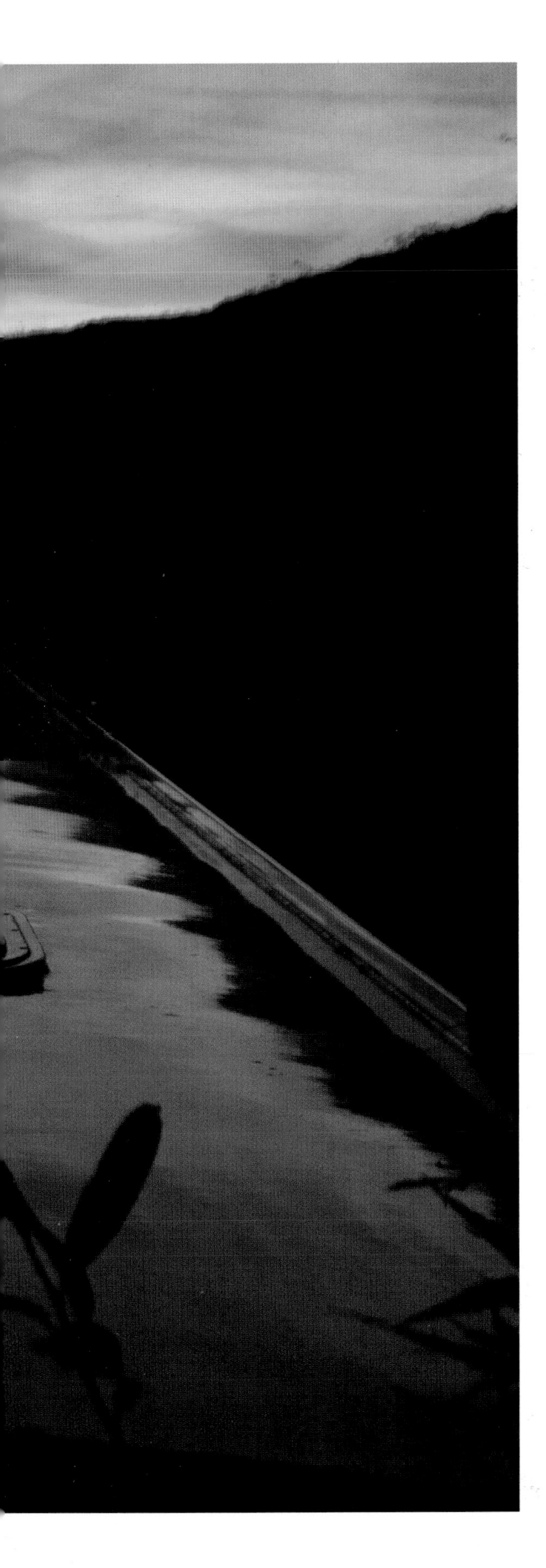

... and FINALLY

Many people, from workmates and family and friends to complete strangers on the towpath, are curious about narrowboat life. They wonder at these colourful, traditional floating toy-boxes. They marvel at how these slow moving – but moving! – vessels can become 'home'.

I know from all those *What's it like* and *How do you do it* questions about living on a boat that it remains a mystery to many. Equally, I am also familiar with the smiles and excitement and interest that accompany most of those questions, and for me this adds to the joy of living afloat. It has made thinking about this alternative way of living on the inland waterways, and photographing its environment, a real pleasure. And I hope this collection of answers to those questions helps encourage a greater understanding of narrowboat life. Who knows, perhaps some of you will discover your own perfect boat and work out the best way to 'do it'.

LEFT *Sunset reflected in a cabin rooftop, near Bugbrooke, Grand Union Canal.*

ABOVE *Still thinking ... about the best boat to call 'home'.*

GLOSSARY

aft located towards the back

barge a flat-bottomed vessel wider than a narrowboat originally designed for the transportation of heavy or bulky goods

bilge/bilges the lowest, inner part of a boat's hull, for example below cabin floors and decks

blacking generally, the process of taking a narrowboat out of the water, pressure washing and cleaning its hull (the surfaces that normally sit under water), then applying coats of special paint – either bitumen or 2-pack epoxy – to protect it from rusting

boat builder someone who designs or constructs a narrowboat shell out of rolled sheets of steel and usually installs its diesel engine and ballasting

boat fitter someone who 'fits-out' the interior of a narrowboat shell, including the construction of its floor, cabin walls and ceilings, installation of windows, doors, electrics and plumbing, design and construction of built-in furniture, cabinetry and woodwork, and puts in appliances

boatman's cabin the small living quarters at the stern of a traditional working narrowboat. Modern reproductions are often sumptuously decorated in traditional style and usually contain a small boatman's stove, a bed that folds into a cupboard and a cupboard that folds down as a table

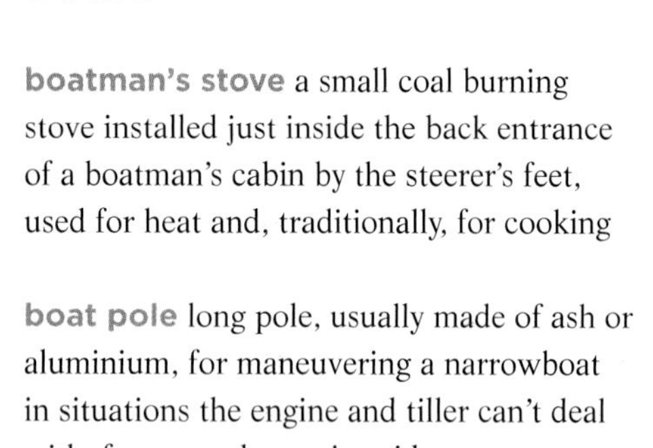

boatman's stove a small coal burning stove installed just inside the back entrance of a boatman's cabin by the steerer's feet, used for heat and, traditionally, for cooking

boat pole long pole, usually made of ash or aluminium, for maneuvering a narrowboat in situations the engine and tiller can't deal with, for example moving sideways across a double lock or extracting the boat from shallows

bow front, pointy end of a boat

broker person or business that sells boats

Buckby can traditional can of fresh water kept on a narrowboat's cabin roof. Today they are known for their elaborate roses and castles decoration

bullseye thick, round, convex glass lens fitted into the roof of a narrowboat to allow extra light into the cabin

butty unpowered narrowboat, towed by a 'motor'

cabin main bedroom in a boat; more generally, any room in a boat

calorifier insulated tank that heats and stores domestic hot water. The water may be transfer-heated in a variety of ways, including from: an engine's cooling circulation system; a central heating type boiler; and/or a 230-volt immersion heating element

cant low, flat section or rail around the edges of bow and stern decks, sometimes incorporating ornamental scrolls

chandler (chandlery) a person (or shop) that sells supplies for boats

continuously cruising living and travelling from place to place in a progressive manner by boat, not staying in one place for more than 14 days

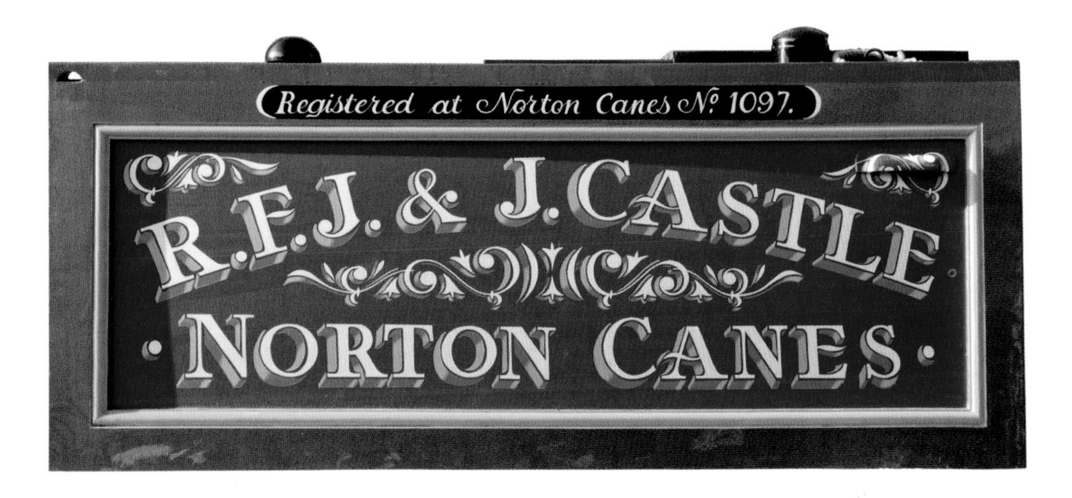

cruiser boat with flared bow made in a variety of lengths and widths, usually of GRP (fibreglass), with inboard or outboard engine and driven by steering wheel. They usually need to be insulated for full-time liveaboard use

Danforth anchor a relatively lightweight and compact hinged anchor that folds flat, so is easy to store

Dutch barge large, flat-bottomed boat, usually with a covered wheelhouse, originally designed to carry cargo on inland or estuary waters, converted for liveaboard or leisure use. Alternatively, a modern replica of such a vessel

Elsan disposal point plumbed receptacle for disposing of waste from portable toilets, often free of charge

fit-out see **boat fitter**

fore located towards the front

galley kitchen

gangplank a board or plank put between a boat and land so that people can get on and off

gongoozler a boating term for non-boating people attracted to canals and boats

gunwale (pronounced 'gunnel') the upper side decks of a narrowboat (usually 4-5 inches wide). The width and height of gunwales also affect the interior layout of a narrowboat, for example: lower gunwales allow for larger windows above them; higher gunwales allow for wider beds below them

hatch aperture in the wall or roof of a boat, or the opening and closing cover for it, for example side hatch, sliding hatch

Houdini hatch roof hatch, usually glazed

inland waterways include tidal and non-tidal rivers, canals, large and deep lakes, and lochs. The UK has over 4,000 miles of inland waterways

inverter an electronic device that changes direct current (DC) to alternating current (AC). On a boat it will typically 'invert' 12v DC power stored in batteries into 230v AC power suitable for operating household electrical appliances

jetty a small pier at which a boat can be moored

leisure batteries a bank of batteries, separate from the engine starter battery, used to store energy for operating a boat's pumps, lights, domestic appliances, etc

lock a chamber with gates on either end used for raising and lowering boats between stretches of water on canals and rivers

longboat Viking longboats (or longships) had very shallow draughts and were strong and flexible enough to cross open ocean, so could go almost anywhere. There have been very few longboats on the inland waterways for about a thousand years

marine fridge/freezer compact, 12v fridge and/or freezer specifically designed for marine use

mooring place to tie up a boat, for example on the bank of a canal or river, in a marina, beside a dock, on a pontoon or at the end of a jetty

- **leisure mooring** a non-liveaboard mooring
- **offside mooring** canal mooring on the opposite side to the towpath
- **online mooring** linear mooring, where boats are tied up end-to-end along the bank
- **residential mooring** a liveaboard mooring

motor motorized narrowboat of a working pair, that tows a non-motorized 'butty'

mushroom vent air vent on a boat cabin's roof shaped like a mushroom

narrowboat (one word) on the UK's inland waterways this generally refers to modern boats around 7-foot wide used for leisure and living aboard

narrow boat (two words) usually used by purists to refer to an original working boat around 7-foot wide

pigeon box small, gabled ventilation aperture in the roof of a narrowboat with hinged panels (often glazed with tiny portholes). A much larger version of the pigeon box, found on widebeams and Dutch barges, is a 'dog box', whose prime function is to let in natural light from above

pontoon a floating dock in a marina or on a river. Finger pontoons extend outwards like fingers; inline pontoons follow the shore

port nautical term; narrowboaters usually use 'left'

pound stretch of canal between locks

pump-out station facility for emptying a pump-out toilet tank

reach stretch of river between locks

roses and castles traditional British folk art that originally decorated a working canal family's narrowboat, furniture and paraphernalia. The origins of the roses & castles theme remains elusive

rubbing strake steel strips welded to a narrowboat hull's sides to provide protection

rudder steel plate mounted below the waterline directly behind the propeller for steering a boat

scumbling painted imitation wood grain, traditionally used to decorate the interior of a boatman's cabin; also used on external steel surfaces to replicate decking and trim traditionally built of wood

single-hander person navigating and locking a boat on their own

starboard nautical term; narrowboaters usually use 'right'

steelwork shell of a narrowboat made of plate steel, including the hull, interior framing, decks, cabin sides and roof

stern back end of a boat

cruiser stern large, open rear deck on a narrowboat, usually protected by a taff rail, with the engine installed beneath it

semi-trad stern (AKA 'semi-trad') essentially a cruiser stern deck enclosed by the extension of the boat's cabin sides, which give some protection from the elements and retains the appearance and lines of a traditional narrowboat

trad stern a small, rounded rear deck based on the style of a traditional working narrowboat. The steerer stands in the hatchway inside the back cabin doors. The engine is positioned either under the stern deck and extends into the back cabin, for example concealed under steps, or further forward in its own engine room

survey (pre-purchase condition survey) a comprehensive inspection of a boat by a marine surveyor made on behalf of the buyer and followed, about a week later, by a written report. The survey will usually include an out-of-water evaluation of a boat's hull – with ultrasonic spot measurements to show plate thickness – stern gear and rudder assembly. It will also assess the boat's internal gas, electric, plumbing and heating systems, cabin build, appliances and engine condition

tiller horizontal tube, usually with a wooden handgrip, used to steer a boat. On a narrowboat it is usually secured with an ornamental tiller pin to an S-shaped 'swan's neck'

tumblehome The slope of a narrowboat's cabin sides inwards toward the roof. Not only does this add to a boat's aesthetic appeal, it also reduces the chance of damaging it against waterways structures

weed hatch a small observation and access hatch with a watertight lid directly over the propeller. Opening this allows you to see and remove anything snagged around the propeller and shaft (such as fishing line, plastic bags, old bed springs)

wind (pronounced as in a blowing wind) to turn a narrowboat around

winding hole a widened section of canal where a narrowboat can be turned around

windlass portable handle used for raising and lowering lock paddles, releasing swing bridges and operating other waterways equipment